100 HIKES in

WASHINGTON'S
GLACIER PEAK REGION:
THE NORTH CASCADES

FOURTH EDITION

Ira Spring & Harvey Manning

THE MOUNTAINEERS BOOKS

Published by
The Mountaineers
1001 SW Klickitat Way, Suite 201
Seattle, WA 98134

First edition 1985. Second edition 1988. Third edition: first printing 1996, second printing 1998, third printing 2001. Fourth edition 2003

Published simultaneously in Great Britain by Cordee, 3a DeMontfort Street, Leicester, England, LE1 7HD

Manufactured in Canada

Editor: Christine Clifton-Thornton
Cover and Book Design: The Mountaineers Books
Layout: Marge Mueller, Gray Mouse Graphics
Cartographer: Gray Mouse Graphics
Photographs: Bob and Ira Spring, unless otherwise noted

Cover photograph: *Sunrise on Dome Peak from White Rock Lakes*
Opposite: *Cub Lake and Dome Peak from Bachelor Meadow*

Library of Congress Cataloging-in-Publication Data

Spring, Ira.
  100 hikes in Washington's Glacier Peak region : the North Cascades /
Ira Spring & Harvey Manning.-- 4th ed.
      p. cm.
Includes index.
  ISBN 0-89886-868-8
  1. Hiking--Washington (State)--Glacier Peak Region--Guidebooks. 2.Hiking--
Cascade Range--Guidebooks. 3. Glacier Park Region
(Wash.)--Guidebooks. 4. Cascade Range--Guidebooks. I. Title: One
hundred hikes in Washington's Glacier Peak region. II. Manning, Harvey.
III. Title.
  GV199.42.W22G537 2003
  917.97--dc21
                        200300712

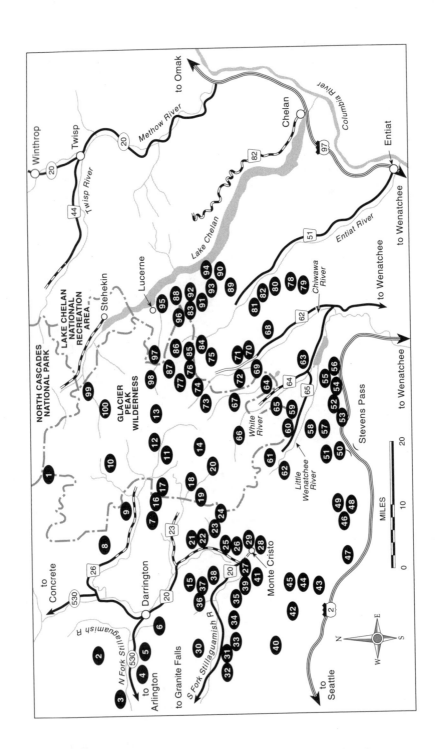

CONTENTS

LEGEND

② US highway		════	freeway or divided highway
⑤③⓪ state highway		▬▬▬	paved road
26 National Forest primary road		▬ ▬ ▬	gravel road
FH7 forest highway		═══	improved road (coarse gravel or dirt)
2040 secondary road (4 digits)		=========	primitive road (jeep road)
689 logging road (3 digits)		------------	trail
790 trail number		┼┼┼┼┼┼┼	railroad
▲ campground		....	cross-country route
backcountry campsite		.▬ ▬.▬.▬	boundary (national forest, national park, wilderness area, or recreation area)
shelter			
ranger station			glacier
building or town			
fire lookout (tower or sitting on ground)			lake
)(pass			marsh

TRAILS AT A GLANCE

On the following pages you will find a quick-view chart listing practical information for every hike in this book, to help you decide which hikes are best for you.

Distance: Indicates in miles the total length of the hike; one-way trips are noted.

Time: The time it might take to complete any hike can vary dramatically from hiker to hiker, depending on their physical fitness and outdoor acumen, the weather, and trail conditions. Times listed here are for an "average" hiker out to enjoy the trail with stops along the way to smell the flowers.

Elevation gain: Indicates the rough cumulative elevation gain in feet one can expect to acquire—in other words, how many feet uphill you'll need to go to complete the hike. Be sure to note the elevation gain of the hike you plan to take in combination with the distance; a 3-mile hike with 2000 feet in elevation gain can be much more strenuous than a 6-mile hike with 2000 feet in elevation gain.

Season: This category indicates the months during which trails tend to be relatively free of snow. Note, however, that in the Glacier Peak region, snowstorms can and do happen in every month. Check weather conditions before you leave for the trail.

Highlight: Indicates the best feature of the hike.

—*The Mountaineers Books*

TRAIL REFERENCE CHART

Hike Number and Destination	Distance (miles)	Hiking Time	Elevation Gain (feet)	Season	Highlight
1 S Fork Cascade River	9	4 hrs	500	June through Oct	Virgin forest along little-used trail
1 Spaulding Mine	10	6 hrs	1500	June through Oct	Seldom-maintained trail, view of cliff-lined cirque below Mount Formidable
2 Finney Peak	6	5 hrs	1600	Mid-June through Oct	Former lookout site, second-growth forest, striking panoramas of the North Cascades
3 Mount Higgins	9	7 hrs	3300	Late June to Nov	A chance to spit a mile from a former lookout site, excellent views
4 Boulder River	9	3 hrs	600	Almost all year	Virgin forest walk, numerous waterfalls
5 Neiderprum Trail	7	7 hrs	3000	July through Sept	Steep, rugged trail on the side of Whitehorse Mountain
6 Squire Creek Pass	10	6 hrs	2300	July through Oct	Virgin forest walk climaxing with view of Three Fingers
7 Circle Peak	4	3 hrs	2100	July to Nov	Trail to former lookout: grand views, meadows, flowers blueberries
8 Huckleberry Mountain	13	9 hrs	4500	July through Sept	Strenuous hike from valley floor to heather meadows, blueberry fields, views
9 Green Mountain	8	6 hrs	3100	Late June through Oct	Hike to lookout with views of Glacier Peak
10 Downey Creek	12½	7 hrs	950	Late June through Oct	Pleasant forest walk beside an active creek
10 Bachelor Meadows	23½	2 to 3 days	4500	Mid-July through Sept	A rugged hike to alpine meadows and dramatic views
11 Milk Creek–Dolly Creek–Vista Creek	33	3 to 5 days	4400	Mid-July through mid-Oct	From lowland forest to alpine meadows on the side of Glacier Peak
12 Image Lake	32	2 to 3 days	4500	Mid-July through Oct	One of the most famous viewpoints in the North Cascades
13 Suiattle River to Lake Chelan	29½	5 to 7 days	5000	Mid-July through Sept	Classic hike across Glacier Peak Wilderness with views, lakes, and meadows
14 Around Glacier Peak N and E section	96 one way	10 days min	15,500	Late July through Sept	A nearly complete loop trail around Glacier Peak with outstanding scenery

TRAIL REFERENCE CHART

Hike Number and Destination	Distance (miles)	Hiking Time	Elevation Gain (feet)	Season	Highlight
15 Peek-a-Boo Lake	6	4 hrs	1200	July through Oct	Small forested mountain lake, good hike for beginners
16 Crystal Lake	8	6 hrs	2200	Late June through Oct	Difficult trail to lakes surrounded by trees and meadows
17 Meadow Mountain–Fire Mountain	21 one way	2 to 4 days	4000	July through Oct	Walk abandoned road and trail to flower fields and views, with longer hikes to lakes and White Chuck River
18 Kennedy Ridge and Hot Springs	18	8 to 10 hrs	3000	July through Oct	Extremely popular hike to hot springs, outstanding views of Glacier Peak
19 Lake Byrne	16	2 to 3 days	3200	Aug through Sept	Steep ascent to an alpine walk with a grand view of Glacier Peak
20 White Chuck Glacier	24	4 days min	2100	Late July through Sept	Long, pleasant hike to meadows below snout of White Chuck Glacier
21 Round Lake viewpoint	10	6 to 8 hrs	3800	July through Oct	Steep climb to alpine meadows and views
21 Lake Byrne	24	3 days min	6500	Aug through Oct	Steep climb followed by sketchy trail through scenic meadows
22 Sloan Peak Meadows	8	7 hrs	2900	Mid-July through Sept	Difficult river crossing leads to climbers' trail up side of Sloan Peak
23 Stujack Pass (Mount Pugh)	10	10 to 12 hrs	5300	Aug through Oct	Strenuous climb to a scenic highpoint on the side of Mount Pugh
24 Bald Eagle Mountain	12	8 hrs	2800	Late July through Sept	Wonderful views of Pride Basin
24 Bald Eagle Loop	24	3 days	4000	Late July through Sept	Miles of ridge-top walking
25 Bedal Basin	6	6 hrs	2200	July through Oct	Bushwack to site of old prospector's cabin
26 Goat Lake	10	5 hrs	1280	Mid June though Oct	Popular hike to lovely subalpine lake surrounded by mountains
27 Gothic Basin	9	9 hrs	2600	Late July through early Oct	Strenuous climb to dramatic views, rocky basin dotted with small lakes
28 Silver Lake	11	8 hrs	2000	July through Oct	Popular destination from Monte Cristo

#	Name					
28	Twin Lakes	17	12 hrs	3500	July through Oct	Demanding hike to two beautiful alpine lakes
29	Glacier Basin	13½	8 hrs	2200	July through Oct	Difficult trail leads to dramatic basin strewn with mining debris
30	Goat Flats	9½	6 hrs	2000	Late July through Oct	Difficult, root-covered trail to lovely alpine meadow and glacier
31	Heather Lake	4½	4 hrs	1200	June to Nov	Moderate to easy hike to subalpine lake at base of towering cliffs
32	Mount Pilchuck	4	4 hrs	2400	July to early Nov	Popular, steep trail to old lookout perched on top of Mount Pilchuck
33	Bald Mountain	20	12 hrs	2500	July through Oct	Historic fire patrol trail along ridge top with occasional views
34	Walt Bailey Trail	8	5½ hrs	1800	July to Nov	Semi-strenuous hike to subalpine lakes
35	What Verlot Forgot to Mallardy Ridge	5	6 hrs	1500	June through Oct	Remains of old fire patrol trail
35	What Verlot Forgot to Marten Creek	5	4 hrs	1400	June through Oct	Hike through tall trees to a brushy ending
35	What Verlot Forgot to Marble Gulch	6	4 hrs	1700	June through Sept	Trail follows route of miners' tramway
36	North Lake	7	6 hrs	1500	Mid-July through Sept	A moderate trail passing Independence Lake to high point overlooking North Lake
37	Perry Creek–Mount Forgotten	8	7 hrs	3100	Mid-June through Oct	Strenuous ascent to subalpine basin, ridge crest, and views
38	Mount Dickerman	8½	8 to 9 hrs	3900	Late July through Oct	Very strenuous hike to meadows, blueberry fields, and tremendous mountain top view
39	Sunrise Mine Trail–Headlee Pass	5	5 hrs	2500	Aug through Sept	Trail starts from a dramatic viewpoint
40	Sultan Basin DNR Trails to Greider Lake	5	3 hrs	1350	June through Nov	Moderate trail to two forested lakes and good campsites
40	Sultan Basin DNR Trails to Boulder Lake	8	5 hrs	2100	July through Oct	Forested lake in a mountainous setting
41	Silver Creek–Mineral City	7	4 hrs	800	most all year	Follow old mine-to-market road up spectacular valley to old mining town site
42	Blanca Lake	8	6 to 8 hrs	2700	July through Oct	Strenuous climb to subalpine meadows and lovely blue-green, glacier-fed lake
43	West Cady Ridge	16	2 to 3 days	3300	Mid-July through late Sept	Moderate to strenuous hike to early season flower fields
44	Bench Mark Mountain Loop	23½	2 to 3 days	4700	Mid-July through Sept	Loop hike through miles of forest and mountain meadows

TRAIL REFERENCE CHART

Hike Number and Destination	Distance (miles)	Hiking Time	Elevation Gain (feet)	Season	Highlight
45 Dishpan Gap Loop	31	3 days	5200	July through Sept	Backpack through vibrant meadows to delightful views on this ridge-top loop
46 Evergreen Mountain Penthouse	2¾	3 hrs	1300	Aug 10 through Oct	Rent a mountaintop fire lookout for a night—but bring your own water
47 Barclay and Eagle Lakes	8½	6 hrs	1700	Late June through Oct	Easy walk to forested Barclay Lake; strenuous climb to subalpine Eagle Lake
48 Scorpion Mountain	9	6 hrs	2300	July through Oct	Famous for the excellence of its flower fields
49 A Peach and a Pear and a Topping	15	2 days	3200	July through Oct	A long hike to three alpine lakes
50 Lake Valhalla	11	6 hrs	1100	Mid-July through Oct	Popular hike to a subalpine lake on the Pacific Crest Trail
51 Lake Janus and Grizzly Peak	17	6 to 8 hrs	1500	Mid-July through Oct	Well-used trail to a friendly lake on the Pacific Crest Trail; continue on for more views
52 Nason Ridge	16	2 to 3 days	4200	Mid-July through Oct	An up and down, down and up hike along Nason Ridge crest; good views
53 Snowy Creek–Rock Mountain	9	6 hrs	3350	Mid July through Oct	Steep climb to an old lookout site with arresting views
54 Rock Mountain	11	8 hrs	4250	Mid-July through Oct	Hot, strenuous climb to a small rocky lake on the side of Rock Mountain
55 Merritt Lake	6	4 hrs	2000	Late June through Oct	Small, pleasant, subalpine lake reached by a moderate climb
56 Alpine Lookout	10	5 hrs	2400	Mid-June through Sept	Manned lookout with a resident population of mountain goats
57 Minotaur Lake	6	5 hrs	2000	Mid-July through Oct	Rough trail leads to two subalpine lakes
58 Heather Lake	6½	4 hrs	1200	July through Oct	Flat, then steep trail to a lovely lake with glacier-ground slabs of granite near the outlet

#	Name	Miles	Time	Elevation	Season	Description
59	Poet Ridge–Irving Pass	7	5 hrs	1900	Mid-June to Oct	Hard route to Poe Mountain, but worth every step
60	Poe Mountain	6	4 hrs	3000	Late June through Oct	Popular hike to former lookout site with meadows and views
61	Meander Meadow and Kodak Peak	16	2 days excellent views	3100	July to Oct	Long valley walk ends in an alpine garden on Kodak Peak;
62	Meander Meadow Loop with side trip	31½	3 to 5 days	5400	July through Sept	Wonderful loop for backpackers, with flower fields and views
63	Dirtyface Peak	9	7 hrs	4000	Mid-June through Oct	A super-strenuous hike to an old lookout site, view over Lake Wenatchee
64	Twin Lakes	8	5 hrs	1000	June through Oct	Easy and popular hike to views of forested Twin Lakes
65	Mount David	16	10 hrs	5400	Mid-Aug to Oct	Extremely strenuous climb to former lookout site, spectacular views
66	Indian Creek – White River Loop	23½	2 or more days	2700	July to Oct	Long valley trek leads to miles of high alpine rambling along the Pacific Crest Trail on the southwest side of Glacier Peak
67	Napeequa Valley via Boulder Pass	26	3 to 7 days	4000	Aug through Sept	Wonderful meadows in the beautiful Napeequa Valley accessed by a difficult creek crossing
68	Basalt Ridge–Garland Peak	9	6 hrs	2500	July to Oct	Hike dry, barren slopes to mountaintop views
69	Schaefer Lake	10	6 hrs	2700	July through Oct	Modest climb to lovely subalpine lake
70	Rock Creek	14	2 days	1800	Mid-June to Oct	Beautiful meadows highlight this valley hike
71	Estes Butte	6	4 hrs	2900	June to Oct	Steep trail to former lookout site, panoramic views
72	Little Giant Pass	9½	9 hrs	4200	Early Aug through Sept	Extremely strenuous climb to dramatic viewpoint; begins with a potentially difficult river ford
73	Buck Creek Pass–High Pass	19	2 to 3 days	3200	July through Oct	Flower gardens all along the way to a 6,000-foot high point overlooking a tiny snowbound lake
74	Chiwawa Basin–Red Mountain	16½	2 days	4100	Mid-July through Sept	Strenuous hike to high alpine meadows, broad views
75	Carne Mountain	7	7	3585	July through Oct	Mighty views and excellent campsites

TRAIL REFERENCE CHART

Hike Number and Destination	Distance (miles)	Hiking Time	Elevation Gain (feet)	Season	Highlight
76 Spider Meadow	15	9 hrs	1600	Mid-July through Oct	A modest walk to some of the largest valley-bottom flower fields in the Cascades
77 Spider Gap–Buck Creek Pass Loop	44	4 to 7 days	7200	Late July to late Sept	A glorious loop through flower fields, passing glaciers, alpine lakes, and some of the greatest views in the Glacier Peak Wilderness
78 Mad River–Cougar Mountain	11	6 hrs	2500	Mid-June through Oct	A strenuous climb to an old lookout site at the edge of a giant burn
79 Mad River–Blue Creek Campground–Mad Lake	16	2 days	1550	July to mid-Oct	See this lovely, moderate trail the Forest Service, without any public hearings, gave to motorcyclists; go on weekdays or early season to avoid machines
80 Mad River Sidetrips	varies	varies	varies	July to mid-Oct	Moderate hikes through alpine meadows from Blue Creek Campground
81 Mad River Hiking Trails	varies	varies	varies	July through Sept	Two motorfree, unmaintained trails into the Mad River Country
82 North Tommy Ridge	13	7 hrs	2900	July through Oct	One-time fire patrol trail, regraded at our expense to motorcycle standards; nice views along the way
83 Duncan Hill from road No. 2920	14	7 hrs	2619	Mid-July through mid-Oct	Long, hot climb to high destination at the crest of the Chelan Mountains; great views
83 Duncan Hill via Anthem Creek Trail	16½	12 hrs	4675	Mid-July through mid-Oct	Extremely strenuous and dry climb to great views
84 Myrtle Lake	8½	4 hrs	600	Mid-June through Oct	Hike a moderate trail to a glacier-carved lake
85 Devils Smokestack	22¾	2 to 3 days	6254	Mid-July through Sept	Excellent views in the Entiat Mountains reached by a strenuous climb
86 Larch Lakes Loops	18	2 to 3 days	3400	Mid-July through Sept	Two small subalpine lakes in a beautiful setting

#	Hike	Miles	Time	Elevation	Season	Description
87	Entiat Meadows and Ice Lakes	28	3 to 5 days	4200	July through October	Long hike to either a beautiful flower meadow or two delicate alpine lakes
88	Big Hill–Pyramid Mountain	18	10 hrs	3000	Mid-July to mid-Sept	Strenuous, high ridge walk to an old lookout site almost a vertical mile above Lake Chelan
89	North Fork Entiat River	16	2 days	2600	July through Oct	Great for beginning backpackers who enjoy rich meadows
90	Pugh Ridge–Pyramid Creek Loop	14	10 hrs	3200	July to mid-Oct	Seldom-used trail to high viewpoint with loop option
91	Fern Lake	15	2 days	2800	Mid-July through Sept	Scramble from the North Fork Entiat River trail to a delightful, rock-bound lake
92	Pyramid Mountain	19	2 days	4300	Mid-July through Sept	Strenuous hike to an old lookout site a vertical mile above Lake Chelan
93	South Pyramid Creek Loop	18	2 to 3 days	3200	July through Oct	Moderate 2-day hike along babbling Pyramid Creek; return via North Fork Entiat River trail
94	Butte Creek–Crow Hill	13	2 days	3400	Early June to mid-Oct	Extremely strenuous climb to Pyramid Mountain trail and views
95	Domke Lake	6	3 hrs	1100	June through Oct	This hike, to a large forested lake, is great for beginners
96	Emerald Peak	16	2 to 3 days	4300	July to Oct	Strenuous climb to flower fields and panoramic views
97	Holden Lake	9	6 hrs	2000	Late July through Oct	Moderate hike to beautiful subalpine lake, ideal for day trips or overnights
98	Lyman Lakes	20	2 to 3 days	2700	July through Sept	Striking scenery, flower-covered meadows, several lovely lakes, and a glacier you can touch
99	Agnes Creek–Lyman Lakes Loop	43	3 to 7 days	4900	Mid-July through Sept	Long valley march to flower fields and lakes; return by way of Holden
100	Pacific Crest National Scenic Trail	98 one way	10 to 15 days	17000	July through Sept	Famous Mexico-to-Canada trail on the crest of the Cascades; forests, meadows, outstanding views

HEALTHY TRAILS MAKE HEALTHY PEOPLE

This book does more than describe paths to beautiful destinations in the Cascade Mountains. It also offers paths to good health.

Physical activities such as walking and hiking improve physical and mental health; reduce risk of major diseases including heart disease, high blood pressure, diabetes, obesity, and colon cancer; and increase longevity. The U.S. Surgeon General recommends people of all ages include a moderate amount of physical activity in their daily routine. On at least five days of the week, people should expend at least 150–200 additional calories daily by performing moderate-intensity activities such as walking.

But during the twentieth century, Americans became less and less physically active. Currently, 30 percent of adults are completely sedentary during their leisure time, and another 30 percent to 40 percent are minimally active. Preventable diseases, such as obesity and diabetes, are increasing dramatically. In the last decade, there was a 61 percent increase in the percentage of Americans who are obese (12 percent to 19.8 percent), and a 49 percent increase in the percentage of American who have diabetes (4.9 percent to 7.3 percent). In 1999, over 13 percent of children age six to eleven were overweight.

But as we encourage Americans to be more physically active, we also should provide them with ample opportunities to be active. We need communities with "physical activity friendly" environments. Part of the solution is building and maintaining the marvelous recreational trails described in this book.

I hope the hikes in this book become part of your pursuit of an active lifestyle. While most of these hikes exceed a moderate amount of activity, the good news is you gain additional health benefits through greater amounts of activity. When you aren't in the backcountry, integrate physical activity into your daily life. Find enjoyable ways to be active, from biking to work, walking a golf course, and playing sports to gardening, kayaking, and dancing—there are many, many pleasant ways to become fit and healthy.

David M, Buchner, MD, MPH
Chief, Physical Activity and Health Branch
U.S. Division of Nutrition and Physical Activity
Centers for Disease Control and Prevention

Introduction

Broad, smooth, well-marked, heavily traveled, ranger-patrolled paths safe and simple for little kids and elderly folks with no mountain training or equipment, or even for monomaniacs dashing from Canada to Mexico. Mean and cruel and mysterious routes through evil brush, over fierce rivers, up shifty screes and moraines to treacherous glaciers and appalling cliffs where none but the skilled and doughty should dare, or perhaps the deranged. Flower strolls for an afternoon, heroic adventures for a week.

A storm side (the west) where precipitation is heavy, winter long, snows deep, glaciers large, peaks sharply sculpted, vegetation lush, and highcountry hiking doesn't get comfortably underway until late July. A lee side, a rainshadow side (the east) where clouds are mostly empties, summer is long, vegetation sparse, ridges round and gentle, and meadows melt free of the white by late June.

Places as thronged as a city park on Labor Day, places as lonesome as the South Pole that Scott knew. Scenes that remind of the High Sierra, scenes that remind of Alaska.

In summary, to generalize about the North Cascades: To generalize about the North Cascades is foolish.

Rules and Regulations

The backcountry in the Glacier Peak section of the North Cascades is mainly administered by the Mt. Baker–Snoqualmie and Wenatchee–Okanogan National Forests. These are "multiple-use" lands, except for the Glacier Peak, Henry T. Jackson, and Boulder River Wildernesses, where the 1964 Wilderness Act guarantees that "the earth and its community of life are untrammeled by man, where man himself is a visitor who does not remain." Mechanized travel, with or without a motor, is banned in Wilderness, meaning no travel device is permitted more complicated than a boot. Horses are allowed where trails are suitable for such masses of flesh. Hikers must acquaint themselves with restrictions on party size and camping before setting out.

Please write for further information:

Mt. Baker–Snoqualmie National Forest
21905 64th Avenue West
Mountlake Terrace, WA 98043

Wenatchee–Okanogan National Forest
215 Melody Lane
Wenatchee, WA 98801-5593

Neither maps nor guidebooks can keep up with all the constant changes by nature and man. When current information about a certain trail is sought, the hiker should visit or telephone the Forest Service ranger station listed in the text. Following are addresses and phone numbers:

Chelan Ranger Station
428 West Wooden Avenue
Chelan, WA 98816
Phone (509) 682-2576

Leavenworth Ranger Station
600 Sherbourne
Leavenworth, WA 98826
Phone (509) 484-5817

Darrington Ranger District
1405 Emmens Street
Darrington, WA 98241
Phone (360) 436-1155

Mount Baker Ranger Station
810 Highway 20
Sedro Woolley, WA 98284
Phone (360) 856-5700

Entiat Ranger Station
2108 Entiat Way
Entiat, WA 98822
Phone (509) 784-1511

Skykomish Ranger District
Skykomish, WA 98045
Phone (360) 677-2414

Lake Wenatchee Ranger Station
22976 Highway 207
Leavenworth, WA 98826
Phone (509) 763-3103

Maps

The maps in these pages are for orientation, not navigation. The U.S. Geological Survey sheets are perhaps the best in the world for meticulous topography. The Green Trails series is the hiker's choice, where available, because the private publisher uses government data as base material and overlays (in green ink) current information, regularly updated, on roads and trails.

The national forests publish recreation maps that are sold at ranger stations.

Clothing and Equipment

No person should set out on a Cascade trail, unless for a brief stroll where the route can't conceivably be lost, lacking warm (wool or equivalent) trousers, shirt and sweater, and hat, plus a windproof and rain-repellent parka, coat, or poncho, plus sturdy shoes or boots and wool socks.

He/she also must have a rucksack to carry the Ten Essentials, a list developed by generations of Mountaineers, often from sad experience.

1. Extra clothing—more than needed in good weather.
2. Extra food—enough so something is left over at the end of the trip.
3. Sunglasses—necessary for most alpine travel and indispensable on snow.

4. Knife—for first aid and emergency firebuilding (making kindling).
5. Firestarter—a candle or chemical fuel for starting a fire with wet wood.
6. First-aid kit.
7. Matches—in a waterproof container.
8. Flashlight—with extra bulb and batteries.
9. Map—be sure it's the right one for the trip.
10. Compass—be sure to know the declination, east or west.

The list was adopted in the 1940s as a teaching device in the club's Climbing Course, to warn novices against overdoing the "going light" theory made famous by John Muir, who would set out for weeks in the High Sierra with little more than a pocketful of rice. The original list was seven. The increase to ten in the 1950s stimulated agitation for an eleventh. The commonest nominee has been "t.p."

A few inventions of the recent past reduce rigors of the wilderness while lessening the human impact on ecosystems. However, the Mr. Toad (of Toad Hall) whose eyes bug out at every new tekky toy has given new life to "going light." The prophet of Minimalism is the late Edward Abbey, who equipped himself for the wilderness sufficiently but not excessively, declaring that he "liked to give Nature a fair crack at him."

Though trails of today are the playpen of the wealthy Mr. Toad, they can still be, as in days of yore (the Great Depression), the spiritual refuge of the poor but honest.

Camping

The laissez-faire of the wilds is defunct. Those wicked old happy days were done in by a refinement of sensitivity and—more importantly—overpopulation. Stewart Udall, Secretary of the Interior under President Kennedy, observed the population of the United States in 1920 had been about the maximum that could be provided the free-swinging, devil-may-care elbowroom of the frontier past. In the 1980s a panel of scholars totted up the pluses and minuses of history and concluded that life in America had been getting better and better up to 1960. Since then it's been downhill, and in wildlands a main reason is the yahoo cry, "If it feels good, do it!" That worked for Dan'l Boone. (He later died.)

On wilderness-edge trails, overnighting is already banned, and will be on others soon. At its best, leave-no-trace weighs on the land; when and where the crowds are madding, the wilds must be reserved for day-hiking re-creation.

At sites where camping is still allowed, the soft soils on the banks of streams and lakes and the gardens bright with flowers and lush with grass must be avoided. If a guardian ranger has not posted a plea, learn the difference between right and wrong and do the right thing.

Some tekky ingenuities can be praised as truly essential for good citizenship. For example, though camps often may be conscientiously sited on tough soils of forests and moraines, they also can be cozy on rock slabs or snowfields if a hiker spreads a sheet of tough plastic, a foam pad, and a sleeping bag atop. (The Therm-a-Rest air mattress is far superior to the pad. The bough bed of the Dan'l Boone past is as heinous as slaughtering the Original Inhabitants to make room for Boonesboro.)

Tents block high winds and frustrate mosquitoes and voyeurs but cost a lot and are heavy, and those now dominating the market are garish violations of Nature's color scheme (forest green and dirt khaki). A tarp is cheap and light and excludes the rain except when it comes sideways. The cheek is pleased by breezes, the nose by flowers, the ears by waterfalls, and the eyes by the heaven of stars. No-see-um netting, light as a feather, can be draped over the head to keep flying bugs at bay.

The wood fire, formerly the supreme pleasure of the mountain night, in the future will be enjoyed mainly in Hell. Seasonal wood is next to totally gone from popular camps; the best of it, silver snags and logs, is scenery too valuable to be wasted on a pot of soup. A single party on a single night may destroy esthetics that took Nature decades to perfect; even where windfall is abundant, the heaps of charcoal will leave black ghosts of vanished fires to haunt hikers to come.

Hikers of the present generation, in being weaned from the free-fire habits of their grandparents, are permitted to burn only at established spots, such as fire rings. If a fire ring is heaped full of rocks, this means it has been "disestablished"; when time of rangers and volunteers is available, the rocks of the ring will be carried off to a nearby talus and the charcoal will be scattered in the brush and the sterile ground will be greened with transplanted turf. (If you have a spare hour, you can help.)

Highland nights may be too chilly to sit out and watch the sunset, but a fire anyway competes with sky colors and shooting stars. If a sweater doesn't stop the shivers, the sleeping bag can be employed as a shawl.

The sleek ingenuities of today's backpacker stoves delight the tekky. There is a price: the weight; the formidable cost. Yes, it is a fun toy. But there is no added nutritional value to hot food. The maxim of Minimalism is, "Though the food is cold, the inner man is hot." The addict deprived of a morning cup of coffee suffers the withdrawal syndrome only a day or two. As for the supper soup, the blood can be warmed by cheese and crackers and a Milky Way.

Water

"Wood water and shelter." The *Boy Scout Manual* of olden days said you couldn't camp without all three and that's why you had to rub sticks together. Two of these items are discussed above. Water, defined as a creek or lake several steps from the campfire, also has been reconsidered. For one thing, the campfire probably isn't there at all. For another, those several steps, taken over and over again by you and succeeding campers, harden a lasting path. A grudging concession is made here to the "essentials" choir: Carry a collapsible, lightweight water bag and camp at a respectful distance. Two bags are better. Carry a couple gallons high on a ridge and escape the crowds that mill around creeks. Solitude. Better views, too.

Needless to say, never wash dishes in streams or lakes. Do that off in the woods or on a rockslide.

Use privies where provided. Where not, eliminate body wastes distant from watercourses. The ethical recommendation of the past has been to dig a shallow hole in the "biological disposal layer," touch a match to the soiled leaves ("t.p." is *not* essential, and the roll should never be handed over to children or other tenderfeet to use without supervision), and cover the evidence. So managed, wastes are digested into the soil in a matter of days.

They are, that is, if not dug up and scattered by wild things wanting salt, a rare commodity in Nature. The new procedure in heavily populated wilds is to double-bag solid wastes for carrying to the nearest privy, at the road or home. Nasty business? Of course. Lacking sewers, most the Third World smells bad. The walls of Yosemite Valley, where extreme climbers hang from ropes for days and nights, also offend.

Our attorney warns us not to guarantee any open water as safe for human consumption. As in the fourteenth century when the Great Pestilence descended on Europe, in the 1970s a vicious little parasite that spends part of its life swimming in water, another part wiggling through the intestinal tracts of wild things, dogs, and people, set off such a panic as Poe wrote about in *The Masque of the Red Death*. The pandemic actually is in the press and the minds of rangers. *Giardia*, identified by microscope in the eighteenth century, were found by Army scientists in World War II to be the culprits putting whole regiments in the sick bay and are present in public water systems of many cities of the world and many towns in America, including some in the foothills of the Cascades. Long before the "outbreak" of "beaver fever" there were the "Boy Scout trots" that on occasion toppled troops. In reality, most humans feel no ill effects from giardiasis (but may become carriers). Others have symptoms that include devastating diarrhea. The reason giardiasis has gone pandemic is that there are more people drinking water in the backcountry. (Some of the most serious cases have been traced to salad bars in city restaurants.)

Giardia can be thanked for raising a warning flag. Jet-trekkers are bringing back from Asia and Africa to our home trails diseases that are no joke, that may not merely upset your digestion but destroy essential body parts.

Boiling water for 10 minutes is 100 percent effective against *Giardia* and company. Better (no fire required) are the iodine treatments such as Potable Aqua or iodine crystals. Filters, another triumph of the tekky tinkerers, doubtless are a blessing when it is necessary to drink from the Ganges. The tourist trekking in from Boston, where the cultivated drink only bottled water (from France), doesn't understand that the murk in North Cascades rivers is not sewage but the bones of clean rocks milled by the glaciers into flour that as "rock milk" gives our wildland water its flavor.

Clerks will try to sell you marvelous machines to go with your trekking sticks and down pajamas and monogrammed Swiss Army knife. Guaranteed by MDs, PhDs, MSs, and MBAs, they are priced at a fortune and up but provide endless fun sitting by a creek and pumping, pumping, pumping. Ask the clerks to put their hands on the Bible and be frank about whether you get your money back when your liver shrivels.

Garbage

Happily, human nature can be improved. When we began this guidebook series, we thundered "BURN BASH AND BURY." Thanks in part perhaps to our sermons, American trails are cleaner today than they have been since Columbus landed. "If you can carry it in full, you can carry it out empty." PACK IT OUT. Enough said.

Pets

The writing is on the wall for dog owners. Pets always have been forbidden on national park trails, and some parts of some wildernesses now are being closed. Dogs belong to the same family as coyotes, and even if no wildlife lets itself be seen, a dog's presence is sensed by the creatures into whose home it is intruding.

Aside from that, some dogs noisily defend an ill-defined territory for their master, "guard" him/her on the trail, snitch undefended bacon, and defecate on the flat bit of ground that the next hiker will want to sleep on.

The hiker who can't go for a walk without his/her best friend must choose trips where friends are permitted and take special care when other folks are around that the friend minds its manners. No barking furies, no bacon hunts.

Theft

A quarter-century ago theft from a car left at the trailhead was rare. Not now. Equipment has become so tekky-fancy and expensive, so much worth stealing, and hikers so numerous, their throngs creating large assemblages of valuables, that theft is a growing problem. Not even wilderness camps are entirely safe; a single raider hitting an unguarded camp may easily carry off several sleeping bags, a couple of tents and assorted stoves, down booties, and freeze-dried strawberries—maybe $1000 worth of gear in one load! However, the professionals who do most of the stealing mainly concentrate on cars. Authorities are concerned but can't post guards at every trailhead.

Rangers have the following recommendations: First and foremost, don't make crime profitable for the pros. If they break into a hundred cars and get nothing but moldy boots and tattered tee shirts, they'll give up. The best bet (but not a guarantee) is to own a second car—a "trailhead car."

Arrive in a beat-up junker with doors and windows that don't close and leave in it nothing of value. If you insist on driving a nice new car, at least don't have mag wheels, tape deck, and radio, and keep it empty of gear. Don't think locks help—pros can open your car door and trunk as fast with a picklock as you can with your key. Don't imagine you can hide anything from them—they know all the hiding spots. If the hike is part of an extended car trip, arrange to store your extra equipment at a nearby motel.

Be suspicious of anyone waiting at a trailhead. One of the tricks of the trade is to sit there with a pack as if waiting for a ride, watching new arrivals unpack—and hide their valuables—and maybe even striking up a conversation to determine how long the marks will be away.

The ultimate solution, of course, is for hikers to become as poor as they were in the olden days. No criminal would consider trailheads profitable if the loot consisted solely of shabby khaki war surplus.

—Harvey Manning

A NOTE ABOUT SAFETY

Safety is an important concern in all outdoor activities. No guidebook can alert you to every hazard or anticipate the limitations of every reader. Therefore, the descriptions of roads, trails, routes, and natural features in this book are not representations that a particular place or excursion will be safe for your party. When you follow any of the routes described in this book, you assume responsibility for your own safety. Under normal conditions, such excursions require the usual attention to traffic, road and trail conditions, weather, terrain, the capabilities of your party, and other factors. Additionally, many of the lands in this book may change because of development or new ownership. Conditions may change, making your use of some of these routes unwise. Always check for current conditions, respect posted private property signs, and avoid confrontations with property owners or managers. Keeping informed on current conditions and using common sense are the keys to a safe, enjoyable outing.

—The Mountaineers Books

1

MIDDLE AND SOUTH FORKS CASCADE RIVER

Round trip to South Fork trail-end: 9 miles
Hiking time: 4 hours
High point: 2200 feet
Elevation gain: 500 feet
Hikable: June through October

Round trip to Spaulding Mine trail-end: 10 miles
Hiking time: 6 hours
High point: 3200 feet
Elevation gain: 1500 feet
Hikable: June through October

Map: Green Trails No. 80 Cascade Pass
Current information: Ask at Mount Baker Ranger Station about trail Nos. 767, 769

Driving directions: Drive Highway 20 to Marblemount and continue east on the Cascade River road. At 16 miles pass Mineral Creek Campground and at 16.6 miles, at a left-turning switchback, find the abandoned South Fork Cascade River road No. 1500(590); park here, elevation 1640 feet.

Standing on a high summit, looking out to horizons and down to valleys, expands the spirit. Standing in a low valley, looking up from forests to summits, gives humility. To know the North Cascades, a person must walk low as well as high. The Middle Fork Cascade valley is one of the "great holes"

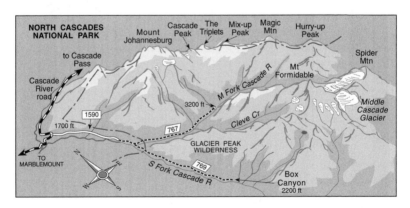

Looking up Middle Fork Cascade River valley

of the range, an excellent place to learn respect. The companion South Fork is one of the grandest wilderness valleys in the range, giant trees rising high—but not so high as the giant, glaciered peaks all around. Expect brush as these trails get very little maintenance.

The overgrown road is still passable to a small four-wheel-drive vehicle, but would ruin a family car. In about 1 mile is a difficult stream crossing. At ½ mile is the start of South Cascade River trail No. 769, elevation 1800 feet.

The first ½ mile is up and down along the river bottom to a junction. The South Fork trail goes straight ahead, crosses the Middle Fork, climbs a bit, and enters the Glacier Peak Wilderness. With modest ups and downs, the way proceeds through magnificent forest to the end of maintained trail at 3 miles from the road, at about 2200 feet. Good camps along the path. An extremely arduous climbers' route continues another 6 miles to Mertensia Pass, 5000 feet.

Back at the junction, the left fork, the Spaulding Mine trail No. 767 (not normally maintained and thus very brushy), climbs steeply up along the Middle Fork beside cascades that are falling down, sometimes seen and always heard. At the 2400-foot lip of the hanging valley (trough, actually), the way gentles out in a superb stand of big trees. At 2 miles is a small creek; leave the trail here and walk several hundred feet down to the riverbank for a look up avalanche-swept Cleve Creek to a glacier on the west ridge of Mount Formidable. Back on the trail, continue upstream in sometimes forest, sometimes avalanche greenery to the trail-end somewhere around 3 miles, 3200 feet. By following gravel bars of the river upstream, or gravel washes of tributary torrents up the slopes of Johannesburg, enlarged views can be obtained of the Middle Cascade Glacier, cliffs of Formidable, and the summits of Magic, Hurry-up, and Spider. Camps abound along the river.

2 | FINNEY PEAK

Round trip: 6 miles
Hiking time: 5 hours
High point: 5083 feet
Elevation gain: 1600 feet
Hikable: Mid-June through October
Maps: Green Trails No. 77 Oso, 78 Darrington
Current information: Mount Baker Ranger Station

Driving directions: For one way to Finney Peak, from I-5 drive Highway 530 toward Darrington. Near milepost 44 go left on Swede Heaven Road 1.8 miles, turn right on road No. 18, cross the pass, and descend Finney Creek to road No. 1735.

For the preferred way, mostly paved, drive Highway 20 to the west side of Concrete, turn right over the Skagit River on the Sauk River–Concrete road, go left about 9 miles, and turn right on road No. 17. Cross Finney Creek. At 13 miles from the Skagit River bridge go left on road No. 1735 another 5.7 miles, to where a nameless little creek has dug a deep trench across the road. Elevation, 3500 feet.

In 1933, when the lookout cabin was built atop the summit jut of rock, the access was a 15-mile trail. In 1968, when we published *100 Hikes in Western Washington*, it had shrunk to 8 miles. Logging roads kept chewing away, and in 1970's first edition of *101 Hikes in the North Cascades*, the trail had only 2½ miles. By 1979's second edition, the scene was stumps, slash, and waist-high brush. However, by poking around I found ½ mile of an abandoned spur road and a short accent through forest would bring me to the still-usable final ½ mile.

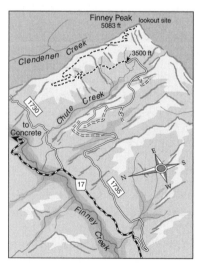

Subsequently I obtained a copy of the Forest Service stipulation that the logger would restore the trail. The loggers apparently forgot and the Forest Service, too, so nothing was done. The views are still there. Better than ever. No longer blocked off by all those old, overmature, dying trees.

A path detours around the gap.

In a scant ½ mile a mudslide must be crossed. Otherwise the clover-carpeted road is good walking. At a Y in 1 mile, go left on an abandoned spur to a deep ditch. Climb some 250 feet through virgin timber to near the top of the ridge. (*Note:* The Forest Service is looking for a better way around this gap.) Find what remains of the old trail, the last few feet blasted from a cliff.

Views from the 5083-foot lookout site include Mount Baker, Whitehorse, the Pickets, and a few hundred other summits up and down the Cascades. Plus clearcuts spacious enough to bring sentimental tears to the eyes of Paul Bunyan and Babe the Blue Ox. Their successors won't find anything of interest. At this elevation, though, for some centuries there could be a sustained yield of Christmas trees.

White Horse Mountain from the top of Finney Peak

3 | MOUNT HIGGINS

Round trip: 9 miles
Hiking time: 7 hours
High point: 4849 feet
Elevation gain: 3300 feet
Hikable: Late June to November
Map: Green Trails No. 77 Oso
Current information: Ask at Darrington Ranger Station about trail No. 640

Driving directions: Drive Highway 530 between Arlington and Darrington to just 0.1 mile west of milepost 38, and then turn left on an obscure and narrow "C Post Road" (SL-0-5500), a Department of Natural Resources logging road. The old trail started right at the river, from a ford that made even horses nervous. This DNR road has obliterated the first 3 miles; the good news is that it gets hikers across the river on a concrete bridge without risking their lives. Across the bridge go left, past spur roads, 2.8 miles to the road-end and Mount Higgins trail No. 640, elevation 1500 feet.

Seen from the bottom of the Stillaguamish valley, Mount Higgins is impressive, the rock strata steeply tilted, the dip slopes appearing to be weathered so clean and smooth as to provide a very rapid (and final) skateboard run. Seen from the top of Higgins, the horizons are equally remarkable. Located near the west edge of the Cascades, the mountain looks north, east, and south to peaks greater and icier than it, and west to towns of the lowlands and islands in the Whulge (the name by which the Original Residents denoted

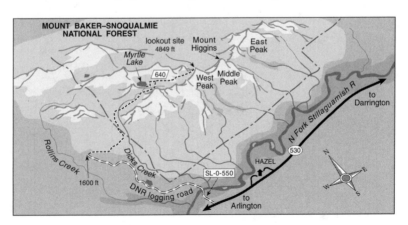

White Horse Mountain, North Fork Stillaguamish River valley

"the saltwater we know"). A stone's throw—4500 feet below—are cornfields and pastures. The hiker has the sensation of teetering on an overhang. This was virtually true of the fire-lookout cabin that from 1926 to 1949 sat atop a cliff on a 4849-foot promontory.

At the road-end (don't be confused by an ATV track that goes straight up), find the trail at the upper end of the parking area. The ascent is very steep, gaining some 1200 feet a mile. The first mile through old clearcuts ends in a deep-woods ravine. At about 2 miles is a tall rock, neatly engraved "S. Strom 8-1917," and on a corner, "K. Neste." Partly in dense forest, sometimes on rockslides, and for a bit through soggy meadow, at 3¼ miles is a side trail to little Myrtle Lake. At 4½ miles the trail reaches the lookout promontory and the breathtaking view. (The summit of the mountain, 5142 feet, will attract only climbers seeking the undying glory that comes from signing a register book.)

About the names on the rock and the mountain: Walter Higgins homesteaded at Hazel, in the valley beneath the peak. Neste was an early settler–prospector. So was Sam Strom, a stubby and pugnacious Darrington Norwegian who acquired a lot of land. The Forest Service built a road on a Sauk Mountain tract Strom thought was his, so he put a gate on it and stood guard with his rifle.

4 | BOULDER RIVER

Round trip: 9 miles
Hiking time: 3 hours
High point: 1550 feet
Elevation gain: 600 feet
Hikable: Almost all year
Maps: Green Trails No. 77 Oso, 109 Granite Falls
Current information: Ask at Darrington Ranger Station
about trail No. 734

Driving directions: Drive Highway 530 east from Arlington 19.8 miles to just beyond milepost 41 and turn right on unsigned road No. 2010. In 1 mile pass DNR's French Creek Campground (no sign). At 2.8 miles keep left at a junction and at 3.7 miles, at the road-end, find the Boulder River trailhead, elevation 950 feet.

See for yourself the only long, lowland, virgin-forested valley left in the Mt. Baker–Snoqualmie National Forest. The Boulder River trail once was part of the Forest Service route over Tupso Pass and down Canyon Creek to the South Fork Stillaguamish road. It was also the shortest way to the fire lookout atop Three Fingers. However, when the Tupso Pass area was clearcut in the 1960s, the trail between Boulder Ford and the pass was abandoned.

The walk is especially good in late spring when the high country is still buried in snow, or in late fall when the maple trees have turned yellow. Views of mountains lacking, a cloudy day is as good as a sunny one.

Trail No. 734 follows a long-abandoned railroad logging grade that ends in ¾ mile, at the edge of virgin forest. At 1¼ miles the way passes an unnamed double waterfall that plunges directly into the river—a favorite picnic spot. In ¼ mile is another lovely waterfall. With more ups than downs,

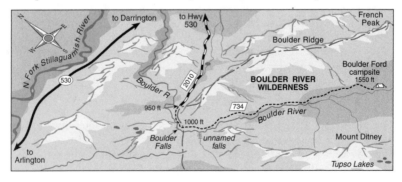

the trail proceeds along the valley, always in splendid forest and always within sound of the river, though it's mostly hidden in a deep canyon. At 4½ miles, the trail ends abruptly in a campsite at Boulder Ford, elevation 1600 feet.

Boulder River and unnamed falls

5 NEIDERPRUM TRAIL

Round trip: 7 miles
Hiking time: 7 hours
High point: 4400 feet
Elevation gain: 3000 feet
Hikable: July through September
Maps: Green Trails No. 78 Darrington, 110 Silverton
Current information: Ask at Darrington Ranger Station
    about trail No. 653

Driving directions: Drive Highway 530 east from Arlington 24 miles.
Where Swede Heaven Road goes left, turn right on Mine Road, passing
several houses. Pavement ends in 0.5 mile in a confusion of driveways;
keep left. At 0.7 mile go left on Forest Road 2030. At 2 miles is the trailhead, signed "Neiderprum Trail No. 653." Elevation, 850 feet.

Built in the early 1900s by Mat Neiderprum as access to his limestone
claims, this trail doesn't go anywhere near the top of Whitehorse Mountain. But it sure goes a long way up in the sky, to a little meadow with close
views of a glacier and airplane-wing views to the Stillaguamish valley,
where cows graze the green pastures and logging trucks rumble through
the town of Darrington. Mr. Neiderprum expended minimum effort on
such frivolities as switchbacks—his trail gains 3600 feet in 3½ miles. Maintenance is skimpy—some log-crawling and bushwhacking must be expected. And there is not much water. Many hikers prefer to do this in
spring, going only to the first good views, turning back when snow grows
deep.
    Though cruelly steep, the first mile is wide and smooth. In the second
mile the tread is so-so (still steep). Then it becomes less a trail than a gully

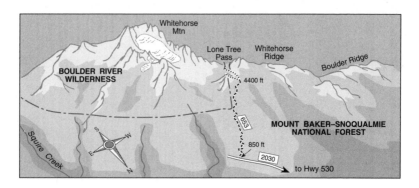

gouged by boots proceeding directly in the fall line, but not always the same line; watch out for spur lines that dead-end. Additional entertainment is provided by logs, mountain ash, huckleberry, salmonberry, and devils club.

Eventually the way enters a brushy meadow and follows a streambed, the first and last water. At roughly 3½ miles, 3800 feet, is a tilted meadow. The alert eye can spot flats excavated for Neiderprum's cabin and tool shed. To the left is a rocky knoll, a delightful place to nurse wounds and enjoy the view down to the pastoral valley, out to peaks of the North Cascades, and up to the summit ice field of Whitehorse. Hikers stop here. Climbers, properly equipped and trained, traverse steep snow slopes to the left and cross Lone Tree Pass.

Whitehorse Mountain

6 | SQUIRE CREEK PASS

Round trip: 10 miles
Hiking time: 6 hours
High point: 4100 feet
Elevation gain: 2300 feet
Hikable: July through October
Map: Green Trails No. 110 Silverton
Current information: Ask at Darrington Ranger Station
about trail No. 654 or 654B

Note: In the winter of 2002 a section of hillside above the Boulder River gave way, blocking the access road. It may take several years before the slide stabilizes, allowing the Forest Service to rebuild the road. For now use the trail from road No. 2060 as described at the end of this hike.

Driving directions: Enter Darrington on Highway 530. Turn right from Madison Avenue onto Darrington Avenue, which becomes Squire Creek road No. 2040. At 1.2 miles is a junction; go left. At 1.7 miles the pavement ends; at 2 miles the road turns left and starts climbing to the road-end at 5.5 miles, elevation 1840 feet.

Hike through lovely forest to a 4000-foot pass with a dramatic view of the seldom-seen cliffs of Whitehorse, Three Fingers, and Bullon—some of the steepest and grandest walls in the western reaches of the Cascades.

Boulder River trail No. 654 immediately boulder hops an unnamed creek and for 1 mile traverses a lovely valley-bottom stand of virgin forest; windows give glimpses of those awesome cliffs. The way then switchbacks steeply upward on rough tread. Whitehorse and Three Fingers tantalize through the trees until approximately 3 miles, at the foot of a huge boulder

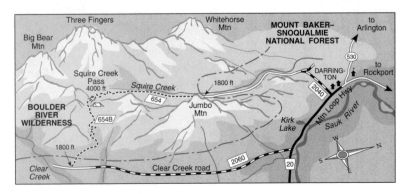

Three Fingers Mountain from Boulder Pass

field, when views open wide and grow more dramatic with each step. At 4½ miles, 4000 feet, the pass is attained. Secluded campsites are scattered about the pretty meadows, but after the snowfields melt the water is chancy and dubious.

A shorter route to the pass—a steep, brushy 2-mile trail, No. 654B, gaining 2200 feet—misses the fine forest and has no exciting views until the pass. From Darrington drive the Mountain Loop Highway 2.3 miles and turn right on road No. 2060. In 5 miles find the trailhead, elevation 1800 feet.

1 CIRCLE PEAK

Round trip: 4 miles
Hiking time: 3 hours
High point: 5983 feet
Elevation gain: 2100 feet
Hikable: July to November
Map: Green Trails No. 111 Sloan Peak
Current information: Ask at Darrington Ranger Station about trail No. 781

Driving directions: Drive road No. 530 north from Darrington or south from Rockport to near the Sauk River bridge and turn off on Suiattle River road No. 26. In 10 miles turn right on road No. 25, over the Suiattle River. In just over 3 miles more go right again on road No. 2700. At 5 miles from the river road go left on road No. 2703 another 6½ miles to the road-end, elevation 3800 feet.

In 1967 the summit lookout cabin was removed and the trail abandoned, but *presently* the path *partly* survives, through meadow flowers, blueberries, and heather to the circle of views from Circle Peak. "Presently" and "partly" are the key words: The vicinity is being clear-cut as high as chain saws can operate without oxygen masks, and 8 miles of trail have been obliterated. Due to major slides, the road may not always be open. The 1950 and 1960 forest maps show a second trail climbing from Crystal Creek to join the Circle Mountain trail near the ridge top. In the 1960s the trail from Crystal Creek on the White Chuck River side was destroyed by a

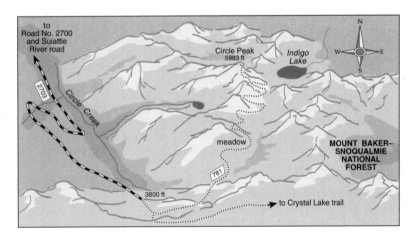

clearcut and never restored. However, a trail of sorts has been established from the Crystal Lake trail (Hike 16) along the top of the clearcut.

From the road-end, climb the edge of the clearcut to find Circle Peak trail No. 638 on the hillside about 150 feet above the road. For most of the way the trail is in decent shape, a testimony to the absence of horses and motorcycles. Nature has been kind, too; surprisingly few logs must be crawled over and only in a few spots has the tread slid out. At about ⅓ mile is a stream, in the first meadow. A long ½ mile more attains the second meadow. At a long 1 mile the way switchbacks up a large meadow where the tread may be hard to find amid the hellebore, aster, bistort, valerian, and other good and bright things. At 1¾ miles the route tops a 5600-foot ridge.

A way trail to a spring used by the lookout switchbacks 200 feet down toward Indigo Lake, ending on top of a cliff some 600 feet above the lake. Stay on the main trail contouring the east slope of the ridge, climbing from a heather meadow to a flower-speckled rock ridge crest and the end of the lookout trail, 5970 feet, 2 miles from the road. Let the eyes swing the circle of peaks—Pugh, White Chuck, Sloan, Green, Huckleberry, and, dominating all, Glacier.

The lookout site isn't far away but is a rock scramble, not recommended for a hiker, and anyhow the 5983-foot summit has little more to offer.

White Chuck Mountain from Circle Peak trail

8 | HUCKLEBERRY MOUNTAIN

Round trip to viewpoint: 13 miles
Hiking time: 9 hours
High point: 5483 feet
Elevation gain: 4500 feet
Hikable: July through September
Map: Green Trails No. 79 Snowking
Current information: Ask at Darrington Ranger Station
about trail No. 780

Driving directions: Drive road No. 530 north from Darrington or south from Rockport to near the Sauk River bridge and turn off on Suiattle River road No. 26. Drive Suiattle River road No. 26 for 14.5 miles and find a small parking place a few feet beyond the Huckleberry Mountain trail No. 780, elevation 1000 feet. Look carefully; this trailhead is very easy to miss.

Most onetime lookout trails of the Cascades have long since had their bottoms amputated by logging trucks, and many their midsections as well, and some have been just about scalped. Clearcuts have climbed so close to timberline that hikers often pass through only the uppermost forest zones. This trail—gloryosky—has survived intact all the way from the valley to the sky. The lower stories are a virgin forest of tall, old Douglas fir and western hemlock, the middle stories are in the zones of silver fir and mountain hemlock, equally virgin, and the top stories are pristine parklands and subalpine meadows wide open to all-around views of craggy peaks and glowing glaciers. Rejoice in the bottom-to-top display of forests of the Cascade west slope. However, don't expect to pack the whole experience into a

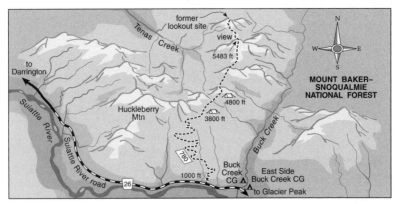

White Chuck Mountain from Huckleberry Mountain

quick afternoon. Indeed, only the best-oiled hiking machines will find the trip practical for a day, and with overnight packs it's a long huffer-puffer.

The well-graded, well-maintained trail gains 800 feet a mile, an ideal steepness for a hiker. The forest shadows minimize sweat and many streams are passed. At 3¾ miles is Fred Bugner Camp, about 3800 feet, with plenty of water all summer. In about 1 mile more, at about 4800 feet, is another campsite with enough water, usually—and probably the last.

At about 5 miles the grade slackens, even drops a bit, contouring below a ridge crest. Views commence, dominated by the spectacular north face of White Chuck Mountain. At 5½ miles, about 5000 feet, the trail sidehills a steep slope. At 6½ miles the trail climbs into meadows and a 5483-foot high point, and enough views to satisfy a hog. Down to the west are the logging roads of Tenas Creek; to the east, the Wilderness-preserved forests of Buck Creek. Across the deep valley are the emerald slopes of Green Mountain, the rocky-snowy cirques of Buckindy and Snowking, and the Pleistocene grandeur of the Glacier Peak Wilderness.

The site of the old lookout is close and the slopes to it invitingly meadowy. Getting there, however, the tread is faint and drops 400 feet from the viewpoint and then climbs 800. A party must begin thinking in terms of a 3-day or 4-day trip, backpacking a gallon of water per person to supply a dry Camp Two.

9 | GREEN MOUNTAIN

Round trip: 8 miles
Hiking time: 6 hours
High point: 6500 feet
Elevation gain: 3100 feet
Hikable: Late June through October
Map: Green Trails No. 80 Cascade Pass
Current information: Ask at Darrington Ranger Station
about trail No. 782

Driving directions: Drive road No. 530 north from Darrington or south from Rockport to near the Sauk River bridge and turn off on Suiattle River road No. 26. Drive Suiattle River road No. 26 almost 19 miles to Green Mountain road No. 2680. Turn left and drive 6 miles to the road-end in a logging patch, elevation about 3400 feet. Find the trail sign above the road several hundred yards before the road-end.

The name of the peak is banal, but few people have ever looked up to it from the Suiattle River valley without exclaiming, "What a *green* mountain!" The trail climbs through these remarkable meadows to the summit, where a restored fire lookout stands with magnificent views to every point of the compass.

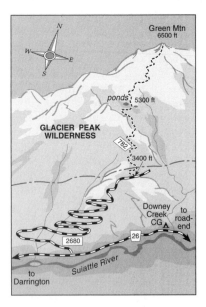

The trail climbs a rather steep mile in mossy forest to a grubby hunters' camp with a year-round spring, then enters the vast meadow system admired from below. First are fields of bracken fern and subalpine plants, then, on higher switchbacks, a feast (in season) of blueberries. Views begin—down to Suiattle forests and out to White Chuck Mountain and Glacier Peak. More meadows, and views of Mount Pugh and Sloan Peak beyond the intervening ridge of Lime Mountain.

At 2 miles, 5200 feet, the trail rounds a shoulder and in ½ mile traverses and drops 100 feet to a pair of shallow ponds amid gardens. Pleasant camps here, and all-summer water; please use established sites away from the ponds. Wood is scarce, so carry a stove. No camping allowed beyond here.

A short way above the pond basin, the trail enters a larger, wide-open basin. Please stay on the trail. The Forest Service is trying to restore the vegetation in erosion channels caused by hasty-footed hikers cutting switchbacks. The summit can now be seen directly above, and also Glacier Peak. Climb in flowers to the ridge and along the crest to the 6500-foot summit, 4 miles.

Look north along the ridge to the nearby cliffs and glaciers of 7311-foot Buckindy. Look up Downey Creek to peaks of the Ptarmigan Traverse from Dome north to Formidable. Look up Milk Creek to the Ptarmigan Glacier on Glacier Peak. Look, look, look.

Green Mountain trail and Glacier Peak

10 DOWNEY CREEK AND BACHELOR MEADOWS

Round trip to Downey Creek: 12½ miles
Hiking time: 7 hours
High point: 2400 feet
Elevation gain: 950 feet
Hikable: Late June through October

Round trip to Bachelor Meadows: 23½ miles
Hiking time: Allow 2 to 3 days
High point: 5900 feet
Elevation gain: 4500 feet
Hikable: Mid-July through September

Map: Green Trails No. 80 Cascade Pass (partly)
Current information: Ask at Darrington Ranger Station
about trail Nos. 768, 796

Driving directions: Drive road No. 530 north from Darrington or south from Rockport to near the Sauk River bridge and turn off on Suiattle River road No. 26. Drive Suiattle River road No. 26 for 21 miles (a bit past Downey Creek Campground) to find the Downey Creek trailhead, elevation 1450 feet.

A pleasant hike through virgin forest along Downey Creek to Sixmile Camp. For those with the energy and ambition, and experience in traveling rough wilderness, it's a tough climb some 5½ miles farther to meadows under 8264-foot Spire Point, with views of deep and blue Cub and Itswoot Lakes, Dome Peak, Glacier Peak, and other icy mountains. Downey Creek trail gets very little maintenance, Bachelor Creek none.

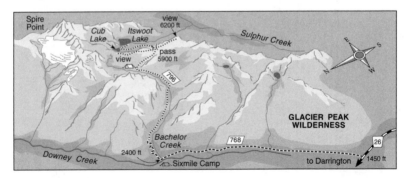

The first mile climbs steadily, then the way levels into easy ups and downs amid tall firs, hemlocks, and cedars, crossing small streams. At 6¼ miles, 2400 feet, the trail ends on the bank of Downey Creek, a good turning point for day-hikers. Six-mile Camp is directly across the creek.

For Bachelor Meadows, cross Downey Creek and proceed onward about ½ mile. Recross Downey Creek and ascend beside Bachelor Creek, initially on a trail that was well graded when built in the days of yore but hasn't seen mattock or pulaski since the CCC went to war. A mile from Downey Creek, the yore is the merest memory. The way becomes simply what boots have trampled, clambering over uncut windfalls, stumbling over roots, and staggering through gooey bogs. After a crossing of Bachelor Creek at about 2 miles, the trail deteriorates to myth in a boulder-cluttered meadow and thickets of slide alder and willow. Blink away sweat and tears for a glimpse of Spire Point. Good campsites begin at about 3½ miles; choose one under trees, spare the fragile heather.

Glacier Peak from a viewpoint along Bachelor Creek

A short but steep 1 mile farther, at 5400 feet, the route abruptly emerges from forest to enter an improbable little valley at a right angle to the main valley. Meadows, water, flat ground for camping, just under Spire Point.

For broader views, continue ½ mile up the trail, quite well-preserved here in this land above the trees, ascending heather fields of the improbable valley south to a 5900-foot pass, from which it drops in ½ mile to 5338-foot Cub Lake and then to 5015-foot Itswoot Lake.

However, don't descend and lose all that elevation; the views are far better on the ridge. From the pass, walk westward ¼ mile along a narrow ridge to a superb view of Dome Peak and the glistening Dome Glacier. A stone's throw below are the two lakes. South is Glacier Peak. A camp on the ridge allows leisurely exploration of meadows eastward to a 6200-foot ridge with an even fuller view of Dome.

11 MILK CREEK–DOLLY CREEK–VISTA CREEK LOOP

Loop trip: 33 miles
Hiking time: Allow 3 to 5 days
High point: 6000 feet
Elevation gain: 4400 feet
Hikable: Mid-July through mid-October
Map: Green Trails No. 112 Glacier Peak
Current information: Ask at Darrington Ranger Station
about trail Nos. 784, 790, 2000

Driving directions: Drive road No. 530 north from Darrington or south from Rockport to near the Sauk River bridge and turn off on Suiattle River road No. 26. Drive Suiattle River road No. 26 for 23 miles to its end, elevation 1600 feet.

A section of the Pacific Crest Trail climbs high across the north flanks of Glacier Peak. Massive flower fields and close-up views of the mountain. Plan to spend an extra day, at least, roaming alpine ridges.

Walk the abandoned road 1 mile to a Y; take the right fork. The Milk Creek trail drops a few steps and crosses the river on a bridge. The way begins in glorious forest; at a mile or so is an awesome grove of ancient and huge cedars, hemlocks, and Douglas firs. Going sometimes level, sometimes uphill, passing cold streams, the path rounds a ridge into the valley of Milk Creek.

The trail enters a broad field of greenery at 3 miles, 2400 feet, with a stunning look up to the ice, a satisfying reward for a short trip. There is a

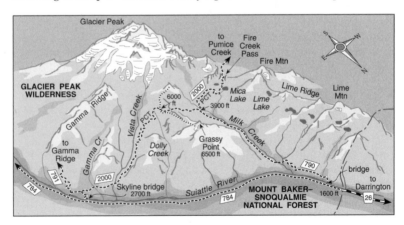

Glacier Creek and Milk Creek valley

pleasant campsite in the forest by the river ½ mile before the field.

From here the trail ascends gently, then passes campsites in the woods and meets the Pacific Crest Trail at 7½ miles, 3800 feet. Turn left at the junction and plod upward on a series of thirty-six switchbacks (growing views of Glacier Peak and toward Mica Lake and Fire Mountain) to the crest of Milk Creek Ridge at 11½ miles, 6000 feet. Here a climbers' route to the summit of Glacier leaves the trail, which traverses the flowery basin of the East Fork Milk Creek headwaters, crosses a ridge into the source of Dolly Creek and, at 14 miles, comes to Vista Ridge and a camp, 5500 feet.

Flower gardens spread in every direction and views are grand north to Miners Ridge, Plummer Mountain, Dome Peak, and beyond. Glacier Peak is too close to be seen at its best. The trip schedule should include one or more walking-around days from the Vista Ridge camp. Wander up the crest to a 7000-foot knoll. Even better, hike north in meadows to 6500-foot Grassy Point, offering views up and down the green valley of the Suiattle River, but especially of the white-glaciered volcano.

From the ridge the trail descends a long series of switchbacks into forest. At 20 miles, 3000 feet, is a campsite by the crossing of Vista Creek. At 21¼ miles is a junction with the Suiattle River trail. At 22 miles, 2700 feet, the trail crosses Skyline Bridge to Skyline Camp and proceeds 11 miles down the valley, reaching the road-end and completing the loop at 33 miles.

12 | IMAGE LAKE

Round trip: 32 miles
Hiking time: Allow 2 to 3 days
High point: 6100 feet
Elevation gain: 4500 feet
Hikable: Mid-July through October
Maps: Green Trails No. 112 Glacier Peak, 113 Holden
Current information: Ask at Darrington Ranger Station
about trail Nos. 784, 785

Driving directions: Drive road No. 530 north from Darrington or south from Rockport to near the Sauk River bridge and turn off on Suiattle River road No. 26. Drive Suiattle River road No. 26 for 23 miles to its end, elevation 1600 feet.

A 2-mile-high volcano, the image of its glaciers reflected in an alpine tarn. Meadow ridges for dream-walking. The long sweep of Suiattle River forests. Casting ballots with their feet, hikers have voted this a supreme climax of the alpine world of the North Cascades and the nation.

Walk abandoned roadway 1 mile to a Y; go left on the Suiattle River trail, largely level, partly in ancient trees, partly in young trees, sometimes with looks to the river, crossing small tributaries, to Canyon Creek Camp, 6½ miles, 2300 feet. At about 9½ miles, 2800 feet, is a creek with a small campsite but no water by midsummer. Just beyond is a trail junction; go left on Miners Ridge trail No. 785. The forest switchbacks are relentless and dry but with occasional glimpses, then spectacular views, out to the valley and the volcano. At 12½ miles are two welcome streams at the edge of meadow country and at 13 miles, 4800 feet, is a junction; campsites here.

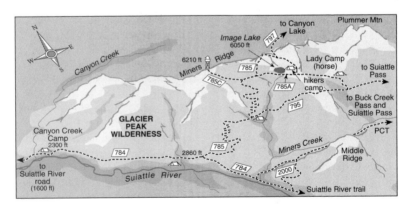

Image Lake and Glacier Peak

Miners Cabin trail No. 795, leading to Suiattle Pass, goes straight ahead from the junction; take the left fork to Image Lake. Switchback up and up, into blueberry and flower meadows, to expanding views, to a junction atop Miners Ridge, about 15 miles, 6150 feet. A ¼-mile trail leads to Miners Ridge Lookout, 6210 feet, the wilderness ranger's headquarters. The main trail goes right ¾ mile, traversing, and then dropping a bit, to 6050-foot Image Lake.

Solitude is not the name of the game here. Indeed, so dense is the summer population that the Forest Service, to protect fragile meadows, has prohibited camping around and above the lake to keep the water pure; it has banned swimming when the water is low. Below the lake ¼ mile is a hikers' camp (no campfires). A mile away at Lady Camp are accommodations for horses and mice. (On a bench above the trail, look for the lovely lady carved in a tree by a sheepherder in about 1916.)

Exploring the basin, climbing the 6758-foot knoll above, visiting the fire lookout, walking the Canyon Lake trail into the headwaters of Canyon Creek—thus one may fill memorable days. By no means omit the finest wandering of all, along the wide crest of Miners Ridge, through flower gardens, looking north to Dome Peak and south across Suiattle forests to Glacier Peak.

Letters can and did make a difference. Kennecott Copper Corporation had planned to dig a ½-mile-wide open-pit mine 1 mile east of the lake at Lady Camp Basin. This blasphemy was prevented by violent objections from citizen-hikers who wrote letters to congressmen and senators.

From Lady Camp the trail drops some 500 feet in ½ mile to a junction with the Suiattle Pass trail, which can be followed 1¾ miles back to the Image Lake trail junction.

13 | SUIATTLE RIVER TO LAKE CHELAN

One-way trip: 29½ miles
Hiking time: Allow 5 to 7 days
High point: 6438 feet
Elevation gain: about 5000 feet
Hikable: Mid-July through September
Maps: Green Trails Nos. 112 Glacier Peak, 113 Holden,
    114 Lucerne
Current information: Ask at Darrington Ranger Station
    about trail Nos. 784, 786, 2000, and Chelan Ranger
    Station about trail Nos. 1256, 1240

Driving directions: Drive road No. 530 north from Darrington or south
from Rockport to near the Sauk River bridge and turn off on Suiattle River
road No. 26. Drive 23 miles, to the Suiattle River road-end, 1600 feet.

A rich, extended sampler of the Glacier Peak Wilderness, beginning in
green-mossy west-side trees, rising to flowers of Miners Ridge and views
of Glacier Peak, crossing Suiattle and Cloudy Passes, descending parklands
of Lyman Lake to rainshadow forests of Railroad Creek and Lake Chelan.
The traverse can be done in either direction; the west-to-east route is described here.

Hike 11 miles on the Suiattle River trail to the 4800-foot junction with
the Image Lake trail (Hike 12). Continue straight ahead on Miners Cabin
trail No. 795, climbing 1¾ miles to a second junction with the Image Lake

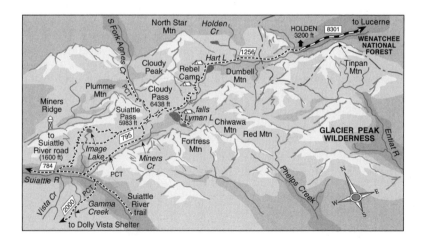

trail, 5500 feet. (The lake can—and should, if time allows—be included in the trip by taking the lake trail, which is 4½ miles from end to end, thus adding some 3 extra miles and about 600 feet of extra elevation gained and lost.) In trees just past the junction are abandoned miners' shacks that are starting to collapse and a spring, a bad-weather campsite. The way now contours, crossing one huge and many small avalanche paths, entering open slopes with grand views to Fortress, Chiwawa, and other peaks at the head of Miners Creek, passing more miners' junk in a small flat. The way briefly joins the Pacific Crest Trail, at 17 miles reaching Suiattle Pass, 5984 feet. A bit before the pass and below the trail is a pleasant camp on a meadow bench.

The trail drops some 300 feet into headwaters of South Fork Agnes Creek and climbs to the most spectacular views and gardens of the trip at 6438-foot Cloudy Pass, 19 miles. (Meadows demand a sidetrip to 7915-foot Cloudy Peak and along the ridge toward 8068-foot North Star Mountain.)

Descend through magnificent flowers, then subalpine forest, to 5587-foot Lyman Lake, 21 miles. Campsites are in the woods north of the lake

Upper Lyman Lake

Lyman Lake

and at the outlet, but camps above, under Cloudy Peak, have better views and fewer bugs. If a campfire is built, use an existing fire ring. From the lake outlet, a hiker-only trail climbs 500 feet to Upper Lyman Lake (Hike 98). At the lake begin bear problems, which continue the full length of the Railroad Creek valley; look to the defense of your good things.

The trail drops past the outlet creek of Lyman Lake, where frothy water pours down long, clean granite slabs, and switchbacks into forests of Railroad Creek; views of Crown Point Falls and Hart Lake. After boggy walking and several bridges, at 24½ miles, 3989 feet, is Rebel Camp and at 25½ miles is Hart Lake. Both have good camping.

The last portion of the route is over blocks of rock under a tall cliff, past tumbling waterfalls, occasional views of high peaks, to beaver bottom and green jungle, and finally a jeep track and baseball field to the abandoned mining town of Holden, 29½ miles, 3200 feet.

Holden Village, Inc., uses the old town as a religious retreat but will sell a hiker of any philosophical persuasion a giant ice cream cone. A road goes 12 miles down to Lucerne, on Lake Chelan, a hot and dusty walk; alternatively, hike trail No. 1240 past Domke Lake to Lucerne (Hike 96). From May 15 to October 15 (check with the Forest Service–Park Service Information Center in Seattle at (206) 470-4060) a bus from Lucerne Resort makes four daily round trips, permitting hikers to catch the boat downlake to Chelan (Hike 96).

14 | AROUND GLACIER PEAK

One-way trip, north and east section: 52 miles
Hiking time: Allow 5 days minimum
High point: 6409 feet (Little Giant Pass)
Elevation gain: 9800 feet
Hikable: Late July through September

One-way trip, south and west section: 44 miles
Hiking time: Allow 5 days minimum
High point: 6450 feet (Red Pass)
Elevation gain: 5700 feet
Hikable: August

Maps: Green Trails Nos. 111 Sloan Peak, 112 Glacier Peak,
   113 Holden
Current information: Ask at Darrington Ranger Station
   about trail Nos. 784, 2000, 789, 790; and Wenatchee
   Ranger Station about trail Nos. 1513, 1518, 1562,
   1507

Driving directions, north and east section: Drive road No. 530 north
from Darrington or south from Rockport to near the Sauk River bridge
and turn off on Suiattle River road No. 26. Drive 23 miles to the Suiattle
River road-end, 1600 feet. Hike 11 miles along the Suiattle River on trail
No. 784 to a junction with Pacific Crest Trail No. 2000. Go left on the
PCT 4½ miles, then right on Middle Ridge trail No. 789 another 5 miles
to Buck Creek Pass.

South and west section: Drive US 2 east from Stevens Pass 19
miles and turn left to Lake Wenatchee. Pass the state park road, cross
the Wenatchee River bridge, and stay left another 4.6 miles to the Lake
Wenatchee Ranger Station. At a big Y go left past the ranger station
and at 6.4 miles from the bridge stay right on White River road No.
6400. At 16.5 miles from the bridge, reach the road-end and parking
area, elevation 2300 feet.

Mount Rainier National Park has the Wonderland Trail; the Glacier Peak
Wilderness offers an equally classic and less crowded around-the-moun-
tain hike. The 96-mile circuit, with an estimated 15,500 feet of climbing,
includes virgin forests, glacial streams, alpine meadows, and ever-changing
views of the "last wild volcano."

The complete trip requires a minimum 10 days, and this makes no al-
lowance for explorations and bad-weather layovers. However, the loop

breaks logically into two sections that can be taken separately. Perhaps the ideal schedule is to do the entire circuit on a single 2-week jaunt, keeping packs to a reasonable weight by arranging to be met midway with additional supplies.

North and East Section: (Two partial alternate routes can be taken; each adds a day and many extra rewards. One is the Milk Creek–Dolly Creek–Vista Creek trail (Hike 11), which adds 12 miles and 3200 feet of elevation

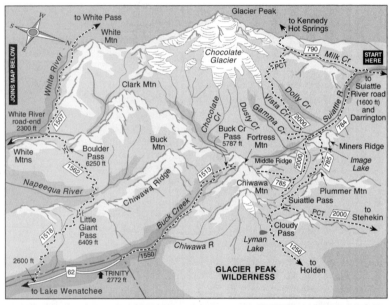

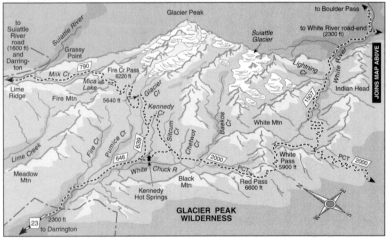

gain to the total. The other is the Image Lake–Miners Ridge trail (Hike 12), which adds 8 miles and 1700 feet of elevation gain.)

Descend 9½ miles from Buck Creek Pass to Trinity (Hike 71) and walk the Chiwawa River road to Little Giant Trail No. 1518. (*Note:* River crossing problems are described in Hikes 70 and 65. Due to the road walking and missing bridges, hikers may prefer to drive between Trinity and the White River trailhead.) Climb 4½ miles over Little Giant Pass and descend 1¾ miles to a ford of the Napeequa River. Cross the river and follow Boulder Pass trail No. 1562 some 22 miles over the pass and down to White River Trail No. 1507. (If this trail is impassable use Indian Creek trail No. 1502, Hike 65.) If the trip is to be broken at this point, hike 3½ miles downstream to the White River road.

The itinerary (excluding the alternates) would be: Day One, 11 miles and a 1150-foot climb to Miners Creek (the best camping is on the river ¼ mile beyond Miners Creek); Day Two, 9½ miles and a 3200-foot climb to Buck Creek Pass; Day Three, descend 3350 feet in 15 miles to Maple Creek; Day Four, climb 3900 feet and descend 2300 feet in 6½ miles to Napeequa River; Day Five, 10 miles to White River road-end, with a climb of 1550 feet and a descent of 3350 feet. However, frequent campsites along the route allow shorter days or different days.

Ptarmigan and alpine flower field

South and West Section: Hike 14¼ miles on White River trail No. 1507 to an intersection with the Pacific Crest Trail. Continue north on the crest 2 miles to White Pass.

From White Pass, contour and climb to Red Pass in 2 miles, then descend the White Chuck River (Hike 20) 7 miles to a junction. For the main route, climb right on the Pacific Crest Trail, crossing headwaters of Kennedy Creek, Glacier Creek, Pumice Creek, and Fire Creek, and reaching Fire Creek Pass in 8 miles (Hike 11).

(If Kennedy Creek is too dangerous to cross, or just for an inviting alternative, go 2 miles from the junction downriver to Kennedy Hot Springs, enjoy a hot (98-degree F) bath, then continue a short ½ mile to the Kennedy Ridge trail (Hike 18)

Indian Head Peak from White Pass

and climb to rejoin the main route; this alternate adds 2½ miles and 800 feet of elevation gain to the total.)

From Fire Creek Pass, the snowiest part of the entire circuit, descend a valley of moraines and ponds past the magnificent cold cirque of Mica Lake, reaching the Dolly–Vista trail junction in 4 miles. Continue 7½ miles down the Milk Creek trail to the Suiattle River road-end (Hike 11).

A possible itinerary would be: Day One, 9 miles and 800 feet in elevation gain to Lightning Creek; Day Two, 9¼ miles with a gain of 2100 feet and a loss of 1000 feet to Glacier Peak Meadows; Day Three, drop 1700 feet and climb 2250 feet on the 9½ miles to Pumice Creek; Day Four, 500 feet up and 900 feet down in 4½ miles to Mica Lake; Day Five, 11 miles and 3800 feet down to Suiattle River road. Again, frequent campsites allow shorter or different days.

15

PEEK-A-BOO LAKE

Round trip: 6 miles
Hiking time: 4 hours
High point: 4300 feet
Elevation gain: 1200 feet in, 400 feet out
Hikable: July through October
Map: Green Trails No. 111 Sloan Peak
Current information: Ask at Darrington Ranger Station
about trail No. 656

Driving directions: Drive Road No. 530 through Arlington to Darring-ton and go right on the Mountain Loop Highway (road No. 20). At 8.8 miles (just short of the Sauk River bridge), turn right on road No. 2080 for 1.1 miles and turn right again on road No. 2081, signed "Peek-a-boo Lake 4 miles." At 4.5 miles from the highway go left on road No. 2086, and at 5.7 miles from the highway find the trailhead at a wide parking area and turnaround, elevation 3000 feet.

A forest trail climbs to a delightful meadow with a spectacular view, and then drops to a lake set in the deep woods of a deep cirque.

The trail begins up the road about 50 feet. Peek-a-Boo Lake trail No. 656 climbs along an old logging grade ⅓ mile, and then narrows to a footpath in virgin forest. Note the stumps with springboard notches from logging operations of the late 1940s.

Relentless switchbacks ascend to a 4300-foot high point from which easy

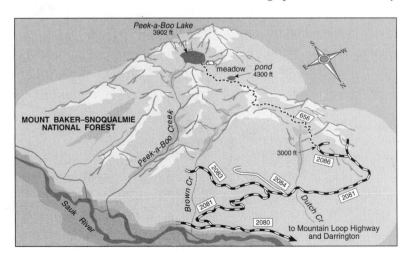

ups and downs lead to a small pond and a pretty meadow. For the trip climax, leave the trail and cross the meadow to the spectacular viewpoint of White Chuck Mountain and Mount Pugh. Look down better than half a vertical mile to the Sauk River and out to the White Chuck River. The glacier-white summit of Dome Peak stands over Meadow Ridge, and Mount Shuksan rises in the distance.

From the meadow the trail deteriorates to a boot-beaten path as it descends 400 feet to the lakeshore and campsites, 3902 feet.

Mount Pugh from Peek-a-Boo Lake trail

16 | CRYSTAL LAKE

Round trip: 8 miles
Hiking time: 6 hours
High point: 4485 feet
Elevation gain: 2200 feet in, 300 feet out
Hikable: Late June through October
Map: Green Trails No. 111 Sloan Peak
Current information: Ask at Darrington Ranger Station
about trail Nos. 657, 638

Note: Wilderness regulations in force at lake

Driving directions: Drive Road No. 530 through Arlington to Darrington and go right on the Mountain Loop Highway (road No. 20). At
roughly 9 miles cross the Sauk River on a concrete bridge. Pass road No.
22 and in 0.2 mile beyond the bridge go left on White Chuck road No.
23 for 6 miles, then left on road No. 2700, signed "Meadow Mountain
Trail 3 miles." At 2.4 miles (not 3, as the road sign says) find the unsigned trailhead on your right, elevation 2580 feet.

A pleasant mountain lake in meadows surrounded by forested ridges,
reached by walking miles of a long-abandoned logging road, a stiff climb
on a fire line, and finally ½ mile of true trail to the lake, which is a meager

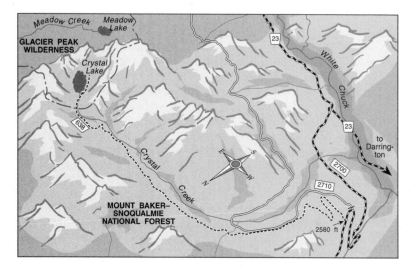

Crystal Lake

¼ mile within Glacier Peak Wilderness. It is permissible to employ vile language discussing the 1960s timber beasts who clearcut-obliterated this and many other trails and never restored them.

The road, formerly No. 2710, now trail No. 657, climbs 450 feet, with glimpses of White Chuck, Pugh, and Glacier to lighten the load, then loses 300 feet. At 1⅓ miles go left on the obscure, overgrown Crystal Creek road. The only sign, almost hidden in brush, is "Road No. (2710)011." (The main road goes to Meadow Mountain, Hike 17.)

The steadily climbing road, now trail No. 638, is brushing in fast and may soon be lost. (Hikers, do a good deed and carry your loppers.) At about 1½ miles from Meadow Mountain trail (road), 3600 feet, the good grade ends in a pleasant campsite beside Crystal Creek. In the next ½ mile the road–trail deteriorates to a muddy rut through the brush, ending at the far end of a clearcut 3½ miles from the car. From here the route goes straight up 500 feet on what was once a fire line. The agony is eased by sound and sight of nearby waterfalls.

At the top of the clearcut the fire line intersects the old Crystal Lake–Circle Peak trail (Hike 7). The ascent continues but the unmolested forest and true trail make the remaining scant ½ mile to Crystal Lake a breeze. Wilderness regulations apply at the lake.

17 | MEADOW MOUNTAIN– FIRE MOUNTAIN

Round trip to 5800-foot viewpoint: 16 miles
Hiking time: Allow 2 days
High point: 5850 feet
Elevation gain: 3500 feet in, 300 feet out
Hikable: July through October

One-way trip to White Chuck River road-end: 21 miles
Hiking time: Allow 2 to 4 days
High point: 6000 feet
Elevation gain: 4000 feet
Hikable: July through October

Maps: Green Trails Nos. 111 Sloan Peak, 112 Glacier Peak
Current information: Ask at Darrington Ranger Station about trail No. 657

Driving directions: Drive Road No. 530 through Arlington to Darrington and go right on the Mountain Loop Highway (road No. 20). Drive the Mountain Loop Highway 9 miles, turn left on White Chuck River road No. 23 for 6 miles, and then go left on road No. 2700 (signed "Meadow Mountain Trail 3 miles"). At 2.4 miles (not 3) find the beginning of the Meadow Mountain road–trail, elevation 2580 feet (Hike 16).

Meadows laced with alpine trees, views to White Chuck forests and Glacier Peak ice, and a long parkland ridge for roaming, plus sidetrips to cirque lakes. But be warned should the sun be shining: there is a 4½-mile road walk to the trailhead with scarcely a tree to cool your brow. The misery is somewhat eased by spectacular views of Mount Pugh and Glacier Peak.

Walk road No. 2710 (now trail No. 657), passing the Crystal Creek road–trail at 1⅓ miles, and cross Crystal Creek to reach the genuine trail at 4½ miles, elevation 3400 feet.

The trail climbs a steep 1¼ miles (but in deep, cool forest) to the first meadow. Cross a bubbling brook in an open basin and choose either of two destinations, both offering splendid views down to the green valley and out to the peaks. For the easiest, follow a faint way trail 1 mile westward toward a high knoll. For the best and the most flowers, hike the main trail 2 miles eastward, climbing to a 5800-foot spur ridge from Meadow Mountain.

For one of the great backpacking ridge walks in the Glacier Peak Wilderness, take the up-and-down trail traversing the ridge east toward Fire

Frost-covered Indian paintbrush

Mountain. Earlier camps are possible, but the first site with guaranteed all-summer water is Owl Creek at 8½ miles, in a bouldery basin to which the trail drops to avoid cliffs of Meadow Mountain.

Going up, then down, then up again, at 10¼ miles the trail touches the 5850-foot ridge crest. For a sidetrip, descend 1 mile northwest on a much-used but not obvious and easily lost path to 5300-foot Diamond Lake. From the east shore, climb a wide gully up the low ridge and descend extremely steep slopes (no trail) to Emerald Lake, 5200 feet. Good camps at Diamond Lake; stay 100 feet from the shores.

The main trail continues along the ridge to a low saddle and proceeds east through patches of trees, grassy swales, sidehill flowers, and views. At 12 miles, beneath Fire Mountain, are charming garden camps near the site

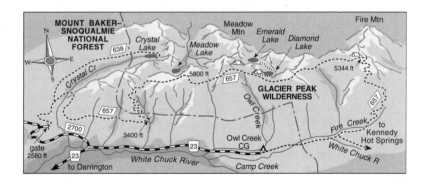

Glacier Peak from the side of Meadow Mountain

of long-gone Fire Chief Shelter. From this area experienced off-trail travelers can find an easy but not obvious route to the summit of 6591-foot Fire Mountain; if the terrain gets steep and scary, you've gone wrong—turn back.

The trail descends an old burn to Fire Creek forests, joining the White Chuck trail at 16½ miles, 1½ miles from the White Chuck River road. By use of two cars, one parked at each road-end, hikers can enjoy a 21-mile one-way trip along the full length of the ridge; a 3-day schedule allows for sidetrips, but more days could easily be spent exploring.

18 KENNEDY RIDGE AND HOT SPRINGS

Round trip to Kennedy Hot Springs: 11 miles
Hiking time: 5 hours
High point: 3300 feet
Elevation gain: 1000 feet
Hikable: May through November

**Round trip to Kennedy Ridge (Glacier Creek camp-
site): 18 miles**
Hiking time: 8 to 10 hours
High point: 5250 feet
Elevation gain: 3000 feet
Hikable: July through October

Maps: Green Trails Nos. 111 Sloan Peak, 112 Glacier Peak
Current information: Ask at Darrington Ranger Station
about trail Nos. 643, 2000

Driving directions: Drive Road No. 530 through Arlington to Darrington and go right on the Mountain Loop Highway (road No. 20). At
roughly 9 miles cross the Sauk River on a concrete bridge. Pass road No.
22 and in 0.2 mile beyond the bridge go left on White Chuck road No.
23 for 10 miles to the road-end parking area and campground, elevation 2300 feet.

Two hikes which can be done separately or combined. A short-and-low trip
leads through tall, old trees, beside a roaring river, to volcano-warmed
waters—the most mob-jammed spot in the Glacier Peak Wilderness. A
long-and-high trip climbs to alpine flowers and a close look at icefalls tumbling from Glacier Peak.

The wide, gentle White Chuck River trail has become—deservedly—
the most popular valley walk in the Glacier Peak area. The way goes
through virgin forest always near and sometimes beside the ice-fed river,
beneath striking cliffs of volcanic tuff, crossing the frothing tributaries of
Fire, Pumice, and Glacier Creeks. At 5 miles, 3300 feet, is a junction with
the hot springs and Kennedy Ridge trails.

Kennedy Hot Springs: In 1976 and in 1990, floods ravaged the White
Chuck River trail to Kennedy Creek. The trail has been restored to the guard
station, hot springs, and camp, 3300 feet. The beautiful forest is the proper
reward of hiking to Kennedy, but an amazing percentage of the 6000 people
who annually sign the register come for the hot (actually only warm)
springs. To satisfy geological curiosity, cross the river on a bridge, turn left,

and in a few yards come to the cruddy, rusty waters seeping from the earth. A tublike pool has been dug, just big enough for three or four people who don't believe in the germ theory of disease. The waiting line gets long at the pool in good weather. It would be a lot shorter if folks knew that in summer the coliform bacteria count exceeds that of the average sewer.

Kennedy Ridge: From the junction at 5 miles, just before crossing Kennedy Creek, climb left on the Kennedy Ridge trail. (A full canteen is barely adequate.) The steep forest way, occasionally glimpsed above, joins the Pacific Crest Trail at 2 miles, 4150 feet. The Crest Trail switchbacks through cliffs of red

Glacier Peak from Pumice Ridge

and gray andesite, then along heather parklands on a moraine crest, swinging left to reach the welcome splash (and campsite) of Glacier Creek at 5250 feet, 4 miles from the White Chuck River trail.

Leave the trail and climb open subalpine forests on the old moraine, then in ½ mile step suddenly out onto raw boulders of a much newer moraine. See the Kennedy and Scimitar Glaciers tumbling down the volcano.

It's a shame to turn back at the edge of so much good highland roaming. Just 1 mile from Glacier Creek, over Glacier Ridge, are the splendid meadows and camps of Pumice Creek, and in 3½ miles more is Fire Creek Pass.

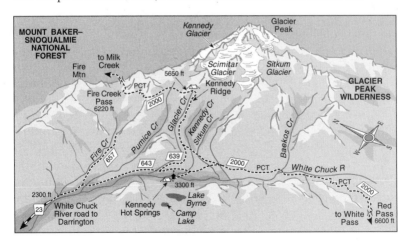

19 | LAKE BYRNE

Round trip: 16 miles
Hiking time: Allow 2 to 3 days
High point: 5544 feet
Elevation gain: 3200 feet
Hikable: August through September
Maps: Green Trails Nos. 111 Sloan Peak, 112 Glacier Peak
Current information: Ask at Darrington Ranger Station
about trail Nos. 643, 774

Driving directions: Drive Road No. 530 through Arlington to Darrington
and go right on the Mountain Loop Highway (road No. 20). At roughly 9
miles cross the Sauk River on a concrete bridge. Pass road No. 22 and in
0.2 mile beyond the bridge go left on White Chuck road No. 23 for 10
miles to the road-end parking area and campground, elevation 2300 feet.

In olden times, when it took 2 full days of hiking up the White Chuck River
just to get to Kennedy Hot Springs, pedestrians never devoted less than a
week to the trip. The glorious forest was savored fully. After sessions of
trail-sweating, the springs were much enjoyed in relative safety, the bath-
ers being few and their diseases not terribly fearsome. However, the cherry
on top of the whipped cream was Lake Byrne and the highland roaming
westward from there. For modern weekenders, however, backpacking to
the lake is something of a horror story. The last chapter, the trail from hot
springs to lake, is short, but *steep*. And spots near the lake where a sleeping
bag can be spread are so few that some campers pitch tents on the lake
itself, which is usually frozen solid all but a few weeks of late summer. No
fires permitted, of course. The recommendation, therefore, is to basecamp

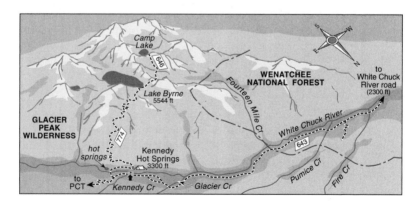

Lake Burne

at Kennedy and day-hike to the lake and the meadow ridges above.

Hike 5½ miles to the patrol cabin at Kennedy Hot Springs (Hike 18) and find a campsite on either side of the White Chuck River, 3300 feet.

From the patrol cabin cross the footbridge to a junction. The left fork goes 100 yards to the warm (80–90 degrees F) springs, in which you might not wish to immerse your own body but which may contain bodies worth looking at. (Ten years ago there was a problem with young rowdies, but nothing recently. Evidently the distance is too far to carry their six-packs.) The right fork climbs a bit, past campsites, and then takes dead aim on the sky, gaining 2200 feet in the next 2½ miles.

The first 1¼ miles from the hot springs are well shaded, with chinks in the green wall giving glimpses of the blinding snows of Glacier Peak. A fairly level and quite brief respite from steepness has heather meadows, a small stream, and possible camping. Then, upward again, the views become bigger and the trail poorer. At 2½ miles from the hot springs, 8 miles from the road, is Lake Byrne, 5544 feet.

The shores are mostly steep heather, rockslides, cliffs, and snowfields. The few campsites are widely scattered around parkland knolls; if you arrive late on a busy weekend, inspect your chosen spot to see whether campers on the other side of the knoll have been using it for other purposes.

For meadows that grow wider and views that expand constantly, take the right fork at the lakeshore and climb 500 feet more to a viewpoint overlooking Camp Lake, set in a deep, cold little bowl where the sun rarely shines and the snow hardly ever melts.

20 | WHITE CHUCK GLACIER

Round trip to Glacier Peak Meadows: 24 miles
Hiking time: Allow 4 days minimum
High point: About 5400 feet
Elevation gain: 2100 feet
Hikable: Late July through September
Maps: Green Trails Nos. 111 Sloan Peak, 112 Glacier Peak
Current information: Ask at Darrington Ranger Station
about trail Nos. 643, 2000.

Driving directions: Drive Road No. 530 through Arlington to Darrington and go right on the Mountain Loop Highway (road No. 20). At roughly 9 miles cross the Sauk River on a concrete bridge. Pass road No. 22 and in 0.2 mile beyond the bridge go left on White Chuck road No. 23. Drive to the White Chuck River road-end, 2300 feet.

Begin beside a loud river in deep forest. Walk miles through big trees; climb to little trees and wide meadows. Roam flowers and waterfalls and moraines to a broad glacier. Wander gardens and ridges. In the opinion of some experts, this is the supreme low-to-high tour of the Glacier Peak Wilderness.

Hike 5½ miles to 3300-foot Kennedy Hot Springs. Ascend steeply, then gently, to join the Pacific Crest Trail at Sitkum Creek, 3850 feet, 7 miles from the road; camping space is available here when Kennedy is full up, as it often is. The Crest Trail continues along the valley, passing the avalanche track and meadow–marsh of Chetwot Creek, fording Baekos Creek, and, at 9½ miles, 4200 feet, crossing a high bridge over the rocky chasm and thundering falls of the White Chuck River.

Now the trail climbs a valley step. Trees are smaller and so is the river, assembling itself from snow-fed tributaries. A little meadow gives promise of what lies above. After more subalpine forest, the way enters the tremendous

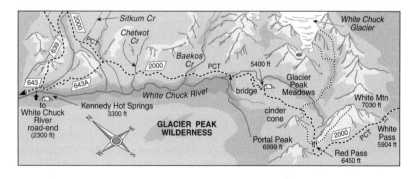

Steaming Kennedy Hot Springs

open basin of Glacier Peak Meadows. At 12 miles, 5400 feet, is the site of the long-gone Glacier Peak Shelter, magnificent campsites everywhere around.

As a base for easy hiker-type explorations, this highland valley of flowers and creeks and snowfields is unsurpassed in the North Cascades.

First off, if your hike is mid-August or later, visit the ice, before it is covered with snow. Climb meadows around the valley corner east, taking any of many appealing routes to a chilly flatland of moss and meanders, to moraines and meltwater, and finally the White Chuck Glacier. The white plateau is tempting, but only climbers with rope and ice ax should venture on its surface.

For another trip, investigate the intriguing White Chuck Cinder Cone, remnant of a volcano smaller and newer than Glacier Peak. Scramble meadows higher to the 6999-foot summit of Portal Peak.

If your visit is in late July or early August, it is flower time on White Mountain. Therefore, hike the Crest Trail 2 miles up a wintry, rocky basin to 6450-foot Red Pass; from here, continue on the trail to White Pass (in early July be careful of the steep snow slopes) or leave the trail and scramble to the summit of 7030-foot White Mountain.

Every direction calls. Invent your own wanderings. The minimum trip to the glacier can be done in 3 days, but any itinerary of less than a week will leave the visitor frustrated, determined to return soon to finish the job at leisure.

Campsites other than those mentioned above are plentiful along the trail and throughout the high basin. However, as a conservation rule to be followed here and everywhere, camp only in established sites, not in the actual meadows, which are so fragile that only a few nights of camping can destroy nature's work of decades.

21 | LOST CREEK RIDGE

Round trip to Round Lake viewpoint: 10 miles
Hiking time: 6 to 8 hours
High point: 5550 feet
Elevation gain: 3800 feet
Hikable: July through October

Round trip to Lake Byrne: 24 miles
Hiking time: Allow 3 days minimum
High point: 6000 feet
Elevation gain: About 6500 feet
Hikable: August through October

Map: Green Trails No. 111 Sloan Peak
Current information: Ask at Darrington Ranger Station
about trail No. 646

Driving directions: Drive Road No. 530 through Arlington to Darring-ton and go right on the Mountain Loop Highway (road No. 20). At 16 miles turn left to North Fork Sauk River road No. 49. Go 3 miles to a small parking area and trail sign, elevation 1849 feet.

A long ridge of green meadows, alpine lakes, and wide views of peaks near and far—one of the most memorable highland trails in the Glacier Peak region. The ridge can be ascended from either end for day trips or overnight

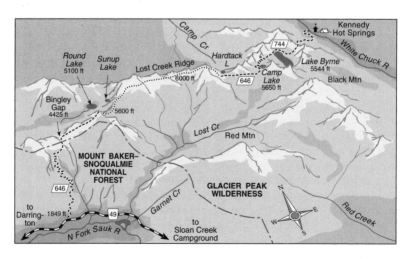

camps, or walked the full length on an extended backpack. However, the middle section of the route is a boot-beaten path, often overgrown. Particularly in the fog and snow, hikers must be careful not to get lost on Lost Ridge (and especially if there is much snow on the ground).

The trail goes gently along the valley ½ mile, then climbs steeply through open woods, with occasional views of impressive Sloan Peak, to 4400-foot Bingley Gap, 3 miles. The way continues some 2 miles up and along the ridge to meadows and a 5600-foot saddle overlooking Round Lake, 5100 feet. (A steep sidetrail descends to the lake and good camps.) Here is the place for day-trippers to have lunch, soak up the scenery, and return home; generally the trail is reasonably snowfree by early July.

Beyond this point is a stretch of route with only a faint tread. The practice used to be to build trail through patches of woods but leave

Sloan Peak—Lost Creek Ridge trail

travelers to find their own way across meadows. Routefinding is easiest when the snow is mostly gone, by late July. Though upsy-downsy, the going is easy and glorious—always near or on the crest, mostly past vast meadows, through open basins, near small lakes, with constant and changing views and a choice of delightful camps. Near Hardtack Lake continuous tread begins. At 11 miles is 5681-foot Camp Lake, set in a cliff-walled cirque; near the lake is a gully that is extremely dangerous when full of snow. The trail climbs to a 6000-foot knob, drops a few feet to the rocky basin of "Little Siberia," then descends to famous Lake Byrne, 12 miles, 5544 feet. Flowers and rocks and waterfalls of the basin and adjoining ridges demand leisurely exploration, ever dominated by the tall white volcano rising beyond White Chuck River forests. However, campsites at Lake Byrne are so small, poor, and overused that exploration should be basecamped at Camp Lake or Kennedy Hot Springs. No campfires permitted at Lake Byrne.

From the lake the trail abruptly drops 2250 feet in 2 miles to Kennedy Hot Springs (Hike 18). If transportation can be arranged, such as by use of two cars, a 19-mile one-way trip can be done; allow 3 days or more.

22 | SLOAN PEAK MEADOWS

Round trip: 8 miles
Hiking time: 7 hours
High point: 4800 feet
Elevation gain: 2900 feet
Hikable: Mid-July through September
Map: Green Trails No. 111 Sloan Peak
Current information: Ask at Darrington Ranger Station
about trail No. 648

Driving directions: Drive Road No. 530 through Arlington to Darrington and go right on the Mountain Loop Highway (road No. 20). Drive 16
miles to North Fork Sauk River road No. 49 and turn left 4.6 miles to the
trailhead, signed "Sloan Peak Climbers' Trail," elevation 1900 feet.

The big-time, big-corporation prospectors of today racket about the sky in
fleets of helicopters and never touch the ground except to drill holes in it
and heap garbage on it. Their predecessors of 100 years ago, earthbound
"dirty miners in search of shining gold," spent half their time building
trails—often steep, but wide and solid enough for pack trains. Hundreds
of miles of trails still in use were engineered by these old-timers, who never
found gold or anything else of value, and earned nothing for their sweat
but a shirt that needed a bath.

One bit of their handiwork, the Cougar Creek trail, climbs from
the North Fork Sauk River to meadows on the side of Sloan Peak. This

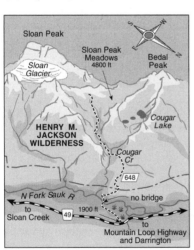

would be a glorious spot to spend a
couple of days roaming, but lacking
dirty miners to maintain it, the trail
has become so mean that hauling
camping gear to the high country
would try the cheerfulness of a
Sherpa. Even as a day trip it's no
simple stroll. Crossing the North
Fork Sauk and Cougar Creek is always difficult and frequently impossible. If in doubt, return to the
car and go someplace else, such as
Lost Creek Ridge (Hike 21).

Walk ½ mile to the river on abandoned road, in several places
flooded by beaver ponds. The
bridge is decades gone and unless a

logjam can be found upstream or down the trip is over—the river is much too deep and swift to ford safely.

On the far side of the river the trail follows an old logging railroad grade ¼ mile, then gains 500 feet up an old clearcut to the old miners' trail. Steep but wide, the relic ascends a long 2 miles to a rotten-log (obviously not permanent) crossing of Cougar Creek between two waterfalls. In the next 2 miles the creek is crossed twice more—or perhaps not at all on a hot day when meltwater is roaring. The way continues relentlessly up, crossing four more creeks, each at the base of a waterfall. (Waterfalls are among the best parts of this hike.)

At a very long 4 miles, elevation 4800 feet, a small meadow invites camping, in views up to Sloan Glacier and the summit cliffs of Sloan Peak and out east to Red Mountain and Glacier Peak. The slopes above the camp meadow invite wandering—which, however, should go only to the first steep snowfield unless the party has climbing gear and skills.

Cougar Creek

23 | STUJACK PASS (MOUNT PUGH)

Round trip to Stujack Pass: 7½ miles
Hiking time: 6 to 7 hours
High point: 5500 feet
Elevation gain: 3600 feet
Hikable: Mid-July through October

Round trip to Mount Pugh: 10 miles
Hiking time: 10 to 12 hours
High point: 7201 feet
Elevation gain: 5300 feet
Hikable: August through October

Map: Green Trails No. 111 Sloan Peak
Current information: Ask at Darrington Ranger Station
about trail No. 644

Driving directions: Drive Road No. 530 through Arlington to Darrington and go right on the Mountain Loop Highway (road No. 20). Drive
12.6 miles to Mount Pugh road no. (2000)095 (may be signed "095").
(*Note:* This road is closed for wildlife protection until June 1.) Turn left 1
mile to the Mount Pugh trail sign, elevation 1900 feet.

Positioned as it is so far west from the main Cascades mass, Mount Pugh's
height and detachment make it strikingly tall and imposing—and an exceptional viewpoint. See out to lowlands of the Whulge (the Original Residents' name for "the saltwater"). See the North Cascades from Baker to
Eldorado to Dome to Bonanza. See nearby Glacier Peak standing magnifi-
cently tall above White Chuck River forests. Closer, see the superb horn of
Sloan and the sharp peaks of the Monte Cristo area. A rare panorama indeed, but not for everyone—the upper portion of the trail once led to a fire
lookout that has long been abandoned and now is climbers' terrain. However, hikers can go most of the way and see most of the horizons.

The steep trail climbs cool forest 1½ miles to tiny Lake Metan, 3180 feet,
and the first looks out. Relentless switchbacks ascend to meadows, 3 miles,
beyond which the trail is not maintained. The only decent camps on the
route are here, but water may be gone by late summer.

Three Fingers and Whitehorse appear beyond valley forests as the trail
switchbacks up talus and flowers to the notch of Stujack Pass, 3¾ miles,
5500 feet. Inexperienced travelers should have lunch and turn back, content with a full bag of scenery.

Those who go beyond Stujack (named for its discoverers, Stuart and

White Chuck Mountain from the side of Mount Pugh

Jackson, U.S. Coast and Geodetic surveyors who mapped the area a century or so ago) must be trained and equipped for steep snow (early summer) and for rock scrambling (all summer) where sections of trail have slid out. The abandoned trail climbs abruptly from the pass to a knife-edge rock ridge, and then picks a delicate way along cliffs above a glacier trough, perhaps vanishing occasionally in snowfields. Part of the trail was dynamited from rock to provide access to the summit lookout; the first cabin was destroyed by lightning and its successor was burned down several decades ago. Steep heather and rock slabs lead to the summit, 5½ miles, 7201 feet.

The summit views are worth the effort for travelers who can use ice ax, hands and feet, and perhaps rope, and thus manage the upper "trail" in safety. The views short of the summit are also worthwhile; be sure to stop, satisfied, when the going gets spooky.

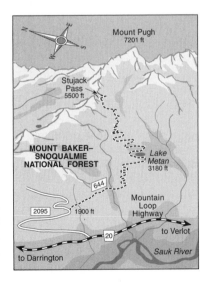

24 | BALD EAGLE LOOP

Round trip: 12 miles
Hiking time: 8 hours
High point: 5200 feet
Elevation gain: 2800 feet
Hikable: Late July through September

Loop trip: 24 miles plus 2½-mile walk on road
Hiking time: Allow 3 days
High point: 6000 feet
Elevation gain: 4000 feet
Hikable: Late July through September

Maps: Green Trails Nos. 111 Sloan Peak, 143 Monte Cristo, 144 Benchmark Mtn.
Current information: Ask at Darrington Ranger Station about trail Nos. 650, 652

Driving directions: Drive Road No. 530 through Arlington to Darrington and go right on the Mountain Loop Highway (road No. 20). Drive 16 miles and turn left on North Fork Sauk River road No. 49. In 6.7 miles, pass road No. (4900)020 to the North Fork Sauk River trailhead, the end of the loop trip. Drive another 2.5 miles to a junction and horse ramp, and go right 0.5 mile more to the road-end at the foot bridge across Sloan Creek, the beginning of Bald Eagle Mountain trail No. 650, elevation 2400 feet, the start of the loop trip. If the loop is planned, unload packs here and park the car back near the campground, where you'll be coming out.

A spectacular day-hike view of Pride Basin and Monte Cristo peaks. Or a several-day looping ramble through miles of subalpine trees and meadows on lonesome trails traveled by more deer and marmots than people. The loop must be carefully planned to end each day at campable ground—and water, which is scarce on the high ridges. After a spot at 1 mile on the abandoned road, the next for-sure water is at Spring Camp, 9 miles. However, early summer normally has snowbanks that cook up nicely in a pot.

Walk 2½ miles on a road converted to trail. Enter forest on a true trail and climb a sometimes muddy 1½ miles to Curry Gap, 4000 feet, and a junction with the Quartz Creek trail. Go left on Bald Eagle trail No. 650, climbing to the 5200-foot level of 5668-foot Bald Eagle Mountain and the turnaround for day-hikers. Dig out the lunch stuff and soak in the views of Pride Basin and the glaciers on the north sides of Kyes, Monte Cristo, and Cadet Peaks.

For the loop, pick up your pack and begin the ups and downs, past Long John Camp (often dry) at 8 miles from the road and Spring Camp at 9 miles. The trail then climbs within a few yards of the crest of 5946-foot June Mountain. Be sure to take the short sidetrip to the summit for views of Sloan Peak, Monte Cristo peaks, Glacier Peak, valleys, and forest. The tread on the north side of June Mountain may be covered by steep, hard snow. Take care.

At 12½ miles is a junction. The trail to the right continues 3 miles to Dishpan Gap and the Pacific Crest Trail. Go left on trail No. 652, dropping 500 feet, and at 14 miles reach 5500-foot Upper Blue Lake, usually frozen until mid-August; the best camps are near the upper lake.

From Upper Blue Lake the trail climbs 500 feet onto Pilot Ridge for 5 miles of some of the finest ridge-walking in the North Cascades.

Alpine flower field from Pilot Ridge

Finally the trail leaves the ridge and drops 3000 feet in an endless series of short, steep switchbacks to a ford and joins North Fork Sauk River trail No. 649, at 11½ miles from Upper Blue Lake reaching Sloan Creek Campground, 24 miles from the start.

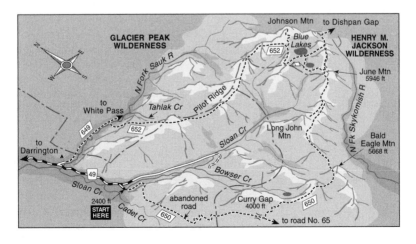

25 | BEDAL BASIN

Round trip: 6 miles
Hiking time: 6 hours
High point: 5000 feet
Elevation gain: 2200 feet
Hikable: July through October
Map: Green Trails No. 111 Sloan Peak
Current information: Ask at Darrington Ranger Station
  about trail No. 705

Driving directions: Drive Road No. 530 through Arlington to Darrington and go right on the Mountain Loop Highway (road No. 20). Drive 17.3 miles (0.8 mile beyond the North Fork Sauk River bridge) and turn left on road No. 4096 for 3 miles to its end and very limited parking, elevation about 2800 feet. Locate trail No. 705 on the uphill side of the road.

Lovely and lonesome alpine meadows beneath the towering south wall of Sloan Peak. The long-abandoned miners' trail gets limited maintenance by volunteers, is rough and sketchy, and is recommended only for experienced hikers who don't mind sweating a bit for the sake of solitude. Don't panic if there are half a dozen cars at the trailhead, which is also the start of a

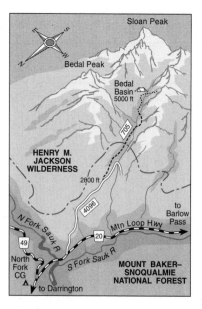

climbing route for Sloan Peak. (Climbers are not dangerous if you do not feed them.)

The trail gains altitude steadily, alternating between cool forest and sun-hot avalanche tracks choked with ferns, salmonberry bushes, and a spicing of nettles. Occasionally the Forest Service sends a brushing crew up the lower trail, which thus is better walking some years than others. If a crew hasn't been along recently, be prepared to foot-probe blindly for the tread in shoulder-high greenery.

At 1½ miles, amid big trees beside the creek, is a campsite much used by Sloan climbers of years past. Cross Bedal Creek here—hopefully on a log. The way gentles out in a broad avalanche area of alder and vine maple and a gathering of tributaries. At 2 miles, recross the creek.

The trail becomes obscure (unless the Forest Service unexpectedly takes up the job started by Harry Bedal many decades ago). The route is steep, ascending an abrupt valley step. Faint tread gains a few hundred feet along the left side of the creek (now quite small), crosses to the right side, and— probably—vanishes. If so, continue upward several hundred feet, cross the creek to the left side, and climb open timber. When the left side gets brushy, cross to forest on the right side and ascend huckleberry slopes to a collapsed mine with a stream flowing from the mouth. About 100 feet higher, rediscover the faint trail, which contours right, into open meadows at the lip of the basin, 5000 feet.

Above is the wall of Sloan. Monster boulders fringe the heather-and-flower floor of the basin. Near a great block of rock on the right side of the meadow are rotten logs of Harry Bedal's cabin, which along about 1940 succumbed to the crushing winter snows. Splendid camps all around. From the pass at the basin head are broad views.

Remains of Harry Bedal's cabin

26 | GOAT LAKE

Round trip: 10 miles
Hiking time: 5 hours
High point: 3161 feet
Elevation gain: 1280 feet
Hikable: Mid-June through October
Map: Green Trails No. 111 Sloan Peak
Current information: Ask at Darrington Ranger Station about trail No. 647

Driving directions: Drive Highway 92 from Everett to Granite Falls. Drive through the town and go left on the Mountain Loop Highway (road No. 20). Pass the Verlot Visitors Center and 20 miles beyond reach Barlow Pass. Drive toward Darrington and at 3.5 miles from the pass, turn right on Elliott Creek road No. 4080 and drive 0.8 mile to the trailhead parking lot and Elliott Creek trail No. 647, elevation 1900 feet.

A subalpine lake beneath cliffs and glaciers, a popular destination with hikers of all ages. Wander beside clear, cold water, investigate artifacts of long-ago mining, and admire snow-fed waterfalls frothing down rock walls. The trail (foot travel only) partly traces the route of a wagon road dating from the late nineteenth century.

There is a choice of two trails. The distance is the same. To the right, The Lower Trail, by far the more interesting, switchbacks down in forest to the raging waters of Elliott Creek and heads upstream. The Upper Trail, the easiest and recommended for beginners, follows an abandoned logging road shaded by young alder trees. At 3½ miles the trails unite and the

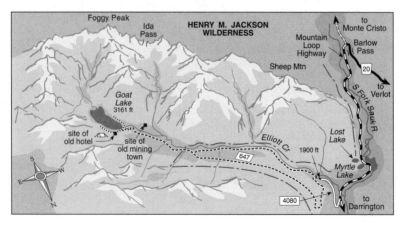

A refreshing dip in Goat Lake

way follows the all-but-vanished route of a wagon road that once served the mining settlement and hotel near Goat Lake.

At approximately 4 miles from the parking area the trail enters the Henry M. Jackson Wilderness. At 4½ miles the trail leaves the wagon road, steepens, and switchbacks upward, reaching the outlet of Goat Lake at 5 miles, elevation 3161 feet.

For an interesting sidetrip, at 4½ miles, where the old wagon route diverges rightward from the trail, cross Elliott Creek to the decrepit remains of a mining settlement. The wagon route then switchbacks and in roughly ½ mile recrosses the creek on risky remnants of a bridge to meet the trail.

Enjoy the views of Foggy Peak. Prowl relics of what was, in the late nineteenth century, a bustling town. In summer sunshine, take a brisk swim.

Beyond the outlet is a nice spot to picnic. The trail continues left around the shore, eventually disappearing in alder and vine maple. On a rocky knoll before the brush is a particularly fine place to sit and stare and eat lunch before going home.

Because campers have overused the lakeshore areas, these are now restricted to picnicking. At the old hotel site are four to six campsites on a knoll above the outlet. Along Elliott Creek is a spacious group campsite; enquire at the ranger station. Fires are prohibited.

27 | GOTHIC BASIN

Round trip from Barlow Pass: 9 miles
Hiking time: 9 hours
High point: 5000 feet
Elevation gain: 2600 feet
Hikable: Late July through early October
Maps: Green Trails Nos. 111 Sloan Peak, 143 Monte Cristo
Current information: Ask at Darrington Ranger Station
about trail No. 724

Driving directions: Drive Highway 92 from Everett to Granite Falls.
Drive through the town and go left on the Mountain Loop Highway
(road No. 20). Pass the Verlot Visitors Center and 20 miles beyond reach
Barlow Pass. Elevation 2360 feet.

A glacier-gouged basin designed for wandering. Rounded buttresses
polished and scratched by ice, sparkling ponds in scooped-out rock, an
arctic-barren cirque lake, loud waterfalls, meadow nooks, old mines, ore
samples, and views of Monte Cristo peaks.

From 1909 to 1912 the Northwest Mining Company operated a 7000-
foot aerial tram from Weden House to a mine just below the basin lip. Little
evidence is left except a few bits of rusty iron, some rotten wood, and the
trail. For years after the railroad fell into disuse, the headwaters of the
South Fork Sauk reverted to wildness. Then, in the 1940s, the American
dream of getting everywhere by car produced a road to Monte Cristo. As
a day-after-Christmas present to pedestrians, in 1980 the Sauk River
washed out long stretches of the road. (In the destruction of silly roads is
the preservation of wilderness.)

Walk the Monte Cristo road 1 mile to the crossing of the Sauk River and

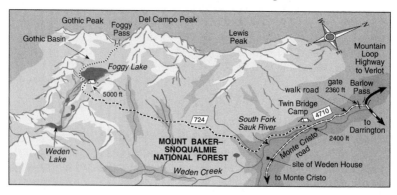

Small tarn on the side of Gothic Peak

just before the crossing find the trailhead on the right-hand side, behind an outhouse, elevation 2400 feet. The miners' trail started from Weden House, ¼ mile farther, but keeping a bridge over the braided channels was nigh impossible. In 1983, therefore, volunteers led by Will Thompson built a path ½ mile along the riverbank to intersect the old trail. Since that time the Forest Service has improved the tread.

The sturdy miners didn't waste effort on switchbacks and the trail is steep all the way. At 1½ miles is a series of three streams rushing down slot gorges possibly snow-filled and dangerous until early August; here, too, are flowers, a mine, and views across Weden Creek to Silvertip Peak. The trail enters brush, the tread gets skimpy and requires some careful walking, and the grade continues to be grueling. "King Kong's Showerbath" demands a halt amid unpleasantness for refreshment. The Consolidated Mine invites a sidetrip. After an especially straight-up and rock-scrambling stretch, the way emerges into a final ½ mile of heather and flowers, traversing the valley wall on meadow shelves.

At 3 miles, 5000 feet, the trail cuts through the ridge into Gothic Basin and ends in a meadow among buttresses. There is a good campsite here and many others throughout the basin. Wood is too scarce to burn; bring a stove or eat cold.

Now, explorations. In the lower basin are flower gardens, artifacts of old-time (and as recent as 1969) prospecting, waterfall gorges, and views down to Weden Creek and across to the Monte Cristo group. Especially fascinating are the rocks: limestone, sandstone, conglomerate, granite, and iron-red mineralized zones, all plucked and polished by the ice, the dominant brownish limestone weathered into oddly beautiful forms. Follow the streambed or the buttress crest 300 feet higher to fish-free Foggy (Crater) Lake, in a solemn cirque under Gothic and Del Campo Peaks. Scramble slabs and talus and blossoms to 5500-foot Foggy Pass between Gothic and Del Campo for higher views.

28 | SILVER LAKE AND TWIN LAKES

Round trip from Barlow Pass to Silver Lake: 11 miles
Hiking time: 8 hours
High point: 4350 feet
Elevation gain: 2000 feet
Hikable: July through October

Round trip to Twin Lakes: 17 miles
Hiking time: 12 hours
High point: 5400 feet
Elevation gain: 3500 feet in, 1000 feet out
Hikable: July through October

Map: Green Trails No. 143 Monte Cristo
Current information: Ask at Darrington Ranger Station
about trail Nos. 708, 708A

Driving directions: Drive Highway 92 from Everett to Granite Falls. Drive through the town and go left on the Mountain Loop Highway (road No. 20). Pass the Verlot Visitors Center and 20 miles beyond reach Barlow Pass. Elevation 2360 feet.

Three beautiful lakes, especially lovely in fall colors. The nearest and easiest, Silver Lake, is tucked in a cirque of cliffs, waterfalls, and meadows. Twin Lakes, 3 grueling miles farther, are twin pools of deep blue beneath the great east face of Columbia Peak.

The authors don't want to hear any hikers whimpering about the December 26, 1980, flood that ripped up the road to Monte Cristo and forced them to walk 4 extra miles, each way. The Christmas flood was the best thing that's happened to this valley since the railroad shut down. The 4 miles now free of automobiles are the most scenic valley walk, forest walk, river walk in the area, with many excellent backpacker campsites, a terrific place to introduce little children to a life away from automobiles. Further, those 4 miles multiplied by two convert certain formerly mobbed day walks to uncrowded wildland backpacks.

Hike the Monte Cristo road 4 delightful miles to a junction. The left is to a campground. Take the right toward the Monte Cristo townsite, cross the Sauk River, and walk past the building to the trailhead, elevation 2800 feet, signed "Silver Lake."

The reconstructed trail climbs through a clearcut to wildland and, in 1½ miles, at 4350 feet, crosses Poodle Dog Pass. Here the Silver Lake and the Twin Lakes trails diverge.

Twin Lakes trail above a sea of fog

For Silver Lake, go right from the pass ¼ mile to the shore, 4260 feet. Camping is permitted but no fires; bring a stove. For the best views and picnics, cross the outlet and climb open slopes 700 feet to a shoulder of Silvertip Peak. Look down Silver Creek toward Mineral City and beyond Silver Lake to the Monte Cristo peaks. In season, graze blue fruit.

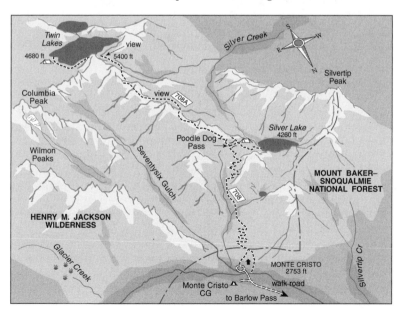

Silver Lake and Silver Peak

For Twin Lakes, go left on a boot-beaten track that follows an old miners' trail. The way is strenuous and rugged, gaining (and partly losing) 1500 feet in the 2½ miles to a viewpoint 650 feet above the lakes. Though the route is well defined it would be easy to lose in snow, so don't go before August. In the first mile, the up-down trail rounds a ridge with views out Silver Creek to logging roads. After dropping to pass under a cliff, at about 2 miles it climbs to a viewpoint over the deep hole of Seventysix Gulch to Wilmon Spires.

Walk on—and scramble along, above cliffs—the ridge crest. Some 150 feet before the highest point of the ridge the trail contours right toward an obvious pass, and at 2½ miles it reaches the view of the lakes, elevation 5400 feet, far enough for most hikers. Make a wrong turn here and you're in cliffs. To reach the lakes go right, descending to the obvious pass and then following the trail down a wide terrace to the lakes. Campsites are plentiful; no fires.

29 | GLACIER BASIN

Round trip from Barlow Pass: 13½ miles
Hiking time: 8 hours
High point: 4500 feet
Elevation gain: 2200 feet
Hikable: July through October
Map: Green Trails No. 143 Monte Cristo
Current information: Ask at Darrington Ranger Station
about trail No. 719

Driving directions: Drive Highway 92 from Everett to Granite Falls.
Drive through the town and go left on the Mountain Loop Highway
(road No. 20). Pass the Verlot Visitors Center and 20 miles beyond reach
Barlow Pass. Elevation 2360 feet.

Meadows and boulders, flowers and snowfields, cold streams for wading
and soft grass for napping, all in a dream basin tucked amid fierce peaks.

Until the flood of December 26, 1980, this was so short and popular a
hike any observer could plainly see the eventual total devastation of the
pristinity. The only salvation in sight was that popularity was generating
unpopularity. Now the hike is long—too long for a rational day or even a
relaxed weekend—and more glorious than it's been since the 1940s, when
the automobile first poked its nose into this valley. It would be a mad, mad
world that reopened the road to Monte Cristo and thus rejected Mother
Nature's gift.

Walk the road, noting the many excellent spots to camp by the river.
Introduce children to wilderness, or basecamp here for day hikes to high
country. At 4 miles the road splits; the left fork goes to a campground. Go
right, on the main drag through Monte Cristo, past the sites of hotels, brothels,

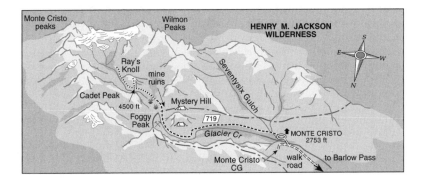

Glacier Basin

and saloons. The road–trail continues 1 more mile to the end, now a scenic campsite.

The "true" trail commences at a moderate grade in open greenery but quickly plunges into Sitka (slide) alder and Alaska cedar and tilts straight up. Stop for a rest on a rock outcrop above a magnificent waterfall before tackling the next stretch—the worst, in sunny summertime blisteringly hot and fly-bedeviled. The "trail" is so eroded by years of snowmelt and boots that, were it not for the alder handholds, the rock slabs and mud walls would require mountaineering equipment. Going up, think how bad it's going to be coming *down*. But there's only ½ mile of the worst (an hour up, an hour down). The track then eases out in a gulch filled with talus, snow, and whistling marmots.

The difficulties are not quite over. When the water is high the trail is flooded and hikers must scramble over boulders. At 4500 feet, 2½ miles from the Monte Cristo townsite, with startling abruptness the way opens into a basin—the meandering creeks, the flat fields of grass and blossoms, and the cliffs and glaciers of Cadet and Monte Cristo and Wilmon Peaks, the sharp thrust of Wilmon Spires.

What to do now? Sit and look, have lunch, watch the dippers. Or roam among boulders and wade sandy creeks and maybe organize a snowball fight. Or climb scree slopes to explore old mines. Or take a loitering walk to Ray's Knoll (named in memory of climber Ray Rigg) and views over the basin and down the valley. Scramblers can continue up an easy gully to a higher cirque with glaciers, moraines, waterfalls, and broader views.

But please be kind to the basin meadows. Walk softly. And camp not in the flower fields but on a flat area partway up tree-covered Mystery Hill, to the right as you enter the basin. No fires; eat sandwiches and yogurt.

30 | GOAT FLATS

Round trip: 9½ miles
Hiking time: 6 hours
High point: 4700 feet
Elevation gain: 2000 feet
Hikable: Late July through October
Maps: Green Trails Nos. 109 Granite Falls, 110 Silverton
Current information: Ask at Darrington Ranger Station
about trail No. 641

Driving directions: Drive Highway 92 from Everett to Granite Falls.
Drive through the town and go left on the Mountain Loop Highway
(road No. 20). In 7 miles go left on paved road No. 41, signed "Tupso
Pass." At 0.8 mile, pavement ends at a junction; keep left, passing several less-used sideroads. At 11 miles, pass the Meadow Mountain trail
(an alternate but longer route). At 17.2 miles find the trailhead at a wide
spot in the road, elevation 2900 feet.

The rock spires and ice fields of Three Fingers Mountain stand virtually at
the west edge of the North Cascades, rising above lowlands and saltwater
(the Whulge, to use the name given Puget Sound by the Original Residents), prominent on the skyline from as far away as Seattle. On a ridge of
the mountain are the lovely alpine meadows of Goat Flats, the most beautiful in the Verlot area. Once upon a time a great network of trails linked
the North and South Forks of the Stillaguamish River. Now most of the
forestland is chopped up by logging roads, the trails ruined or abandoned
or neglected. The hike to Goat Flats follows a small remnant of the old pedestrian network.

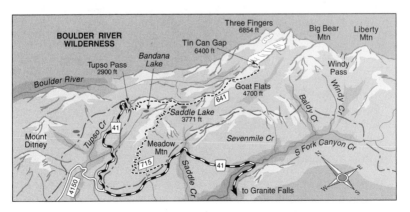

Trail No. 641 is a classic example of how tread can be completely worn out by the combined efforts of hiking feet and running water. The 2½ miles to Saddle Lake are all roots and rocks and gullies, such slow walking that to do them in less than 2 hours is to risk twisted ankles and broken legs. But take the better with the bitter; improving the trail would increase hiker traffic at Goat Flats, already severely overused. So walk carefully, slowly, blessing the roots and rocks and gullies or at least stifling your curses.

At 3771 feet, just across the outlet of Saddle Lake, is a junction with the Meadow Mountain trail and campsites. Go left for Three Fingers and Goat Flats, ascending steep slopes in forests to rolling meadows, acres and acres of blueberries and heather, broken by groves of subalpine trees and dotted with ponds. One in particular, several hundred feet below the trail, offers an excellent camp.

Some 2¼ miles from Saddle Lake the trail enters the meadow plateau of 4700-foot Goat Flats. Near the center is a historic artifact, anciently a patrol cabin, now just a pile of logs. The meadows are paying the price of beauty, suffering badly from trampling. Visitors will want to leave the trail to pick blueberries and seek viewpoints but, as much as possible, should keep to beaten paths. Camping would better be done along the ridge before the flats, and if done here, must be at existing sites. Fires are prohibited everywhere on the route.

Goat Flats and Three Fingers shrouded in clouds

Three Fingers Lookout perched on a narrow bit of cliff

For most hikers the flats are far enough, offering a close-up view of the cliffs and ice of Three Fingers, looks south to Pilchuck, north to White-horse and Mount Baker, west to the Whulge and the Olympics. Campers get the best: sunsets on peaks and valleys, farm and city lights in the far-below lowland night, a perspective on megalopolis and wildness.

For hikers who want more, the trail goes on, traversing meadows and then climbing steeply up a rocky basin to 6400-foot Tin Can Gap, overlooking what the USGS recently has named the Queest-Alb Glacier (wherever that came from). From here a climbers' route drops on steep snow to the glacier, returns to the ridge, and ascends to the base of the pinnacle of the 6854-foot South Peak of Three Fingers, atop which is perched a lookout cabin built in the 1930s. The pinnacle is mounted by a series of ladders. In order to build the cabin the Forest Service dynamited a platform on the summit; tradition says the original summit never was climbed before it was blown away. Tradition also says one lookout was so stricken by ver-tigo he had to telephone Forest Service supervisors to come help him down the ladders. Hikers will not want to go beyond Tin Can Gap.

31 | HEATHER LAKE

Round trip: 4½ miles
Hiking time: 4 hours
High point: 2600 feet
Elevation gain: 1200 feet in, 200 feet out
Hikable: June to November
Map: Green Trails No. 109 Granite Falls
Current information: Ask at Darrington Ranger Station
about trail No. 701

Driving directions: Drive Highway 92 from Everett to Granite Falls.
Drive through the town and go left on the Mountain Loop Highway (road
No. 20). One mile past the Verlot Visitors Center go right on Mount Pilchuck
road No. 42 and drive the 1.2 miles to the trailhead, elevation 1400 feet.

There was a time when this little lake, though just barely subalpine, was
the place where Scout troops from miles around learned to shiver out
mountain nights on the cold, hard ground, and to slap mosquitoes and
burn oatmeal and fall in creeks. In those days, too, it was (and maybe still
is) the most popular outdoor ice-skating rink in the county, thronged in
early winter weeks when the temperature stays well below freezing and
the snow hasn't started to pile up.

Among the attractions was the cirque wall plucked from the substance
of Mount Pilchuck. Another was the fan of avalanche snow below the cliffs,

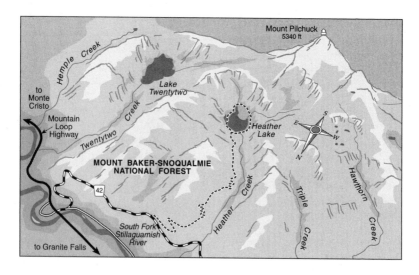

Mount Pilchuck

many a summer never melting out completely. And another was the cathedral of ancient cedars that began at the Stillaguamish River and continued nearly to the lake basin. Then the state superintendent of public instruction, ruler of "school lands" given the state upon admission to the Union, decided the kids needed gymnasiums more than trees and skinned old Nanga Pilchuck down practically to the huckleberry bushes.

But lo, those ancient cedars are again a star attraction. The chain saw was not perfected until better than a decade after the era of World War II. These giants were felled by two-man teams manning the long, limber crosscut saws known as "misery whips." To get above butt-swell and brush, the sawyers were aerialists, standing on springboards set in notches axe-cut in the trunk. Cedar is virtually impervious to rot. The notches therefore remain intact, puzzling children until explained—then in mind's eye they see the loggers balancing-bouncing on skinny boards high in the air, pulling misery whips back and forth and chewing snuice.

The tread of the old trail was moss-soft, a pleasure for the feet. As the trees went, so did the soil, and the path through the second growth has rude and rocky and rooty stretches, despite the occasional spreading of wheelbarrows of wood chips. Happily, as the cirque was neared the loggers lost interest, and from a 2600-foot high point the forest, if not awesome, becomes virgin the final ¼ mile down to the lake, 2395 feet.

Admire the cliffs that conceal Pilchuck's summit, 3000 feet above. A path circles the lake for a good look at a waterfall from snows up there. The avalanche fan arms snowball warriors well into summer or even fall.

Where is the heather? Not at the lake. But there are dippers on the shore. Varied thrushes trilling in the trees.

32 | MOUNT PILCHUCK

Round trip: 4 miles
Hiking time: 4 hours
High point: 5340 feet
Elevation gain: 2400 feet
Hikable: July to early November
Map: Green Trails No. 109 Granite Falls
Current information: Ask at Darrington Ranger Station
about trail No. 700

Driving directions: Drive Highway 92 from Everett to Granite Falls.
Drive through the town and go left on the Mountain Loop Highway
(road No. 20). One mile past the Verlot Visitors Center go right on
Mount Pilchuck road No. 42, at 1.3 miles pass the Heather Lake trailhead,
at 2 miles keep left and also at 4.7 miles. At 6.7 miles is the trailhead, a
bit short of the road-end, elevation 3100 feet.

A peak on the exact west edge of the range, prominent on the mountain
horizon seen from the lowlands, offering broad views west over farms,
towns, cities, and the Whulge (as the Original Residents called Puget
Sound) to the Olympics, and views east to the Cascades from Baker to
Rainier. Plus a museum on the summit, established by the Everett Mountaineers in 1989 in the preserved fire lookout cabin.

Though the trail is simple and safe, an alarming number of hikers stray,
stumble, or tumble and must be rescued. When the fog rolls in, or the trail
is lost in snow, or a "shortcut" dead-ends, the cliffs await.

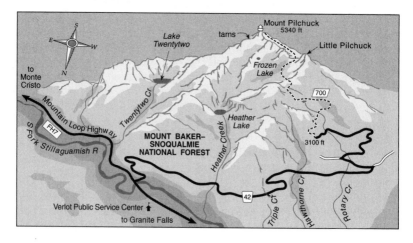

The trail ascends in gorgeous old-growth forest, skirts the edge of a 1977 clearcut, and switchbacks across the top of the ski slopes of the abandoned tow hill. The trail rounds the base of Little Pilchuck and climbs heather and ice-polished rock slabs to a saddle, where an insidious shortcut tempts. The true and proper and safe trail sidehills and then switchbacks ½ mile up southwest slopes to the summit.

Views from the restored lookout cabin are magnificent—lowland civilization in one direction, mountain wilderness in the other. Immediately below sheer cliffs is Frozen Lake, set in a snowy and rocky cirque. For those with leftover energy, an easy way trail descends 200 feet east along the ridge top to a group of picturesque tarns.

Lookout on top of Mount Pilchuck

33 | BALD MOUNTAIN

Round trip to viewpoint: 7½ miles
Hiking time: 4 hours
High point: 4100 feet
Elevation gain: 1700 feet
Hikable: July through October

Round trip to Walt Bailey Trail: about 20 miles
Hiking time: 12 hours
High point: 4500 feet
Elevation gain: 2100 feet
Hikable: July through October

Maps: Green Trails Nos. 110 Silverton, 142 Index
Current information: Ask at Darrington Ranger Station
about Bald Mountain trail

Driving directions: Drive Highway 92 from Everett to Granite Falls. Drive through the town and go left on the Mountain Loop Highway (road No. 20). At 4.6 miles past the Verlot Visitors Center go right on Schweitzer Creek road No. 4020, signed "Bear Lake Trail" and "Bald Mountain Trail." At 2.3 miles from the highway turn right on road No. 4021, signed "Bald Mountain." In 1.5 miles more, go left on road No. (4021)016 for 0.2 mile. At about 4 miles from the Loop Highway reach a large Department of Natural Resources sign and parking lot, elevation 2400 feet.

A fine, high route traverses the 7-mile ridge separating Sultan Basin and the South Fork Stillaguamish River. Walk the complete way, partly in views of valleys, lakes, and peaks, and partly in deep forest. Or just visit the scenic climax—a dozen small lakes in huckleberry-heather meadows near the summit of 4851-foot Bald Mountain. This climax can also be attained from the Walt Bailey Trail (Hike 34). Two cars permit an excellent one-way trip.

Walk a road-become-trail a long 1 mile to the veritable trail, which proceeds from old clearcut into old virgin forest, much of the way on puncheon. At ¾ mile pass a sidetrail to Beaver Plant Lake, and in a scant mile reach a Y. The right fork goes a short bit to Upper Ashland Lake and camps. Keep left.

The trail climbs around the end of Bald Ridge in grand forest, at 3½ miles topping a 3950-foot saddle with views through the trees of Three Fingers, the Stillaguamish valley, and Clear Lake, directly below. At about 4 miles the trail, to pass under cliffs, switchbacks down and down 500 feet to the head of Pilchuck River; here is the first water since the lakes area. The

Island Lake from the Bald Mountain trail

lost elevation is regained and at about 6½ miles reaches a 4400-foot saddle under the 4851-foot highest peak of Bald Mountain. Here begin those promised meadows.

At 7½ miles is a fork. The left fork dead-ends at a clearcut. The right fork joins the Walt Bailey Trail, which drops a scant mile to Cutthroat Lakes, a dozen or more delightful tarns and ponds. Campsites are plentiful, but in late summer running water may be hard to find. The lakes are easier to reach on the Walt Bailey Trail (Hike 34).

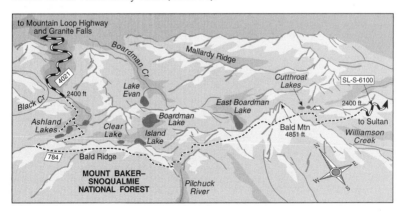

34 | WALT BAILEY TRAIL

Round trip: 8 miles
Hiking time: 5½ hours
High point: 4200 feet
Elevation gain: 1800 feet
Hikable: July to November
Maps: Green Trails Nos. 110 Silverton, 142 Index (trail not
on maps), and USGS Mallardy Ridge (trail not shown
on any map)
Current information: Ask at Darrington Ranger Station
about the Walt Bailey Trail

Driving directions: Drive Highway 92 from Everett to Granite Falls.
Drive through the town and go left on the Mountain Loop Highway
(road No. 20). At 7.1 miles beyond the Verlot Visitors Center go right on
Mallardy Ridge road No. 4030. At 1.5 miles turn right again on road No.
4032. Avoid sideroads that may look better than the main road and
drive to the road-end at 5.7 miles, elevation 3080 feet. Only two or
three cars can be parked at the trailhead. More space is 0.3 mile back.

A rough-and-tumble trail to the dozen-odd Cutthroat Lakes scattered about
heather-covered meadows on Bald Mountain. For a much longer trail to
Cutthroat Lakes, see Hike 33.

The trail was constructed entirely by volunteer labor, primarily seventy-
three-year-old Walt Bailey and his "young" friends Warren Rush and Ken
Countrymen (a former companion in the CCC). Lacking trail-building machines and dynamite, they took the path of least resistance; the ups and

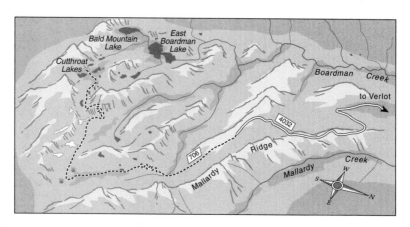

One of the Cutthroat Lakes

downs to avoid trees, rocky areas, and marshes are many and the tread on steep hillsides skinny. If a Forest Service trail crew had done the job the trail would be wide, have a relatively even grade, and little mud. However, it would have cost $200,000, which could take ten to fifteen years to squeeze from a tight budget.

The trail leaves overgrown clearcut for virgin forest, climbing steadily, steeply at times. At about 1 mile it drops a bit, crosses a small creek, and starts up again, often in bogs, to a 3680-foot high point of small heather and blueberry glades. The way drops 200 feet to a lovely meadow at 1¾ miles and continues down another 200 feet to pass under a cliff, crosses a rockslide, and starts up—and down—and up some more. About 4 miles from the road is the first of the Cutthroat Lakes, at 4200 feet. Others lie beyond, some with campsites having metal fire rings and toilets.

35 | WHAT VERLOT FORGOT

Round trip to Mallardy Ridge: 5 miles
Hiking time: 6 hours
High point: 3800 feet
Elevation gain: 1500 feet
Hikable: June through October
Map: USGS Mallardy Ridge (trail not shown)

Round trip to Marten Creek: 5 miles
Hiking time: 4 hours
High point: 2800 feet
Elevation gain: 1400 feet
Hikable: June through October
Map: USGS Silverton (trail not shown)

Round trip to Marble Gulch: 6 miles
Hiking time: 4 hours
High point: 4200 feet
Elevation gain: 1700 feet
Hikable: June through September
Map: USGS Silverton (trail not shown)

Current information: Ask at Darrington Ranger Station

Driving directions, Mallardy Ridge: Drive Highway 92 from Everett to Granite Falls. Drive through the town and go left on the Mountain Loop Highway (road No. 20). At 7.1 miles beyond the Verlot Visitors Center go right on road No. 4030 for 6 miles to unmarked trail No. 705, located just where the road swings through a gap in the ridge, elevation 2800 feet.

Marten Creek trailhead: Drive the Mountain Loop Highway east 9.3 miles from the Verlot Public Service Center. A few feet beyond the Marten Creek bridge find Marten Creek trail No. 713, elevation 1415 feet.

Marble Gulch trailhead: Drive the Mountain Loop Highway to within 1 mile of Silverton and find a suitable place to ford.

Until the decades after World War II, a trail network of some 50-odd miles radiated from the South Fork Stillaguamish River—Canyon Creek, Coal Creek, Bear Creek, Boardman Lakes, Mallardy Ridge, Granite Pass, and Everett's Boy Scout camp at Kelcema Lake. Logging roads obliterated many miles. More were abandoned when no longer needed by forest patrolmen or by the miners (prospectors) who built many of them. Less than half the near-Verlot mileage remains intact. A curious person might ask why this is so, considering that the crowds swarming on the "official" trails of the Verlot vicinity make them so overcrowded that a person pausing to sniff a flower is liable to get trampled.

Are you in a mood to be peaceful and quiet? Try the three abandoned trails noted here. Solitude is 99.9 percent guaranteed.

Mallardy Ridge: Of a 14-mile loop that started and ended at the river, 2½ miles along the top of Mallardy Ridge survive.

Wiped out in places by clearcuts and never reestablished, the trail is easy to lose. If you do, go back and search. It is extremely important to stay on the correct track (the correct ridge!). After the final clearcut the way becomes surprisingly free of blowdowns and easy to walk, following ups and downs of the crest. Climb off the trail to high points to see Sperry and Vesper Peaks and the red-rock south wall of Big Four Mountain.

Sperry Mountain from Mallardy Ridge

Marten Creek: This surviving stretch of the old Granite Pass trail, which crossed to join the Kelcema Lake–Deer Pass trail, is a delightful walk through tall trees. The peaks tower. So does the brush!

The first mile is on an abandoned, extremely steep mining road. At 1½ miles the trees thin and brush fills the gaps. Salmonberry, thimbleberry, devils club, and vine maple grow waist high, shoulder high, and over your head. At about 2½ miles a small campsite beside Marten Creek is a good turnaround. The old mine apparently was across the creek, its secrets now guarded by jungle. At the valley head, Three Fingers Mountain can be seen poking its head over Granite Pass.

Marble Gulch: A tramway once carried ore from a mine at the headwaters of Williamson Creek up to and over Marble Pass and down to the Stillaguamish. The miners' trail began at Silverton and switchbacked under the tram to the pass, then proceeded 10 miles down to the Sultan River. Private property has blocked access from Silverton; a hiker therefore must wade the Stillaguamish River, only safely possible in late summer.

On the far side, scout around for the trail on the east side (left) of Marble Creek. Much of the way is a bushwhack; only bits and pieces of the original tread survive. The best views are a short way up the ridge above the pass.

36 | NORTH LAKE

Round trip: 7 miles
Hiking time: 6 hours
High point: 5070 feet
Elevation gain: 1500 feet in, 900 feet out
Hikable: Mid-July through September
Map: Green Trails No. 110 Silverton
Current information: Ask at Darrington Ranger Station
about trail No. 712

Driving directions: Drive Highway 92 from Everett to Granite Falls.
Drive through the town and go left on the Mountain Loop Highway
(road No. 20). Pass the Verlot Visitors Center and 15 miles beyond go
left on Coal Lake road No. 4060. Drive the 4.7 miles to its end at Independence–North Lake trail No. 712, elevation 3600 feet.

A steep and at spots difficult trail to heather meadows, tarns, and a lake
surrounded by forest, flowers, and cliffs. No wilderness protection carries
with it no wilderness restrictions, which may or may not enhance the wilderness experience.

A start on excellent tread soon deteriorates to huge boot-tripper roots
and shin-barking rocks. A loss of about 200 feet is made up, and then some,
in the 1 mile or so to Independence Lake, 3700 feet. Round the left shore to
campsites at the inlet. Select from the confusion of paths the North Lake
trail, which switchbacks steep slopes to the right, largely on tread almost

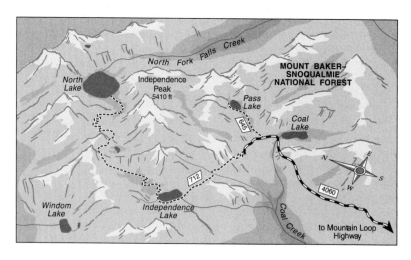

lost in a field of flowers. Elevation is gained relentlessly, 1300 feet in 1½ miles. A huge Alaska cedar with twin tops must be a record-holder, if considered a single tree. Across the valley is red-topped Devils Thumb.

The way eventually drops a bit, crosses a small meadow, and climbs to a divide overlooking Murphy Creek. Viewpoint paths go this way and that. Keep right and at 4800 feet enter heather meadows and pass two small tarns, one large enough to provide good camping. Another 200-foot climb tops a saddle overlooking North Fork Fall Creek valley. A bit farther is a view down to North Lake, 700 feet below. The trail works its way through the heather over, around, and under glacier-scoured cliffs and past small tarns and then descends 700 feet to the lakeshore, 4158 feet, 3½ miles from the road. Camping at the lake is very limited. The best places are near the tarns. About 100 yards before arriving at the lake a toilet is left of the trail.

Tarn on saddle above North Lake

37 | PERRY CREEK–MOUNT FORGOTTEN

Round trip to meadows: 8 miles
Hiking time: 7 hours
High point: 5200 feet
Elevation gain: 3100 feet
Hikable: Mid-June through October
Map: Green Trails No. 111 Sloan Peak
Current information: Ask at Darrington Ranger Station
about trail No. 711

Driving directions: Drive Highway 92 from Everett to Granite Falls. Drive through the town and go left on the Mountain Loop Highway (road No. 20). At 15.3 miles past the Verlot Visitors Center, go left on Perry Creek road No. 4063 for 1 mile to the road-end, elevation 2100 feet. Very limited parking.

A valley forest famed for its botanical richness, a small alpine meadow, a waterfall, and views of the impressive south wall of Big Four Mountain and the white volcano of Glacier Peak. Come early for flowers, come late for blueberries.

The trail traverses a steep hillside, now in forest, now in a grand display of ferns and flowers, boulder-hops a frenzied creek, and at 2 miles climbs above Perry Creek Falls. Pause to look over the top of the falls—but don't trust the handrail. A few feet farther the way crosses Perry Creek on boulders.

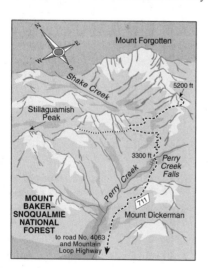

Elevation is gained steadily in old-growth timber, which at 3½ miles yields to a field of heather and lupine dotted by subalpine trees. The trail switchbacks up forests on the slopes of Mount Forgotten. Near the top of the switchbacks an abandoned trail branches off left, contouring then climbing ½ mile to the ridge top near Stillaguamish Peak and ending on a cliff above South Lake. The main trail goes right, enters lush, fragile meadows, and disappears at about 5200 feet, 4 miles.

Novice hikers should turn back here, well rewarded by views of Glacier Peak, seen at the head of the long valley of the White Chuck River, and closer views of Big Four, Twin Peaks, Mount Dickerman, and the long ridge of Stillaguamish Peak.

Experienced off-trail travelers can continue onward and upward a mile, climbing very steep heather slopes, then scrambling broken rock, to the 6005-foot summit of the peak and more views.

Perry Creek Falls

38 MOUNT DICKERMAN

Round trip: 8½ miles
Hiking time: 8 to 9 hours
High point: 5723 feet
Elevation gain: 3900 feet
Hikable: Late July through October
Map: Green Trails No. 111 Sloan Peak
Current information: Ask at Darrington Ranger Station
about trail No. 710

Driving directions: Drive Highway 92 from Everett to Granite Falls.
Drive through the town and go left on the Mountain Loop Highway
(road No. 20). At 16.3 miles past the Verlot Visitors Center, go left to the
large trailhead parking area almost opposite the Big Four Ice Cave parking area, elevation 1710 feet.

All too few trails remain, outside wilderness areas and national parks,
which begin in valley bottoms and climb unmarred forests to meadows.
The way to Dickerman is strenuous, but the complete experience of life
zones from low to high, plus the summit views, is worth every drop of
sweat.

Trail No. 710 doesn't fool around. Switchbacks commence in ¼ mile, up
and up and up through lovely cool forest; except perhaps in late summer,
several small creeks provide pauses that refresh. Tantalizing glimpses
through timber give promise of scenery above. A bit past 2 miles the tree
species of lower elevations yield to Alaska cedars and subalpine firs. Then

the forest thins as the trail traverses
under leaping cliffs. Near here, in a
sheltered hollow to the west, is a
snowmelt lakelet reached by a faint
path; camping is possible.

The next ½ mile passes through
one of the most popular blueberry
fields in the Cascades; grazing hikers may find progress very slow indeed. In the fall, photographers find
the blazing colors equally obstruc-
tive. Here, too, the horizons grow.

The final mile is somewhat
steeper, switchbacking meadows
to the broad summit, as friendly
a sack-out spot as one can find.

Abrupt cliffs drop toward Perry Creek forests, far below. Beyond are Still-aguamish Peak and Mount Forgotten. To the east rise Glacier Peak, the horn of Sloan Peak, and all the Monte Cristo peaks. Across the South Fork Stillaguamish River are rugged Big Four Mountain and the striking rock slabs of Vesper Peak.

Snow tracks after a late summer snowstorm

39 SUNRISE MINE TRAIL–HEADLEE PASS

Round trip: 5 miles
Hiking time: 5 hours
High point: 4600 feet
Elevation gain: 2500 feet
Hikable: August through September
Map: Green Trails No. 111 Sloan Peak
Current information: Ask at Darrington Ranger Station
about trail No. 707

Driving directions: Drive Highway 92 from Everett to Granite Falls. Drive through the town and go left on the Mountain Loop Highway (road No. 20). At 17.7 miles beyond the Verlot Visitors Center, go right on Sunrise Mine road No. 4065 for 2.3 miles to the road-end and trailhead, elevation 2100 feet. (The final ½ mile often is blocked by a slide.)

"Theirs not to reason why, Theirs but to do and die: Into the valley of Death rode the six hundred."

Judging by the avalanche debris, the narrow valley ascended by the Sunrise Mine trail must be bombarded by snow, rock, and broken trees from

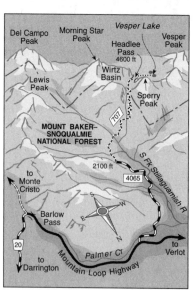

the first snowfall in October until all the snow has slid from surrounding peaks sometime after mid-July. Hikers may feel they *are* the Light Brigade as they trudge into the valley, but if they make sure not to do so until the heavy artillery has ceased for the summer, the risk is no greater than on any other steep, rough, and often snow-covered terrain. The happy demise of the Monte Cristo road has put that area's several popular trails much deeper in de facto wilderness, glory be; as a consequence, more and more hikers with limited time have been doing the Sunrise Mine trail. Best that they (you) be warned what to expect.

In the first ½ mile through forest

Headlee Pass trail

the root-and-rock trail crosses four creeks, including—on a slippery log—the incipient South Fork Stillaguamish River. The second ½ mile, still rough, switchbacks steeply up a fern-covered hillside, rounds a corner, and levels briefly as the trail enters the steep, narrow valley of death or whatever.

Avalanche fans may remain unmelted all summer, or even for years. Just because you're technically "on" a trail, don't be silly about steep, hard snow. Unless the way is clear, be satisfied with the valley view of peaks piercing the sky.

The miners who built the trail begrudged time that could be spent more entertainingly digging holes in the ground and sought to gain maximum elevation with minimum distance. No fancy-Dan 10-percent grade for *them*—the final mile, gaining 1200 feet to Headlee Pass, is 15 to 20 percent, ideal for hikers who also have no time to waste. The last 500 feet is in a slot gully where the grade has to be remade every summer by unpaid volunteers.

Headlee Pass, 4600 feet, is a thin cut in the ridge with rather limited views, confined by cliffs on three sides and snowy Vesper Peak to the west. The trail continues a short distance beyond the pass to an end at the edge of a giant rockslide; at one time it went to Sunrise Mine. A faint way trail crosses the slide to tiny Vesper Lake, often snowbound even on Labor Day.

40 | SULTAN BASIN DNR TRAILS

Round trip to Greider Lakes: 5 miles
Hiking time: 3 hours
High point: 2932 feet
Elevation gain: 1350 feet
Hikable: June through November

Round trip to Boulder Lake: 8 miles
Hiking time: 5 hours
High point: 3706 feet
Elevation gain: 2100 feet
Hikable: July through October

Map: Green Trails No. 142 Index

Driving directions: Drive US 2 to Sultan and on the east side of town, near the top of the hill, turn left on a road signed "Sultan Basin Recreation Area." From the west the sign is obscured, and there is no turn lane; if you are unable to get off the highway—safely—on the first pass, circle around and try again, cautiously.

Drive Sultan Basin road 13 miles to Olney Pass, entry to the Everett Watershed. Visitors please register here. Car camping is forbidden in the watershed, but trail camping is allowed from June 15 through October 15. However, be certain to use the toilet facilities so authorities will have no reason to prohibit backpackers in the future.

Proceed a few feet from the pass to a three-way junction. Take the middle road, No. 61, and drive past three access roads to the reservoir. The Greider Lakes trailhead is at 7 miles, elevation 1550 feet; and the Boulder Lake trailhead is at 8.3 miles, elevation 1600 feet.

Due to faulty mathematics when it entered the Union in 1889, Washington failed to receive the full land grant due from the federal government. The error belatedly was noticed and the U.S. Forest Service handed over a large tract in the Mount Pilchuck–Sultan River area. Even more belatedly, the state Department of Natural Resources commenced providing Forest Service-style recreational opportunities. Among the fruits of the new policy are two superb trails in the Sultan Basin leading to lovely subalpine lakes.

Greider Lakes: Two delightful cirque lakes ringed by cliffs. Excellent campsites at both.

Find the trail in a large parking area. The path immediately enters forest, passes a picnic area and nature trail, and starts switchbacking up a very steep hillside. The tread is rough with boulders, roots, and even some

Big Greider Lake

short stairways, which are not easy for short-legged people. At 2 miles, 2900 feet, reach Little Greider Lake and campsites. Cross the outlet stream and continue another ½ mile to Big Greider Lake and more campsites. Toilets at both lakes.

For greater views, go right near Big Greider Lake and climb 600 feet in ¾ mile to a dramatic viewpoint.

Boulder Lake: The boulders are on the far side of the lake. The near side—the trail side—is meadows and forests.

The trailhead, elevation 1600 feet, is on an abandoned, badly eroded old logging road, now trail, that gains 800 feet in 1 mile. The angle moderates on true though rough trail across a brushy rockslide to forest at 1½ miles. The tread improves as it switchbacks to a steep sidehill marsh at 3 miles, traversed on puncheon. At 4 miles is the lake, 3706 feet.

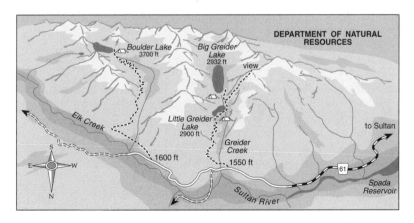

41 | MINERAL CITY

Round trip to Mineral City: 7 miles
Hiking time: 4 hours
High point: 2173 feet
Elevation gain: 800 feet
Hikable: Most all year

Maps: Skykomish Ranger District and Green Trails No. 143
Monte Cristo
Current information: Ask at Skykomish Ranger Station

Driving directions: From Seattle take US 2 east to the Index exit. Go
9.2 miles up the Index–Galena Road and just past the Howard Creek
bridge take a left on road No. 6330, cross over the North Fork Skykomish bridge, and in 0.1 mile go right on Snohomish County Mine-to-
Market Road No. 6335. It is possible to drive another 1.5 miles, but
between 0.2 mile and 0.6 mile the road is badly eroded and passable
only to four-wheel-drive vehicles. A deep wash stops cars 600 feet from
a barricade that marks the road-end, elevation 1400 feet.

Walk a road, gated by a perpetual rock slide, to the site of once-prosperous
Mineral City, which boasted two hotels. *Note:* The rock slide may be active
and dangerous, and all the bridges are rotting and could collapse. Take this
hike at your own risk.

At the road-end, the way turns into a trail and shortly enters a massive
two-part rock slide. Landowners of the numerous claims along the way
have scratched a thin tread across the slides that changes from year to year.

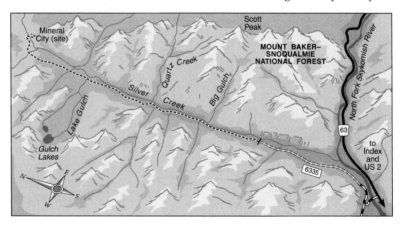

Old mine shaft along Silver Creek

Except for a few blowdowns to climb over, and the rotting bridges, beyond the second slide the old roadbed is a joy. The way is in sound of the deep Silver Creek gorge and mostly in sight. At 3.5 miles reach the site of Mineral City. There is nothing left of the hotels and mill that once stood at Mineral City. However, it makes a good campsite. The old trail that continued on to Poodle Dog Pass is brushed in.

Partly in Henry M. Jackson Wilderness

42 | BLANCA LAKE

Round trip: 8 miles
Hiking time: 6 to 8 hours
High point: 4600 feet
Elevation gain: 2700 feet in, 600 feet out
Hikable: July through October
Map: Green Trails No. 143 Monte Cristo
Current information: Ask at Skykomish Ranger Station
about trail No. 1052

Driving directions: Drive east from Everett 35 miles on the Stevens
Pass Highway (US 2) to the Index junction and go left on the North Fork
Skykomish River road 14.5 miles to a four-way junction. Turn left on
road No. 63 (easy to miss) for 2 miles and turn left again to the Blanca
Lake trailhead sign and parking area, elevation 1900 feet.

The rugged cliffs of Goblin (also called Kyes), Monte Cristo, and Columbia
Peaks above, the white mass of the Columbia Glacier in the upper trough,
and the deep waters of ice-fed Blanca Lake filling the lower cirque. A steep
forest climb ending in grand views, with further explorations available to
the experienced off-trail traveler. This is a popular trip for day-hiking, but
camping is too limited and cramped to be recommended.

Trail No. 1052 immediately gets down to the business of grinding out
·elevation, relentlessly switchbacking up and up in forest. At 3 miles the
way reaches the ridge top at 4600 feet, the highest point of the trip, and at
last enters the Henry M. Jackson Wilderness. In a few hundred yards is
shallow little Virgin Lake, amid meadows and trees of a saddle on the very
crest. Acceptable camping here for those who don't wish to carry packs
farther, but no water in late summer.

Now the trail goes down, deteriorating to a mere route as it sidehills
through trees with glimpses of blue-green water, dropping 600 feet in 1

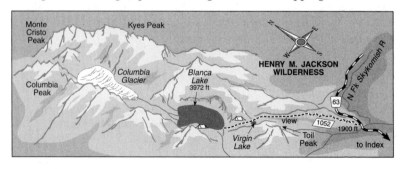

Clockwise from upper left: Pacific Crest Trail near White Mountain; Glacier Peak and Image Lake; Glacier Peak from Green Mountain; marmot

Overleaf: Cub Lake and 8860-foot Dome Peak

Lyman Lake and Chiwawa Mountain, Spider Gap on the left

Above: Sloan Peak and wild flowers; *right:* Glacier Basin

Dome Peak and deer from near White Rock Lake

Flower garden

Twin Lakes near Monte Cristo

Above: Cutthroat Lake near Granite Falls; *right:* small falls at Silver Lake

Above: Silver Peak from Twin Lakes trail; *left:* Fortune Pond

Above right: Silver Lake near Monte Cristo; *below:* mountain daisy

Above: Pacific Crest Trail near Kodak Peak; *left:* tiger lily

Meadows along the Pacific Crest Trail near Indian Head Peak

Above: Moon setting over Buck Mountain; *below:* Lyman Glacier; *right:* Ice River Falls

Napeequa River Valley from Little Giant Pass

Air view of Columbia Glacier, Blanca Lake, and Kyes Peak

mile and reaching the 3972-foot lake at the outlet. Relax and enjoy the wind-rippled, sun-sparkling lake, ¾ mile long, the Columbia Glacier, the spectacular peaks. Do not camp on the lakeshore. A bench to the right has a site and by crossing the outlet stream and following a boot-beaten path toward the head of the lake several more can be found. No fires permitted; carry a stove.

Experienced hikers can explore the rough west shore to the braided stream channels and waterfalls and flowers at the head of the lake. For a spectacular view of lake and mountains, hike to the top of 5128-foot Toil Peak, the first of two wooded bumps between Virgin Lake and Troublesome Mountain. On the highest point of the trail above Virgin Lake find a faint path traversing heather meadows southward, climbing, at times steeply, to the summit.

43 WEST CADY RIDGE

Round trip to viewpoint: 8 miles
Hiking time: 5 hours
High point: 4761 feet
Elevation gain: 2200 feet
Hikable: Mid-June through September

Round trip to Bench Mark Mountain: 16 miles
Hiking time: Allow 2 to 3 days
High point: 5816 feet
Elevation gain: 3300 feet
Hikable: Mid-July through late September

Maps: Green Trails Nos. 143 Monte Cristo, 144 Benchmark
Current information: Ask at Skykomish Ranger Station about trail No. 1054

Driving directions: Drive east from Everett 35 miles on the Stevens Pass Highway (US 2) to the Index junction and go left on North Fork Skykomish River road 14.5 miles to a four-way junction, just before the North Fork bridge. Turn left and drive 4.6 miles on road No. 63 to West Cady Ridge and Quartz Creek trailheads, elevation 2500 feet. In a few years the road will be closed at this point and the North Fork trailhead will also start here.

A splendid stroll in early summer through miles of mountain meadows and groves of subalpine firs and mountain hemlocks. If snow permits, go all the way to where once was the Bench Mark Mountain Lookout, at 5816 feet. If not, as in springtime, do as much as lingering winter permits and delight in the first burst of flowering.

Find West Cady Ridge trail No. 1054 on the south side of the road

Ripe blueberries

Harvesting blueberries

and head upstream, cross the river on a sturdy bridge, and start climbing virgin forest. Long switchbacks change to short ones as the trail leaves the big trees and ascends the spine of a narrow ridge to a saddle at 3600 feet. The trail gains another 600 feet on a broad ridge crest, through fields of waist-high huckleberries (grazing begins in late August). The views already are sensational, but don't give up yet. At about 4 miles from the car is a heathery 4761-foot high point in views north to Columbia and Kyes Peaks, northeast to Glacier Peak, and west to Jacks Pass and rugged peaks of the Eagle Rock Roadless Area. Enjoy for an hour or a whole day.

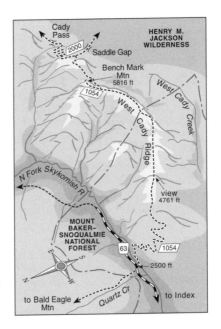

But the fun has only begun. The trail follows the ridge crest eastward, 4 more miles of meadows and forest, each high point adding more views, climaxing on 5816-foot Bench Mark Mountain.

44 | BENCH MARK MOUNTAIN LOOP

Loop trip: 23½ miles
Hiking time: Allow 2 to 3 days
High point: 5816 feet
Elevation gain: 4700 feet
Hikable: Mid-July through September
Maps: Green Trails Nos. 143 Monte Cristo, 144 Bench-mark
Current information: Ask at Skykomish Ranger Station about trail Nos. 1051, 1053, 1054, 2000

Note: There is a difficult river crossing on this trip. Unless the summer has been dry and the river is low, you may want to take Hike 45 instead.

Driving directions: Drive east from Everett 35 miles on the Stevens Pass Highway (US 2) to the Index junction and go left on the North Fork Skykomish River road 14.5 miles to the four-way junction just before the North Fork bridge. Turn left and drive 4.6 miles on road No. 63 to West Cady Ridge and Quartz Creek trailheads, elevation 2500 feet. In a few years the road will be closed at this point and the North Fork trailhead will also start here.

Even if the road is still open beyond here, this starting point is recommended because the 1.4 miles to the end, elevation 3000 feet, are barely drivable, if at all. If they are, loopers could unload packs there, drive 1.4 miles back to where the loop will end at West Cady Ridge trailhead, and walk the 1.4 miles back to the packs.

Climb virgin forest to the Pacific Crest Trail, amble relaxed and happy through a glory of flowers, and loop back down in fine old forest. Camp as many camp nights as you have to spare at a succession of magnificent to heavenly sites.

Hike North Fork trail No. 1051 to the junction at 1½ miles, 3200 feet, with Pass Creek trail No. 1053. Staying on the main trail, in 2½ miles more cross the river by boulder-hopping or logjam clambering. Both may be life threatening in high water, but survivors can hold prayers for the departed at a splendid campsite on the far bank, or a mile farther at a commodious camp in a huckleberry farm.

The way now turns up and up, to Dishpan Gap on the Pacific Crest Trail, 5600 feet, 7½ miles from the road. Here the easy ambling begins, 4 miles south in Trapp Family meadows to Wards Pass and Lake Sally Ann, Cady Pass, and at ½ mile past the pass, the end of the Pass Creek trail, 4200 feet. Continue on the Crest Trail 2¼ miles and at 4900 feet turn for home on

Mount Rainier from Bench Mark Mountain

West Cady Ridge trail No. 1054. A little way along is a steep snowfield that may not melt out until late July. A detour is then advisable to the highest point of the ridge, 5816-foot Bench Mark Mountain, and the views that in olden days a fire lookout scanned for smokes, and if there were none, filled his eyes with Sloan, Monte Cristo peaks, Glacier, Baker, and Rainier.

The 4 miles up and down meadows and parkland of West Cady Ridge will submerge memories of the Cascade Crest idyll. Then the ridge comes abruptly to an end and it's down, down you go in short switchbacks to the river road.

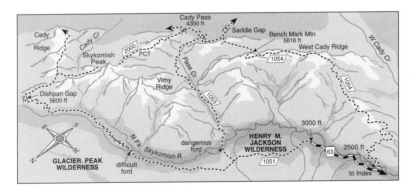

45 | DISHPAN GAP LOOP

Loop trip: 31 miles
Hiking time: Allow 3 days
High point: 5800 feet
Elevation gain: 5200 feet
Hikable: July through September
Map: Green Trails No. 144 Benchmark
Current information: Ask at Skykomish Ranger Station
about trail Nos. 1050, 650, 2000, 1054

Driving directions: Drive east from Everett 35 miles on the Stevens
Pass Highway (US 2) to the Index junction and go left on North Fork Sky-
komish River road 14.5 miles to a four-way junction, just before the
North Fork bridge. Turn left and drive 4.3 miles on road No. 63 to the
Quartz Creek–Cady Ridge trailheads, elevation 2500 feet.

Dishpan Gap rates four trips in this book. The flowers, views, and campsites are marvelous, though really no better than other loops. And this one
is longer. Ah, but easier on the mind. No near tragedies at river crossings,
no shuffling of cars, just roaming the ridges with a banjo on your knee. To
be sure, steep snowbanks may be a fright, even in late summer. But these
are, after all, mountains. If you lack an ice ax, stay down in the trees. Those
dainty little ski poles that "trekkers" use in the Himalaya don't cut it here.

The first leg of this loop follows Quartz Creek trail No. 1050 in woods

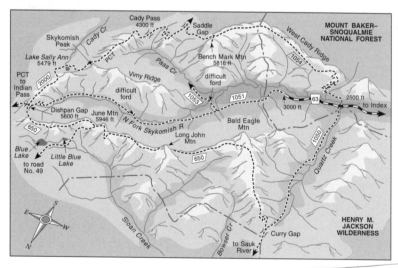

4½ miles to Curry Gap. Turn right on trail No. 650 toward Bald Eagle Mountain (Hike 24) and climb into ridge-top meadows. In 8½ up-and-down miles is a junction. The left fork drops to the two Blue Lakes and camping. Go straight ahead 3 miles to Dishpan Gap and the Pacific Crest Trail at 5600 feet, about 16 miles from the road.

The second leg heads south 4 miles on the Pacific Crest Trail (Hikes 44 and 62) through flower-bright meadows, past Wards Pass and Lake Sally Ann, and down into the timber of 4300-foot Cady Pass. From there the Crest Trail switchbacks in meadows toward Saddle Gap. A few feet shy of the gap turn right on West Cady Ridge trail No. 1054 (Hike 43) and hike 9 miles back to the starting point.

Pride Basin from Bald Eagle Mountain

46 EVERGREEN MOUNTAIN PENTHOUSE

Round trip: 2¾ miles
Hiking time: 3 hours
High point: 5587 feet
Elevation gain: 1300 feet
Hikable: August 10 (when the gate opens) through October
Map: Green Trails No. 143 Monte Cristo
Current information: Call Skykomish Ranger Station (phone (360) 677-2414) to ask about trail No. 1056 and the lookout rental

Driving directions: Drive east from Everett 35 miles on the Stevens Pass Highway (US 2) to the Index junction and go left on North Fork Sky-komish River road 14.5 miles to a four-way junction, just before the North Fork bridge. Turn left on North Fork Skykomish Road No. 63 to 2800-foot Jack Pass. (Or you can drive Beckler River road No. 65 to the pass.) From there take road No. 6550 for 1 mile and go left on road No. 6554. At 2.8 miles are Evergreen Creek and a gate that is kept closed until August 10 to protect nesting sites of the marbled murrelet. The road reaches the trailhead 9 miles from Jack Pass, at an elevation of 4250 feet.

Honeymoon (or whatever) in a penthouse amid flowers and an all-around view of wild peaks. Be warned: There's no elevator, it's a walk-up. No running water, either. In fact, no water. Carry a couple gallons or dehydrate. Built in 1935, the Evergreen Mountain fire lookout was abandoned in 1980 but somehow escaped being burned down by federal lawyers, who considered this species of structure an "attractive nuisance." From 1990 to 1997

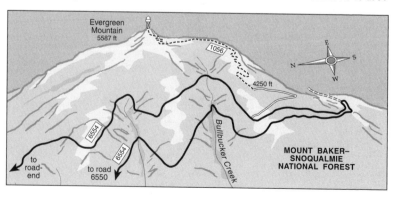

Evergreen Mountain

some 4600 man (youth) hours were devoted by Seattle Explorer Search and Rescue to repairing the building. It is now available for nightly rental to hikers.

The sunrises and sunsets are gorgeous. Gales are thrilling. Try to get a reservation for a five-star thunderstorm, the sort where the lookout used to put plugs in his ears and perch on an insulated stool, his feet off the floor, and watch the little cookstove glow cherry red from lightning strikes.

The trail is only a bit over 1¼ miles, substandard for our book, but gains enough elevation fast enough to get up a huff and a puff, what with carrying those gallons of water plus the watermelon and six-pack of root beer. Scout around for a snowfield to chill the root beer while you gaze that way to peaks of Columbia, Kyes, and Monte Cristo, but especially Glacier Peak (especially nice in the alpenglow), and other ways to the Eagle Rock Roadless Area (expected soon to become part of a new Sky Peaks Wilderness), to Daniels and Rainier, and to such a maze of peaks east that you don't have enough maps to identify them all.

The trail steeply ascends a skinny ridge ½ mile through a clearcut, now old (but wasn't there when we did our first *100 Hikes*), to the prelogging tread. At a scant 1 mile the trail vanishes in flowers as views expand to box the compass. The door of the lookout is locked. Do you have the key?

47 | BARCLAY AND EAGLE LAKES

Round trip to Eagle Lake: 8½ miles
Hiking time: 6 hours
High point: 3888 feet
Elevation gain: 1700 feet
Hikable: Late June through October
Map: Green Trails No. 143 Monte Cristo
Current information: Ask at Skykomish Ranger Station
about trail No. 1055

Driving directions: Drive east from Everett 41 miles on the Stevens
Pass Highway (US 2) to the town of Baring and go left on 635th Place
NE, cross railroad tracks, and go 4.3 miles on road No. 6024 to the trail-
head, elevation 2200 feet.

For many years Barclay Lake was among the most popular low-elevation
hikes in the Cascades, passing through pleasant old forest to the base of
the tremendous north wall of Mount Baring, a good trip in early spring
and late fall when higher country was deep in snow. The wall remains, and
the lake, but not much forest. Tragically, the walk to Barclay Lake no longer
deserves, by itself, inclusion in this book. However, there is still Eagle Lake,
amid trees, meadows, and peaks, offering a staggering cross-valley look at
the north wall of Baring, a legend among climbers and to date ascended
only once.

The trail, with minor ups and downs and numerous mud holes, meanders through what remains of the forest of Barclay Creek, in 1½ miles
reaching Barclay Lake, 2422 feet, and at 2¼ miles ending near the inlet
stream. Camping is possible at several spots along the shore. Enjoy the

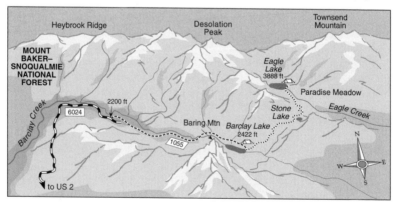

Paradise Lake

neck-stretching look up and up the precipice of 6123-foot Baring Mountain.

At the lake head, just where the trail leaves the water by a small campsite, find a meager, unsigned path climbing 1000 feet straight up steep forest. For a bit the way is on rockslide, then briefly levels and resumes climbing beside another rockslide. The grade abruptly flattens at a viewpoint above Stone Lake and contours to 3888-foot Eagle Lake. By the shore is a cabin, kept locked. For more views, and for meadows, an experienced roamer can scramble up the steep slopes of 5936-foot Townsend Mountain.

Now then. As you are sitting in Paradise Meadow nursing bruises and sprains and wiping sweat from your eyes, you may be hailed by a fisherman who is astounded at your suffering and stupidity, inasmuch as he is just an hour from his car, parked on a logging road up Eagle Creek. And you go home and write a letter demanding to know why this guidebook has put you through this ordeal. Well, what makes it an ordeal is not the steep climb, which enriches the wilderness experience, but learning a road is so near (though not by trail—it's a brush route). Why isn't the road gated, banning public vehicles, and thus placing Eagle Creek back in deep wilderness where it belongs?

48 | SCORPION MOUNTAIN

Round trip: 9 miles
Hiking time: 6 hours
High point: 5540 feet
Elevation gain: 2300 feet in, 300 feet out
Hikable: July through October
Maps: Green Trails No. 143 Monte Cristo, 144 Benchmark
Current information: Ask at Skykomish Ranger Station
  about trail No. 1067

Driving directions: Drive east from Everett 49 miles on the Stevens Pass Highway (US 2) to the town of Skykomish. Just 0.2 mile beyond town, turn left on Beckler River road No. 65. At 6.8 miles turn right on road No. 6520, once signed "Johnson Creek" and "Johnson Ridge Trail." At a junction 1.7 miles from the Beckler River road, keep straight ahead at a junction, and at 5.6 miles turn right on No. 6526 to its end, some 7 miles from the Beckler River, elevation 3600 feet. (Don't be confused by a spur road 0.3 mile from the road-end.)

Looking for views from an easy trail? A sociable family stroll? Scratch Scorpion. Even the access road, carved into a steep hillside stripped bare of trees, is difficult and mean, and there is no water except in your canteen. For solitude, of course, these are plus factors. Moreover, the logging didn't molest the fields of wildflowers that progress from yellow glacier lilies of snowmelt time to lupine and paintbrush of high summer. Peakful horizons, you bet. Physical fitness fanatics seeking a nice view—and a good sweat—will find Scorpion just what the aerobics manual prescribes.

Trail No. 1067 begins on ½ mile of abandoned road. Keep left at a switchback, reaching real trail at ¾ mile, on the ridge top. Windfalls obscure the

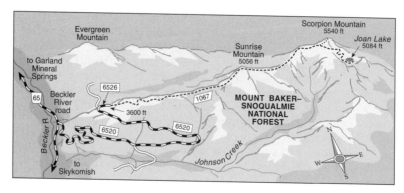

way but detouring is no problem. If the seldom-walked tread is lost, just follow the forested ridge top. Openings in the trees occasionally offer glimpses south of rocky 6190-foot Mount Fernow. At 2¼ miles the trail crosses the top of 5056-foot Sunrise Mountain, with a view of Glacier Peak, and drops about 300 feet before climbing nearly to the top of 5540-foot Scorpion Mountain at 4 miles. Leave the path at its highest point and ascend the ridge a few hundred feet to the summit's lush carpet of grass and flowers and a grand panorama of the Cascades.

The trail continues around the south shoulder of the mountain and drops 500 feet to tiny Joan Lake at 4½ miles, a popular mosquito rendezvous. Volunteers have partially reopened 5½ miles of an old trail from Scorpion Mountain to Captain Point and Scenic.

Johnson Ridge

49 A PEACH AND A PEAR AND A TOPPING (LAKES, THAT IS)

Round trip to Pear Lake: 15 miles
Hiking time: Allow 2 days
High point: 5300 feet
Elevation gain: 3200 feet in, 500 feet out
Hikable: July through October
Map: Green Trails No. 144 Benchmark
Current information: Ask at Skykomish Ranger Station
   about trail No. 1057

Driving directions: To approach from the east, drive US 2 east from Stevens Pass 19 miles and turn left to Lake Wenatchee. From the upper end of Lake Wenatchee, drive 6 miles on Little Wenatchee River road No. 65, turn left on road No. 6700, cross the river, and in 0.6 mile go right on road No. 6701, following the river upstream. In 4.7 miles turn left onto road No. (6701)400. At 4 miles past the junction with road No. (6701)400, find Top Lake trail No. 1506. From the more popular west, drive east from Everett 49 miles on the Stevens Pass Highway US 2 to the town of Skykomish. Just east of town turn north on Beckler River road No. 65. At 6.8 miles turn right and go 4.4 more miles on Rapid River road No. 6530 to Meadow Creek trail No. 1057, elevation 2100 feet.

Savor flower and heather gardens ringing three alpine lakes and a spatter of ponds along the Pacific Crest Trail. And if you feel the call for whipped cream on top, get that at a third lake with a full horizon of valleys and mountains.

Beginning in the Evergreen Mountain burn of 1967, now all silver snags and shrubbery and young trees, the trail gains almost 1000 feet switchbacking out of Rapid River valley. At about 1½ miles the burn is left and forest entered. The grade moderates and contours into Meadow Creek drainage, crossing

Bear paw print on the side of Fortune Pond

Upper Fortune Pond

the creek at 3 miles by hopping boulders (there aren't really enough). At 3¾ miles recross the creek and climb steeply from Meadow Creek into the West Cady Creek drainage. At 6½ miles reach the lower of the two Fortune Ponds, 4700 feet.

In another 1¼ miles, cross 5200-foot Frozen Finger Pass, between West Cady Creek and Rapid River, and drop to 4809-foot Pear Lake, there intersecting with the Pacific Crest Trail 8 miles from the car. Do not camp within 200 feet of the shores here or at Fortune Ponds. The meadows are so fragile, and so damaged, you really ought to sling a hammock in the trees. Peach Lake, at the same elevation over the ridge south, is best reached by sidehilling off-trail around the ridge end and below cliffs, passing narrow Grass Lake. Top Lake is attained via ½ mile more on the Crest Trail and another ½ mile on trail No. 1506. For the promised land of views, leave the trail at Fortune Ponds and ascend Fortune Mountain, 5903 feet.

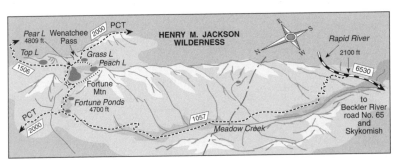

50 | LAKE VALHALLA

Round trip: 11 miles
Hiking time: 6 hours
High point: 5100 feet
Elevation gain: 1100 feet in, 400 feet out
Hikable: Mid-July through October
Map: Green Trails No. 144 Benchmark
Current information: Ask at Lake Wenatchee Ranger
Station about trail No. 2000

Driving directions: Drive US 2 to Stevens Pass, elevation 4061 feet, and park in the lot at the east end of the summit area. Find the trail between the utility substation and a green A-frame building.

North of Stevens Pass, the Pacific Crest Trail passes a succession of meadowy alpine lakes. First in line is Lake Valhalla, set in a cirque under the cliffs of Lichtenberg Mountain.

The way begins along the original grade of the Great Northern Railroad, used when trains went over the top of the pass; the right-of-way was abandoned after the Wellington Disaster and upon completion of the first Cascade Tunnel (predecessor of the present tunnel) early in the last century.

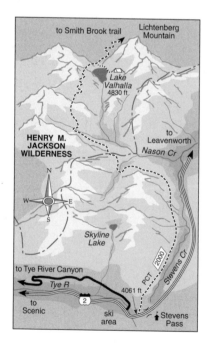

From the open hillside, views extend beyond the pass to ski slopes and down Stevens Creek to Nason Creek and far east out the valley. Below is the roar of highway traffic. In 1½ miles the gentle path rounds the end of the ridge and into the quieter drainage of Nason Creek.

The main trail descends a bit to cross a small stream, climbs a ridge, and at 3½ miles enters a basin of meadows and marsh, with a fine campsite. Staying east and below the Cascade Crest, the way ascends gently to a 5100-foot spur and drops to the rocky shore of the 4830-foot lake.

Heavily used camps crowd the

forest near the inlet. The best sites are near the outlet, where the terrain is less fragile. No fires are permitted, of course; carry a stove. For explorations, continue north on the Pacific Crest Trail (Hike 100), climbing heather meadows to the summit of 5844-foot Lichtenberg and broad views, or hike on as far as time and energy allow.

A much shorter (5½ miles round trip) but less scenic approach is via the Smith Brook trail (Hike 51), which joins the Pacific Crest Trail at Union Gap 1 mile from the road. The Crest Trail leads south from the Gap 1¾ miles to Lake Valhalla.

Lake Valhalla

51 | LAKE JANUS AND GRIZZLY PEAK

Round trip to Grizzly Peak: 17 miles
Hiking time: 6 to 8 hours
High point: 5597 feet
Elevation gain: 1500 feet in, 600 feet out
Hikable: Mid-July through October
Map: Green Trails No. 144 Benchmark
Current information: Ask at Lake Wenatchee Ranger
　Station about trail Nos. 1590, 2000

Driving directions: Drive US 2 east 4 miles from Stevens Pass and turn left on Smith Brook road No. 6700. Cross the Nason Creek bridge, turn left, and follow the road 3 miles toward Rainy Pass and the Smith Brook trailhead, elevation 3800 feet.

A beautiful alpine lake and a long ridge trail, sometimes in Western Washington and sometimes in Eastern Washington and sometimes straddling the fence. An easy but spectacular stretch of the Pacific Crest Trail. The trip can be done in a day, but at least a weekend should be planned—the lake is inviting and so is "looking around the next corner."

Climb 1 mile on trail No. 1590 to 4680-foot Union Gap and the junction with the Pacific Crest Trail. Turn right, dropping 600 feet down the west side of the crest to round cliffs of Union Peak, then regaining part of the elevation to 4146-foot Lake Janus, 2½ miles from the Gap.

The trail goes through pleasant forest in the far-off sound of Rapid River and the lake is everything it should be—sparkling water surrounded by meadows and tall trees and topped by the bright green slopes of 6007-foot Jove Peak. Numerous camps are available, but finding one vacant is a rare

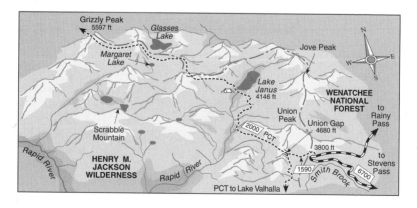

Glasses Lake and Heather Lake

chance on weekends. Forget wood fires; carry a stove or eat cold.

From the lake the trail enters forest on smooth and easy tread, climbs 1100 feet in 1½ miles to the Cascade Crest (good camps here), contours around the Eastern Washington side of a small hill, and ducks around a corner back to Western Washington, a process repeated frequently on the way to Grizzly Peak. Carry water; there's little to be found here.

Every turn of the crest-wandering trail offers new views. Look east down to Lake Creek and Little Wenatchee River drainage and across to nearby Labyrinth Mountain. Look north to Glacier Peak. Look west down to the Rapid River and out to peaks above the Skykomish. At 2½ miles from Lake Janus is a glimpse of Margaret Lake, some 400 feet below the trail. A scant ½ mile beyond is a view down to Glasses Lake and larger Heather Lake; this is a good turnaround point for day-hikers.

At about 5¼ miles from Lake Janus, the trail climbs within a few feet of the top of 5597-foot Grizzly Peak and more panoramas. The trail also goes close to the summit of a nameless peak with a view of Glacier Peak; succumbing to this temptation will lead to further temptations on and on along the Pacific Crest Trail.

52 | NASON RIDGE

One-way trip: 16 miles
Hiking time: Allow 2 to 3 days
High point: 6400 feet
Elevation gain: 4200 feet
Hikable: Mid-July through October
Map: Green Trails No. 145 Wenatchee Lake
Current information: Ask at Lake Wenatchee Ranger Station about trail No. 1583

Driving directions: The trip is best done with two cars. Leave one at the Snowy Creek trailhead and drive to the Round Mountain trailhead.

Snowy Creek trailhead: Drive US 2 east 4 miles from Stevens Pass and turn left on Smith Brook road No. 6700. Cross Rainy Pass and about 5 miles from the highway, at a major switchback, go straight ahead on road No. 6705 another 3.6 miles to a crossing of Snowy Creek and the trailhead, elevation 3531 feet.

Round Mountain trailhead: Drive US 2 east 17 miles from Stevens Pass to 0.3 mile beyond the Nason Creek Rest Area. Pass a driveway to a lodge and turn left on Butcher Creek road No.6910 (not signed but marked with a row of mailboxes). Cross Nason Creek, avoid side roads to private homes. Cross Nason Creek again, enter national forest land in a short mile, and start climbing. At 4.6 miles from the highway, go right on road No. 6910170. At 4.8 miles reach Round Mountain trail No. 1529, elevation 3900 feet.

The magnificent journey the length of Nason Ridge, through forest and wide-sky highlands from Snowy Creek to near Lake Wenatchee, is a prime tour for experienced navigators. Unfortunately, the last 6½ miles to Lake Wenatchee are so muddled by logging roads and harassed by motorcycles as to be no fun; the 16 miles between Snowy Creek and Round Mountain road, though, are superb.

Climb a steep 1000 feet in 1½ miles to the junction with Nason Ridge trail No. 1583 on Round Mountain and go left up a wooded ridge to within ¼ mile of 6237-foot Alpine Lookout (well worth the detour). From the lookout the trail drops to Merritt Lake (Hike 55) and campsites, 9 miles from the start.

Still in timber, the trail continues downward. In 1 mile keep right at a junction with the Merritt Lake trail. Ascend forest to a 5400-foot high point and drop to a crossing of Royal Creek and campsites at 4900 feet. Now the way climbs into meadowland, passing tiny Crescent Lake, 5500 feet, to a 6000-foot high point and skirts Rock Lake to a junction with the Rock

The summit ridge of Rock Mountain

Mountain trail (Hike 54), 12 miles from the car. Camp in established sites in the trees near Crescent and Rock Lakes and not in the fragile meadows surrounding them.

Endless switchbacks take the trail to the 6400-foot shoulder of Rock Mountain, followed by a final drop to the Snowy Creek trailhead.

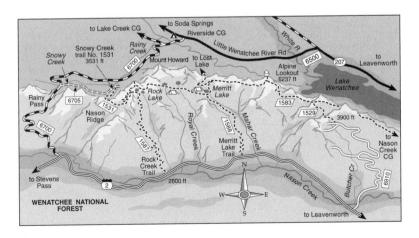

53 | SNOWY CREEK–ROCK MOUNTAIN

Round trip: 9 miles
Hiking time: 6 hours
High point: 6852 feet
Elevation gain: 3350 feet
Hikable: Mid-July through October
Map: Green Trails No. 145 Wenatchee Lake
Current information: Ask at Lake Wenatchee Ranger
Station about trail No. 1583

Driving directions: Drive US 2 east 4 miles from Stevens Pass and turn left on Smith Brook road No. 6700. Cross Rainy Pass and about 5 miles from the highway, at a major switchback, go straight ahead on road No. 6705 another 3.6 miles to a crossing of Snowy Creek and the trailhead, elevation 3531 feet.

Forest, meadows, and switchbacks through the sky lead to the summit of Rock Mountain. This is a much more civilized route than the Rock Mountain trail (Hike 54). It starts 900 feet higher and has cool shade for hours after the other is so hot you can hear the ants sizzling.

Snowy Creek trail No. 1531 heads into magnificent old-growth forest. At 2 long miles, 4600 feet, is a fine campsite in upper Snowy Creek Basin, a

Clark's nutcracker

Ridge leading to the top of Rock Mountain

large flat meadow enclosed by a horseshoe of cliffy peaks. Tread vanishes in the meadow then reappears halfway across, on the left. The next 2 miles (steep and dry) enter trees, leave them for flower fields, and gain 2000 feet to the summit ridge of Rock Mountain. Here is a junction with the Nason Ridge–Rock Mountain trail. Go left on the crest to the lookout site atop Rock Mountain, 6852 feet, and the glorious views described in Hike 54.

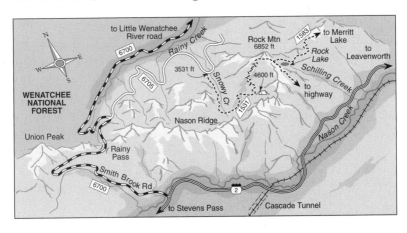

54 | ROCK MOUNTAIN

Round trip: 11 miles
Hiking time: 8 hours
High point: 6852 feet
Elevation gain: 4250 feet
Hikable: Mid-July through October
Map: Green Trails No. 145 Wenatchee Lake
Current information: Ask at Lake Wenatchee Ranger
    Station about trail No. 1587

Driving directions: Coming from the east, drive US 2 west 8.8 miles from the Nason Creek Rest Area. From the west, cross Stevens Pass and drive 8.5 miles (0.4 mile past the Highway Department buildings). Near milepost 73 find a small parking area and the Rock Mountain trail sign, elevation 2600 feet.

Broad meadows and a cold little lake enhance Rock Mountain, the scenic climax of Nason Ridge. However, the person who chooses this route to the top, rather than Snowy Creek (Hike 53), must be young and stubborn or old and ornery. The trail is very steep, despite ninety-five switchbacks. It lies on a south slope swept clean of shade trees by fire and avalanche. No water—unless you swallow a few thousand of the flies which, in season, fling themselves into your gasping mouth.

Rock Mountain trail No. 1587 begins on a powerline service road. In about ⅓ mile go left and climb steeply to the highest powerline pylon, at about ⅔ mile, 3000 feet.

True trail commences, narrow and rocky, switchbacking up the naked bones of the mountain. Views, of course, begin immediately and never quit. The massive high bulk of the Chiwaukum Mountains, across the valley,

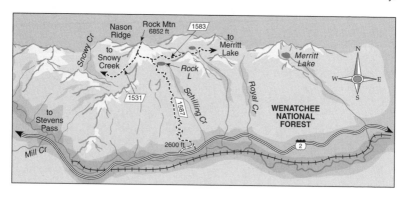

Rock Lake

dominates. A bit to the west, the green slopes of Arrowhead Mountain and Jim Hill Mountain grow greener the higher you climb. At about 3½ miles, 5000 feet, the wayside vegetation shifts to the subalpine—blueberries, heather, and shrubby Christmas trees (mighty thin shade). At 4½ miles, 6000 feet, is a junction with the Nason Ridge trail.

For Rock Lake, turn right on the ridge trail, contouring several hundred feet above the lake. The snowfields that generally fill the basin until late July may be mighty tempting to feet that have been flying for hours on the sunny side of the ridge. Don't camp in the fragile meadows by the lake inlet. Find nice sites in the trees just above and to the northeast of the shore.

For Rock Mountain turn left on the ridge trail, switchbacking, then following a spur ridge, and switchbacking again to the summit ridge and a junction with the Snowy Creek trail (Hike 53). Steep snow may force a party to detour or call it a day or call Mountain Rescue.

The summit ridge makes for an easy walk to the old lookout site atop Rock Mountain, 6852 feet, 5½ miles from the highway. The views extend north to Sloan Peak and Glacier Peak, south to the tip of Mount Rainier rising above Mount Daniel, and straight down 1000 feet to Rock Lake.

55 | MERRITT LAKE

Round trip: 6 miles
Hiking time: 4 hours
High point: 5003 feet
Elevation gain: 2000 feet
Hikable: Late June through October
Map: Green Trails No. 145 Wenatchee Lake
Current information: Ask at Lake Wenatchee Ranger
Station about trail No. 1588

Driving directions: Coming from the east, drive US 2 west 6 miles from the Nason Creek Rest Area. From the west, drive east 11.4 miles from Stevens Pass to 3.3 miles beyond a cluster of highway department buildings. Near milepost 76, turn north on road No. 657 for 1.6 miles to the road-end and the start of Merritt Lake trail No. 1588, elevation 3000 feet.

Merritt Lake is a delightful tarn ringed by subalpine forest and enclosed by 6000-foot peaks.

Fishermen, botanizers, and esthetes swarm. Nearby is another not so popular lake—the largest on Nason Ridge—that goes by the name of "Lost." Some hikers do indeed become lost, and wounded, too, because the trail is unmaintained, difficult, and treacherous, definitely not for the inexperienced wayfarer.

The trail switchbacks up through a scattering of splendid old ponderosa pine and Douglas fir. At 2 miles, skirt a boulder field and cross a small

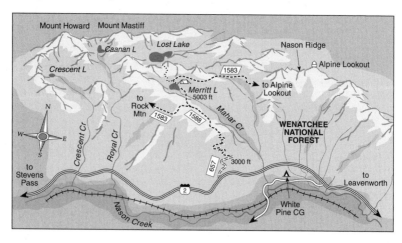

creek. At 2½ miles is a junction with Nason Ridge trail No. 1583 (Hike 52) and at 3 miles, Merritt Lake, 5003 feet. Numerous camps lie in the woods, handy to an open-air privy. Campers will want to carry a stove; the scene was picked clean of good burning wood by fishermen a couple of generations ago. Better to eat cold as nature intended.

For Lost Lake, follow the Nason Ridge trail up and away from Merritt Lake a very scant ½ mile to a junction. The ridge trail ascends right, to the Alpine Lookout. Go left on the unmarked Lost Lake route, climbing to a 5500-foot pass. Look down—this is the best view a hiker will have. If going on, descend, initially at an easy grade but soon in a steep draw, sharing the trail with a creek. People with slippery shoes and a tendency to easily break bones shouldn't try it. The route is straight down to the lake, 4930 feet. Aside from fish, there isn't much to see. Keep in mind the 650-foot climb on the return; add 3 miles and 3 hours to the round trip.

Merritt Lake

56 | ALPINE LOOKOUT

Round trip: 10 miles
Hiking time: 5 hours
High point: 6237 feet
Elevation gain: 2400 feet
Hikable: Mid-June through September
Map: Green Trails No. 145 Wenatchee Lake
Current information: Ask at Lake Wenatchee Ranger
Station about trail Nos. 1529, 1583

Driving directions: Drive US 2 east 17 miles from Stevens Pass to 0.3 mile beyond Nason Creek Rest Area. Pass a driveway to a lodge and turn left on Butcher Creek road No. 6910 (not signed but with a row of mailboxes). Cross Nason Creek, avoid spur roads to private homes, cross Nason Creek again, enter national forest land in a scant mile, and start climbing. At 4.6 miles from the highway go right on road No. 6910-170. At 4.8 miles reach Round Mountain trail No. 1529, elevation 3900 feet.

Nason Ridge has a reputation as the definition of "grueling." That, of course, is only accurate insofar as it refers to certain stretches of certain trails. This route, for example, hardly gets up enough sweat for a hiker to notice there is no water. Yet the views are broad, the flowers pretty. Moreover, chances are very good of spotting mountain goats in the small no-hunting area around Alpine Lookout. Further, as one of the last lookouts still active for fire detection, Alpine is a living vignette of history. The 1994 Round Mountain fire damaged part of this trail, but in a few years the black will turn to the silver of bleached snags amid the rainbow of flower fields.

The first 1½ miles are typical Nason, climbing steeply to meet Nason

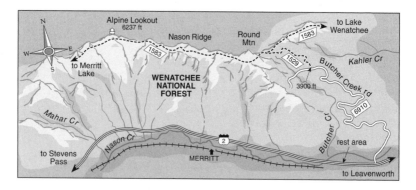

Ridge trail No. 1583, at 5300 feet. Go left. The next 3 miles are also less than perfect joy because the Forest Service currently gives motorcycles free run to the lookout junction. The trail (wheel road) contours the side of Round Mountain and gains almost 1000 feet to the junction. A short wheelfree spur leads to Alpine Lookout, 6237 feet, 5 miles from the road.

The views are north to cliffs of Dirtyface Mountain above waters of Lake Wenatchee, and south to the Stuart Range, Chiwaukum Mountains, and other peaks of the Alpine Lakes Wilderness.

The best times to see goats are early and late in the day. Don't wander about searching. Sit still, be quite, and wait for them to come near. Don't visit the lookout sanctuary during hunting season, when your presence might frighten the animals out of their small safe spot into the rifle sights.

Mountain goat at Alpine Lookout

57 | MINOTAUR LAKE

Round trip: 6 miles
Hiking time: 5 hours
High point: 5550 feet
Elevation gain: 2000 feet
Hikable: Mid-July through October
Map: Green Trails No. 144 Benchmark
Current information: Ask at Lake Wenatchee Ranger
   Station about trail No. 1517

Driving directions: Drive US 2 east from Stevens Pass 19 miles and turn left to Lake Wenatchee. Pass the state park roads. At 1.8 miles beyond the Lake Wenatchee Ranger Station go left on Little Wenatchee River road No. 65 for another 6.2 miles, turn left again, cross the river on road No. 6700 for 6.2 miles, then go right on road No. 6704 (this junction also can be reached from the Smith Brook–Rainy Pass road No. 6700, Hike 51) and drive 1 more mile to the trailhead, elevation 3800 feet.

Minotaur Lake lies in a Grecian setting. Above and beyond are the rock walls of 6376-foot Labyrinth Mountain. Below is Theseus Lake. Heather meadows and subalpine firs complete the mythological scene. No longer

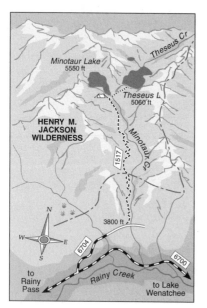

are seven girls and seven boys annually given in sacrifice to Minotaur, but each year visitors pay (in season) a tribute to the gods as the bugs take a libation of blood. *Note:* The Forest Service signs this trail as a "route."

Minotaur Lake trail (route) No. 1517 is maintained but muddy. The way switchbacks up a hill, drops to cross an unnamed creek, and becomes a fishermen's path shooting straight up. There is no formal tread, only the groove scoured by many pounding boots, gaining 1500 feet in the next mile. Views are limited to a few glimpses out through trees. At the end of the long, steep, dry ascent the trail turns downvalley ½ mile, losing 100 feet, then turns again and heads

Theseus Lake

up Minotaur Creek. Forest gives way to highland meadows, and at 3 miles is 5550-foot Minotaur Lake.

In trees around the shore are several good campsites, a mob scene on weekends. Dine on crackers and cheese or carry a stove; the last firewood was burned up in 1937. Cross the outlet and walk a few yards northeast to see 5060-foot Theseus Lake; a very steep path leads down to more good camps (no fires here, either) and the shores of the lake. Minotaur Lake has extensive, but fragile, heather and huckleberry meadows. Please limit use to existing trails and established campsites.

For broader views of mountains west to Stevens Pass, north to Glacier Peak, and east beyond Lake Wenatchee, scramble easily to open ridges above the lakes and wander the crests.

58 | HEATHER LAKE

Round trip: 6½ miles
Hiking time: 4 hours
High point: 3953 feet
Elevation gain: 1200 feet
Hikable: July through October
Map: Green Trails No. 144 Benchmark
Current information: Ask at Lake Wenatchee Ranger
Station about trail No. 1526

Driving directions: Drive US 2 east from Stevens Pass 19 miles and turn left to Lake Wenatchee. From the upper end of Lake Wenatchee, drive 6 miles on Little Wenatchee River road No. 65, turn left on road No. 6700, cross the river, and in 0.6 mile go right on road No. 6701, following the river upstream. In 4.7 miles turn left onto road No. (6701)400. In 300 feet keep right and in another 2.3 miles reach the trailhead at the road-end, elevation 2800 feet.

Waters of the ½-mile-long lake-in-the-woods reflect rocks and gardens of Grizzly Peak. A family could be happy here for days, prowling about from a comfortable basecamp. So could doughty adventurers seeking more strenuous explorations. The bad news is that on summer weekends it's often impossible to find a campsite.

The trail is a constant joy (nearly). The minor ups and downs of the first 1½ miles, netting only 100 feet in elevation, ease muscles into their task. Having done so, it turns stern, crossing Lake Creek on a logjam and heading up seriously, leaving no doubt as to why horses are forbidden. At about 2 miles is the boundary of the Henry M. Jackson Wilderness. In 2½ miles, after gaining 900 feet, the grade relents and joy resumes in the last ¾ mile

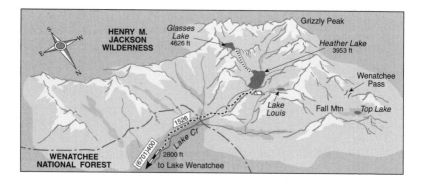

to Heather Lake, 3953 feet, with fine camps and a cozy privy.

The bare schist near the lake outlet displays the grinding done by the glacier that plucked out the lake basin. Once these slabs were smooth, but eons of erosion have eaten away the polish, leaving only the grooves.

Attractive to the ambitious navigator with map and compass, a way trail rounds the left side of the lake. At the far end follow a small stream south, climbing 700 feet in ½ mile to Glasses Lake, 4626 feet, so named because from neighboring peaks it looks like a pair of eyeglasses. No fires at either lake. The only heather at Heather Lake is all the women named Heather who make a pilgrimage to visit their namesake lake.

Heather Lake

59 | POET RIDGE–IRVING PASS

Round trip to "The Bump": 6 miles
Hiking time: 4 hours
High point: 6000 feet
Elevation gain: 1900 feet
Hikable: Mid-June to October

Round trip to Poe Mountain: 7 miles
Hiking time: 5 hours
High point: 6000 feet
Elevation gain: 1900 feet
Hikable: Mid-June to October

Map: Green Trails No. 144 Benchmark
Current information: Ask at Lake Wenatchee Ranger
Station about trail Nos. 1545, 1543

Driving directions: Drive US 2 east from Stevens Pass 19 miles and turn left to Lake Wenatchee. Pass the state park road, cross the Wenatchee River bridge, stay left another 4.6 miles to the Lake Wenatchee Ranger Station. Go another 1.8 miles to a Y, then left on No. 65, Little Wenatchee River road. Drive Little Wenatchee River road No. 65 for 9.6 miles (exactly 1 mile past Soda Springs Campground). Go right on road No. 6504. At 4.3 miles from the river road go right at an unmarked junction. Drive another 2 miles and find Irving Pass trail No. 1545 at a switchback and road-end, elevation 4200 feet. (In 2002, in places, the road was a tunnel through brush. Before scratching a nice new car, check at the ranger station.)

Hike a difficult path, more a route than a trail, to a viewpoint bump on Poet Ridge in the Wenatchee Mountains, or, as many do, continue on to Poe Mountain. However, if Poe is the destination, most hikers find Hike 60 easier, though it starts at a lower elevation.

The trail climbs a very steep 700 feet in what the sign says is ½ mile to Irving Pass, 4900 feet. Straight ahead from the junction here is the abandoned Panther Creek trail. Go left, climbing steeply a smart ¼ mile to a second junction (unmarked). The right-hand trail contours down to Cockeye Creek and a pleasant camp.

Keep to the crest on ever-deteriorating tread, climbing over and around bumps atop Poet Ridge. Views begin to open up in another ½ mile as the trail crosses the top of steep meadows. At approximately 3 miles from the road the trail passes below the 6000-foot "The Bump" on Poet Ridge and

Trail along Poet Ridge looking toward Poe Mountain

starts down. Views now include the Wenatchee Range, Nason Ridge, Mount Stuart, Mount Rainier south, and peaks of Poet Ridge north. This is the time for a decision. What you will see atop 6015-foot Poe Mountain is practically the same as what you see here, so if the 15 extra feet are of no interest, call it a day and wander up the boot-beaten path to "The Bump."

If you must get Poe, from the high point follow the trail across a green bench, drop 100 feet to a timbered saddle, and contour around Poe Mountain, losing another 200 feet. Join trail No. 1520 (Hike 60) and climb to the 6015-foot top.

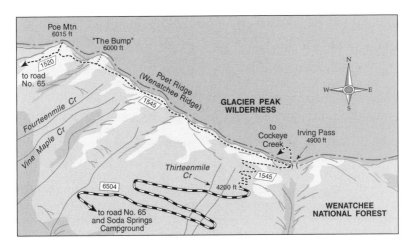

60 | POE MOUNTAIN

Round trip: 6 miles
Hiking time: 4 hours
High point: 6017 feet
Elevation gain: 3000 feet
Hikable: Late June through October
Map: Green Trails No. 144 Benchmark
Current information: Ask at Lake Wenatchee Ranger
Station about trail No. 1520

Driving directions: Drive US 2 east from Stevens Pass 19 miles and turn
left to Lake Wenatchee. Pass the state park road, cross the Wenatchee
River bridge, stay left another 4.6 miles to the Lake Wenatchee Ranger
Station. Go another 1.8 miles to a Y, then left on No. 65, Little Wenatchee River road, 14.8 miles to its end, elevation 3000 feet. (The last 2.8
miles are very primitive, winding around big old-growth trees.)

What the map calls "Wenatchee Ridge" is unofficially known as "Poet
Ridge," due to a government mapmaker of yore having named its various
high points Bryant Peak, Longfellow Mountain, Poe Mountain, Irving
Peak, and Whittier Peak. Discriminating students of literature call it
"Poetaster Ridge" and lament the taste of government mapmakers of yore.
Poe is not the highest of the lot but has so commanding a view it was once

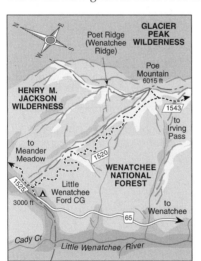

the site of a lookout cabin. The pan-
orama includes the Little Wenatch-
ee River valley from Meander
Meadow to Soda Springs, forests of
Nason Ridge, and mountains of the
Cascade Crest. Views in other direc-
tions are blocked by various poets.
Glacier Peak, Sloan, Monte Cristo,
Hinman, and Rainier can be seen
above distant ridges.

The two trails to Poe Mountain
are the same length. The better
choice on a hot day would be the
ridge route, reached from road No.
6504, starting at an elevation of 4200
feet (Hike 59). The direct route from
the west described here should be
done early in the morning before

the sun blisters the trail. Carry water; there's none along the way save dewdrops.

Walk ⅛ mile on Little Wenatchee River trail No. 1525 and turn right on poorly marked Poe Mountain trail No. 1520. The rate of gain is about 1000 feet per mile, ideal for getting there firstest with the mostest rubber left on the lugs. Shade trees are scarce but views are plentiful, enlarging at each upward rest stop. Just below the top the way joins the ridge trail, No. 1543, for the final ¼ mile to the meadowy summit.

Poet Ridge and Glacier Peak from Poe Mountain

61 | MEANDER MEADOW AND KODAK PEAK

Round trip to Meander Meadow: 12 miles
Hiking time: 7 hours
High point: 5400 feet
Elevation gain: 2400 feet
Hikable: July to October

Round trip to Kodak Peak: 16 miles
Hiking time: Allow 2 days
High point: 6121 feet
Elevation gain: 3100 feet
Hikable: July to October

Map: Green Trails No. 144 Benchmark
Current information: Ask at Lake Wenatchee Ranger
Station about trail No. 1525

Driving directions: Drive US 2 east from Stevens Pass 19 miles and turn
left to Lake Wenatchee. Pass the state park road, cross the Wenatchee
River bridge, stay left another 4.6 miles to the Lake Wenatchee Ranger
Station. From the ranger station drive 1.8 miles, then go left 14.8 miles
on Little Wenatchee River road No. 65 to its end at the Little Wenatchee
Ford Campground and trailhead, elevation 3000 feet, and find Little
Wenatchee River trail No. 1525.

Perhaps the easiest way in the Wenatchee area to sample the glories of the
high country. A forest-and-meadow valley floor, a steep-and-hot struggle,

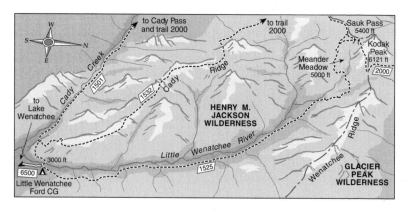

Pacific Crest Trail around Kodak Peak

and finally a superb little basin of grass and flowers and slow deep meanders of the headwaters stream. Above lie parklands of the Cascade Crest
and endless easy wandering with views to everywhere.

In ⅛ mile pass the Poe Mountain trail junction. The first 4 miles are gently up and down, a net gain of only 700 feet, alternating between forest and
glade and frequent stream crossings. The easy part ends at the edge of a
vast meadow; here are a small creek and a campsite. The next 2 miles, gaining 1300 feet, may require courage and fortitude in the heat of the afternoon sun in fly season. The way climbs grass and brush, through
sometimes-soggy greenery. Once above the meadow, in a mix of trees and
avalanche paths, the tread is distinct but steep. Fortunately, the views grow
with every step. At 6 miles the trail drops a short bit into the basin of 5000-
foot Meander Meadow; the camps are splendid and so are the hours of
flower-walking.

The trail crosses a meandering fragment of the Little Wenatchee River
and climbs another open mile and 500 more feet to a ridge and trail fork.
Go either way—north or south of a small hill—to join the Pacific Crest Trail
at 5400-foot Sauk Pass.

The junction with the Crest Trail gives the first view of Glacier Peak and
marks the boundary of the Glacier Peak Wilderness. Walk north 2½ miles
to a 5630-foot saddle on the east ridge of Kodak Peak. Climb a boot-beaten
path through blossoms another ½ mile to the 6121-foot summit and start
cranking film through the Kodak. For more exploring, see Hike 60.

The return trip can be made by going south 2 miles on the Crest Trail
and then left on Cady Ridge trail No. 1532 some 5 miles to the starting
point, or by way of Cady Pass (Hike 62).

62 CADY PASS–MEANDER MEADOW LOOP

Loop trip: 17½ miles
Hiking time: Allow 3 to 5 days
High point: 4600 feet
Elevation gain: 1600 feet
Hikable: July through September

Loop with side trip: 31½ miles
Hiking time: Allow 3 to 5 days
High point: 6450 feet
Elevation gain: 3000 feet
Hikable: July through September

Map: Green Trails No. 144 Benchmark
Current information: Ask at Lake Wenatchee Ranger Station about trail Nos. 1501, 1525, 2000

Driving directions: Drive US 2 east from Stevens Pass 19 miles and turn left to Lake Wenatchee. Pass the state park road, cross the Wenatchee River bridge, and stay left another 4.6 miles to the Lake Wenatchee Ranger Station. At 1.8 miles beyond the ranger station, go left 14.8 miles on Little Wenatchee River road No. 65 to its end, near Little Wenatchee Ford Campground, elevation 3000 feet.

A loop hike splendid in its own right, and a sidetrip, if desired, to White Pass along what some argue is the most beautiful segment of the entire Pacific Crest National Scenic Trail, certainly one of the longest meadow walks anywhere in the Cascade Range.

Trail No. 1501 drops to a bridge over the Little Wenatchee River. In ¼ mile, pass the Cady Ridge trail and at 3½ miles find a nice camp beside Cady Creek. Follow the creek 5 miles, gaining 1700 feet (including ups and downs) to wooded and

Sloan Peak

waterless 4300-foot Cady Pass. Turn right (north) on the Pacific Crest Trail, climbing 1300 feet in 2 miles to break out above timberline on the divide between Cady Creek and Pass Creek. Now the way goes around this side or that of one small knoll after another, alternating between Eastern Washington and Western Washington. Then comes a traverse along the east slope of 6368-foot Skykomish Peak. At 2½ miles from Cady Pass (8 miles from the road) is 5479-foot Lake Sally Ann, a charming little tarn amid cliff-bordered meadows, very fragile and, in the past, badly abused. Camping with stock is now banned, as are fires within 200 feet of the lake.

Less than 2½ miles farther is an intersection with the Cady Ridge trail and another camp in a broad meadow. Climb a waterfall-sparkling basin to 5680-foot Wards Pass and roam parkland atop and near the crest past Dishpan Gap to 5450-foot Sauk Pass, 5½ miles from Cady Pass (2½ miles from the road), and a junction with trail No. 1525, the return route by way of Meander Meadow (Hike 61). For a basecamp, descend meadows to the

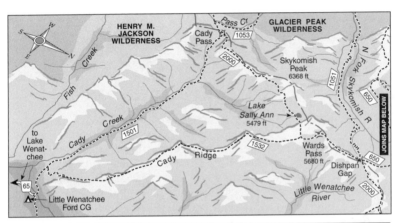

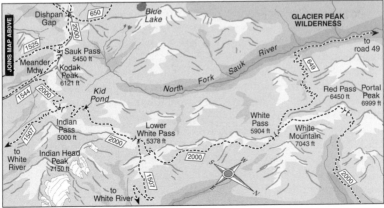

Meander Basin

campsites or proceed on the crest a mile farther to superlative spots.

For the sidetrip, continue on the Crest Trail 7 miles, with more flower-covered meadows and a spectacular view of Glacier Peak from 6450-foot Red Pass. The way goes up (1900 feet) and down (900 feet) the ridge top, totaling for the round trip 14 miles of hiking and 2400 feet of climbing—worth it.

The sidetrip begins by traversing green slopes of Kodak Peak to a saddle. (Take a few minutes to carry your camera to the 6121-foot summit.) Descend across a gorgeous alpine basin and down forest to mostly wooded Indian Pass, 5000 feet, 12½ miles from Sauk Pass. Find pleasant campsites at the pass—but usually no water except in early summer.

Climb forest and gardens around the side of Indian Head Peak to tiny Kid Pond and beyond to 5378-foot Lower White Pass, and a junction with the White River trail. The next 1½ miles go through the climax meadows, past Reflection Pond, and into flower fields, culminating at 5904-foot White Pass. Follow the Crest Trail another 1½ miles to Red Pass for dramatic views of Glacier Peak and the White Chuck Glacier.

Having done (or not) the sidetrip, finish the loop from Meander Meadow by following trail No. 1525 down 2 miles of flowers and another 4 miles of meadow and forest.

63 | DIRTYFACE PEAK

Round trip: 9 miles
Hiking time: 7 hours
High point: 5984 feet
Elevation gain: 4000 feet
Hikable: Mid-June through October
Map: Green Trails No. 145 Wenatchee Lake
Current information: Ask at Lake Wenatchee Ranger
Station about trail No. 1500

Driving directions: Drive US 2 east from Stevens Pass 19 miles and turn left to Lake Wenatchee. Pass the state park road, cross the Wenatchee River bridge, and stay left another 4.6 miles to the Lake Wenatchee Ranger Station. Just before the station, turn right on a paved service road (unmarked in 2001), curve behind the station, make a switchback, and find the trailhead, elevation 2000 feet.

A stiff climb, cruelly hot in sunny and windless weather, to a deserted lookout site with an airy view over Lake Wenatchee and into the Glacier Peak Wilderness. The last 2½ miles are dry; carry lots of water. For hikers who don't mind a few small snowpatches, this is a fine mid-June trip.

The trail is mostly in very good shape, wide and smooth, but steep, very steep, gaining about 1000 feet a mile. (The trail sign says the peak is 4 miles, but the distance is definitely 4½ or 5 miles or more.) In the first mile are several creeks. At ½ mile intersect an abandoned logging road, follow it a scant ½ mile to its end, and pick up the trail again. Here is a good campsite in the woods, and also the last water.

The way relentlessly climbs seventy switchbacks (we counted them) to the summit ridge. At about switchback forty-five, the trail leaves the tall

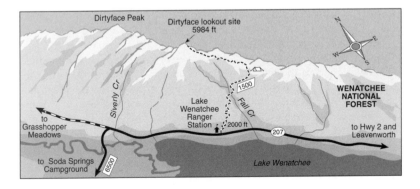

Lake Wenatchee from Dirty Face Lookout site

ponderosa pine and enters subalpine trees and flowers—and glorious
views of the lake. From the crest it is almost ½ mile and eleven more switchbacks (for a total of eighty-one) to the old lookout site, at 5984 feet.

Enjoy views west to Nason Ridge, north up the Napeequa River to Clark
Mountain, Chiwawa Ridge, and the Chiwawa valley, and east to endless
hills. Below and to the left is Fish Lake, and directly beneath, Lake Wenatchee. At the head of the latter, note the vast marshes and the meandering streams; at one point the White River comes within a few feet of the
lake but snakes back another ½ mile before entering. Ant-sized boats can
be seen on the lakes, and cars on the highways.

In early July the rock gardens are snowfield-brilliant in blossoming
phlox. In late summer and fall the upper trail offers blueberries to sate a
perhaps gigantic thirst.

64 | TWIN LAKES

Round trip: 8 miles
Hiking time: 5 hours
High point: 2825 feet
Elevation gain: 1000 feet
Hikable: June through October
Map: Green Trails No. 145 Wenatchee Lake
Current information: Ask at Lake Wenatchee Ranger
Station about trail No. 1503

Driving directions: Drive US 2 to Coles Corner between Stevens Pass
and Leavenworth. Turn north on Lake Wenatchee road No. 207. Pass the
state park road, cross the Wenatchee River bridge, and stay left. Pass the
Lake Wenatchee Ranger Station to a big Y. Stay right another 6.2 miles.

A forest walk past magnificent cedar trees to two large, shallow lakes used
by the state as a fish hatchery; no fishing allowed. The trail is so rough and,
in places, so very steep, that horses are banned.

A few feet from the road the trail tips steeply upward, gaining 250 feet
up a cliff in a long ¼ mile. A short sidetrip leads to a dramatic viewpoint
where several dogs have fallen off. Hold onto the kids and look down to
the Tall Timber Ranch and Presbyterian Church Camp, and upvalley to
7431-foot Mount David. The trail then contours a hillside, entering Glacier
Peak Wilderness in ¾ mile. In dropping to near the Napeequa River, 1 mile

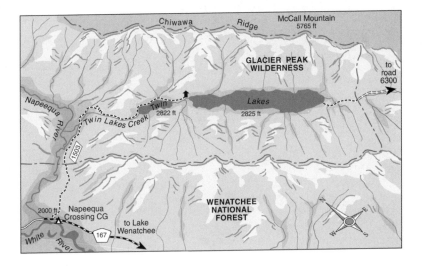

from the road, the trail loses all but 30 feet of the 250 feet gained in elevation.

The way levels, passes a swamp (maybe a beaver pond), and then climbs steadily up Twin Lakes Creek. At about 2¾ miles a narrow gorge requires a short bit of hands-and-feet rock-scrambling. At 3¼ miles is the first and smallest of the Twin Lakes, elevation 2822 feet.

Brush fences off the water. For views, follow the trail around the north shore to bare rock, or a bit farther to where beavers have gnawed down a large tree. In a scant 4 miles are a cabin built in 1949 by the State Game Department and a view of the 2-mile-long second Twin Lake, 2825 feet. Again the water is beyond reach.

State Game Department cabin, built in 1949

65 | MOUNT DAVID

Round trip: 16 miles
Hiking time: 10 hours
High point: 7431 feet
Elevation gain: 5400 feet
Hikable: Mid-August to October
Map: Green Trails No. 145 Wenatchee Lake
Current information: Ask at Lake Wenatchee Ranger
Station about trail No. 1521

Driving directions: Drive US 2 east from Stevens Pass 19 miles and turn left to Lake Wenatchee. Pass the state park road, cross the Wenatchee River bridge, and stay left another 4.6 miles to the Lake Wenatchee Ranger Station. At a big Y go left past the ranger station and at 6.4 miles from the bridge stay right on White River road No. 6400. At 16.5 miles from the bridge reach the road-end and parking area, elevation 2300 feet.

Climb a real mountain, 7431 feet high. However, though the ascent is lengthy and strenuous, the cliffy summit, where climbers would otherwise rope up, has a trail blasted to a long-abandoned lookout site. (The cabin is gone, but the stone privy remains.) Enjoy panoramic views out over countless peaks and down almost a vertical mile to the river. It's best not to try the hike until August, when snow has melted from the steep and potentially dangerous gullies. The trail is dry, so carry plenty of water.

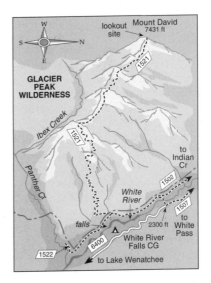

Cross the White River on a horse bridge signed "Indian Creek Trail." On the far side enter the Glacier Peak Wilderness and turn downstream on a trail signed "Mt. David" and "Panther Creek." In 1 long mile from the bridge, where the river trail keeps left, turn right on the Mount David trail.

There is a big bundle of elevation to gain and the trail gets at it immediately. At ⅓ mile from the river trail, cross the last reliable stream. In 1 mile the tread is difficult to find in slide alder and vine

Trail to Mount David: Look carefully for the trail zigzagging toward the summit

maple of an avalanche slope. From here the trail is well graded. Relentless switchbacks grind up and up through forest to the ridge crest at 4½ miles.

The final 3½ miles follow ups and downs of the ridge, sometimes sidehilling around high points, switchbacking up one gully then moving to the next. Around several cliffs the trail has eroded away but is considered safe—but you are the judge. Views grow: south to Lake Wenatchee, Mount Daniel, and Mount Rainier and north to Clark Mountain.

Snow remains on slopes directly under the summit rocks until late August—a good reason for doing the trip no earlier. Tread is very obscure in a talus here and may easily be lost. If so, climb to the ridge and find the way where it crosses to the south side of the peak. The last few hundred feet have been blasted from cliff and improved by cement steps. Once there was even a guardrail, but it's gone now. Hikers suffering from acrophobia will be happier to settle for a conclusion somewhat short of the absolute top, 8 miles from the road.

Views are long to all horizons. Glacier Peak, 12 miles away, dominates, but careful study identifies many other mountains of the Cascade Crest; off west, above the head of Indian Creek, is Sloan Peak. Look down and down to the Indian Creek trail, crossing streamside meadows.

The only possible campsite is a flat meadow at about 5200 feet. The meadow is some 500 feet below the trail, reached by a spur descending from a short bit past the 4-mile marker.

66 | INDIAN CREEK AND RED PASS

Round trip to Indian Pass: 23½ miles
Hiking time: 2 or more days
High point: 5000 feet
Elevation gain: 2700 feet
Hikable: July to October

Round trip to Red Pass: 40 miles
Hiking time: 5 days
High point: 5500 feet
Elevation gain: 3200
Hikable: July to October

Maps: Green Trails Nos. 144 Benchmark, 145 Wenatchee
Lake, 112 Glacier Peak
Current information: Ask at Lake Wenatchee Ranger
Station about trail Nos. 1502, 2000; if trying for the
loop, ask about stream crossings on trail No. 1507

Driving directions: Drive US 2 east from Stevens Pass 19 miles and turn left to Lake Wenatchee. Pass the state park road, cross the Wenatchee River bridge, and stay left another 4.6 miles to the Lake Wenatchee Ranger Station. At a big Y go left past the ranger station and at 6.4 miles from the bridge stay right on White River road No. 6400. At 16.5 miles from the bridge reach the road-end and parking area, elevation 2300 feet.

A long forest walk to the climax of flowers and views along the Pacific Crest Trail. Combined with White River trail No. 1207, this used to be a 28-mile loop trip, one of the Cascade's greatest. For years the Forest Service fought a losing battle with slides and floods trying to kept the White River trail open. A major effort by the Forest Service and volunteers to reopen the trail is planned for 2003 and 2004.

Cross the river on the horse bridge and turn upstream on Indian Creek trail No. 1502, following the White River a long 2 miles. The way then crosses Indian Creek on a bridge and tilts, gaining 800 feet in 1¾ miles. Trail and creek abruptly level off at a nice campsite, 3200 feet, 4 miles from the road. This is a dandy turnaround for a day hike or a short overnighter, though there are several other good camps in the next 3 miles.

The next 2 miles from the 3200-foot camp go up and down a lot, from solid ground to horse-churned mud holes, but make a net elevation gain of zero. The next 5 miles compensate by climbing moderately but steadily to

Crest Trail on the side of Indian Head Peak

Indian Pass, 5000 feet, 11 miles from the road. The camps here usually have no potable water after early summer.

Climb from parkland forest of the pass to flowers of the 5500-foot high point on the side of Indian Head Peak. Drop a bit to Lower White Pass, 5378 feet, and meet White River trail No. 1507 at a scant 1½ miles from Indian Pass.

It would be a shame, having walked this far, not to romp through the gardens a little. Indeed, if you can't allow an extra day or two to hike north on the Pacific Crest Trail—1 mile or 2, or the 4½ miles all the way to Red Pass—why bother?

For now the best way back to the road end is the way you came. However, a loop is possible, and when the White River trail work is done it will be the recommended route. For the loop, descend from Lower White Pass on the White River trail No. 1507. Some 4 miles from the pass a bridge over the river has been washed

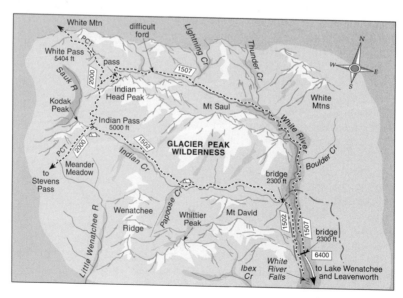

out. The footlogs (belly logs?) are slick. The alternative is to ford, which can be hazardous in high water, which lasts until mid-August. Consider the advantages of hiking counterclockwise, in order to confront the raging torrent on the way in, when you can readily turn back. Farther along are several long stretches of the sort of brush that thrives where avalanches forbid forests to do so. One stretch is 2 miles long. If you think you don't like it when the bushes are soaked with rain, wait until you've tried it in a blazing sun when the flies are so hungry they're eating the mosquitoes. Except for *that*, the way lies in cathedral stands of ancient-growth forest.

At 15 miles from Lower White Pass the loop returns to the road, for a total of 28 miles plus the side-romp north on the Cascade Crest.

Indian Creek

67 NAPEEQUA VALLEY VIA BOULDER PASS

Round trip to Napeequa ford: 26 miles
Hiking time: Allow 3 to 7 days
High point: 6250 feet
Elevation gain: 4000 feet in, 2000 feet out
Hikable: August through September
Maps: Green Trails Nos. 145 Wenatchee Lake, 113 Holden
Current information: Ask at Lake Wenatchee Ranger
Station about trail Nos. 1507, 1562

Driving directions: Drive US 2 east from Stevens Pass 19 miles and turn left to Lake Wenatchee. Pass the state park road, cross the Wenatchee River bridge, and stay left another 4.6 miles to the Lake Wenatchee Ranger Station. At a big Y go left past the ranger station and at 6.4 miles from the bridge stay right on White River road No. 6400. At 16.5 miles from the bridge reach the road-end and parking area, elevation 2300 feet.

The Napeequa River has craftily designed its fabled "Shangri La" to keep people out. The stream exits a valley via a cliff-walled gorge that has never had any sort of trail and enters the valley from glaciers and precipices inaccessible to all except climbers. Each of the only two reasonable hiker accesses is over an exceedingly high pass and a wide, deep, swift river. Hikers may well climb to the top of Boulder Pass, drop to the floor of Napeequa valley—and find themselves cut off from the meadows by the Napeequa River. Then, if they get across the flood alive, they can expect to be sucked dry of blood by flies as big as the flowers and as numerous. Pretty pictures don't tell the whole story.

Hike White River trail No. 1507, a pleasant, virtually level 4 miles

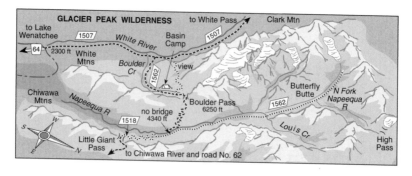

Napeequa valley

through lovely virgin forest to Boulder Pass trail No. 1562. Subsequent mileages are from this junction, 2550 feet.

The well-graded trail climbs steadily. In about 2½ miles is a crossing of Boulder Creek, hazardous in high water. At 4 miles is 5000-foot Basin Camp, under the walls of 8676-foot Clark Mountain. This is a logical and splendid spot to end the first day—and also a grand base for an extra day exploring a very faint path west to a 6150-foot saddle overlooking the White River. To find the path, cross the creek from camp to a point just under a slab of red rock on the opposite side of the valley. Even without tread the going is fairly easy up open meadows.

From Basin Camp the trail climbs 2½ miles to 6250-foot Boulder Pass, the meadowy saddle to the immediate east of Clark Mountain. Look down into the Napeequa valley and over to Little Giant Pass (Hike 72). The hike to here, 10¼ miles from the road, makes a strenuous but richly rewarding 2- to 3-day trip. You may well decide to say the heck with Shangri La and drowning.

Switchback down some 2000 feet in 2¼ miles to the valley floor—and trouble—at 4340 feet. The Forest Service is unable to keep a bridge across the swift-flowing Napeequa River, which perhaps can be safely forded at this point in late August. But many summers it's never less than very risky.

If you manage to cross, explorations are limited only by the time available. Follow the trail up the wide, green valley floor, probably the floor of a Pleistocene lake, 5 or 6 miles; good camps are numerous. In ½ mile look to glaciers on Clark Mountain. In 2 miles pass under the falls of Louis Creek. Wander on and on, higher and higher, better and better, to trail's end in the moraines and creeks of Napeequa Basin, a deep hole half-ringed by dazzling glaciers, one of which tumbles nearly to the basin floor.

68 | BASALT RIDGE–GARLAND PEAK

Round trip: 9 miles
Hiking time: 6 hours
High point: 6351 feet
Elevation gain: 2500 feet
Hikable: July to October
Maps: Green Trails Nos. 145 Wenatchee Lake, 146 Plain,
114 Lucerne
Current information: Ask at Lake Wenatchee Ranger
Station about trail Nos. 1530, 1515

Driving directions: Drive US 2 between Stevens Pass and Leavenworth
and turn north on the Lake Wenatchee road. Cross the Wenatchee River
bridge and go straight ahead on Chiwawa Loop Road (county road No.
22) 1.4 miles, then left on the Chiwawa River road 9.4 miles, then right
on road No. 6210, signed "Chikamin Trail." Drive another 5.8 miles and
find trail No. 1530 on a steep curve, elevation 3900 feet (don't mistake
this for trail No. 1539, at approximately 4 miles).

The trail along Basalt Ridge to the Garland Peak area of the Entiat Mountains gives views across Rock Creek to Old Gib Mountain and beyond to
the ice-gleaming spires of Clark Mountain and Glacier Peak. There are four
ways to reach Basalt Ridge: the hard way, by way of Minnow Creek; over
the top of Basalt Peak; 5 miles up Rock Creek (Hike 70); and the terribly
steep (but short—only 1½ miles) access described here.

The trail starts steep, relents briefly, and reverts to type, henceforth
showing little mercy. In 1¼ miles the trail climbs 1200 feet to a 5200-foot

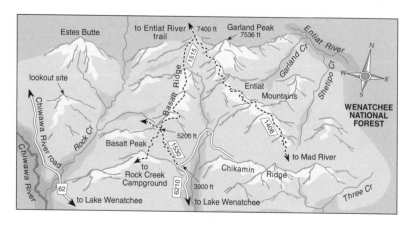

saddle and an unsigned junction with Basalt Ridge trail No. 1515. Several hundred feet uphill to the left is the signed junction with the access trail from Rock Creek. Go right, along the saddle, losing about 50 feet then climbing a moderately steep, rocky slope, emerging from trees to buckbrush. This gives way to meadows that are almost all stones.

At about 3 miles from the road the way attains a high point, 6351 feet, with views big enough to satisfy the day-hiker—who by now will have been laboring 2 or 3 or 4 hours. Overnighters will continue, losing about 200 feet, gaining them back, and contouring the slopes of a knob to a 6500-foot saddle at the edge of a huge pumice field (deposited by Glacier Peak 12,000 years ago). Descend a way trail 500 feet to campsites—and the only water of the trip—below Garland Peak.

For explorations, continue on the Basalt Ridge trail to the Garland Peak trail (Hike 86) and proceed north or south.

Basalt Ridge and Garland Peak

69 | SCHAEFER LAKE

Round trip: 10 miles
Hiking time: 6 hours
High point: 5131 feet
Elevation gain: 2700 feet
Hikable: July (if a safe crossing can be found) through October
Map: Green Trails No. 145 Wenatchee Lake
Current information: Ask at Lake Wenatchee Ranger Station about trail No. 1519

Driving directions: Drive US 2 between Stevens Pass and Leavenworth and turn north on the Lake Wenatchee road. Cross the Wenatchee River bridge and go straight ahead on Chiwawa Loop Road (county road No. 22) 1.4 miles, then left on the Chiwawa River road 13.4 miles to upstream 0.2 mile from the Rock Creek Information Center and campground to Schaefer Creek trail No. 1519, elevation 2474 feet.

A forest trail leads to a sparkling lake amid rocky ridges. First, however, a person must get to the trail, which lies on the far side of the Chiwawa River, safe to wade only in late summer. So, is the good old logjam still in place? It moves every winter. Thereby hangs the decision. Logjams come and go with every flood, but this one was here in 1983 and still in place in 2001. Well, almost—in high water the logs do not reach all the way across.

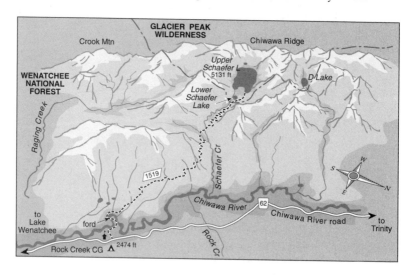

The trail drops to the river, hoping as it does that the logjam is still there and safe to cross. On the far side the way pokes along the Chiwawa valley floor a magnificent mile of spruce and cedar forest. It then hits the valley wall and begins a long sidehill up woods, with a couple of short switch-backs and occasional glimpses to snowy summits of Red Mountain, Dumbell, and Seven-Fingered Jack. At about 2½ miles a corner is rounded into the valley of Schaefer Creek, passing a possible camp just short of 3 miles and at 3½ miles crossing the creek on a sturdy bridge, 4100 feet.

The trail now does business, climbing 1000 feet in 1¼ miles (at 4½ miles is the boundary of Glacier Peak Wilderness). The ascent slackens, passing Lower Schaefer Lake and a shallow pond, and reaching Upper Schaefer Lake at 5 miles, 5131 feet.

Schaefer Lake

70 | ROCK CREEK

Round trip: 14 miles
Hiking time: Allow 2 days
High point: 4300 feet
Elevation gain: 1800 feet
Hikable: Mid-June to October
Maps: Green Trails Nos. 113 Holden, 145 Wenatchee Lake
Current information: Ask at Lake Wenatchee Ranger
Station about trail No. 1509

Driving directions: Drive US 2 between Stevens Pass and Leavenworth
and turn north on the Lake Wenatchee road. Cross the Wenatchee River
bridge and go straight ahead on Chiwawa Loop Road (county road No.
22) 1.4 miles, then left on the Chiwawa River road for 14.8 miles. Just
before the Rock Creek bridge, find Rock Creek trail No. 1509 on the
right side of the road, elevation 2515 feet.

Looking for a spot just like Spider Meadow (Hike 76), except with the flowers outnumbering the hikers? This forest trail leads to campsites at the edge
of Rock Creek Meadow, not as big as the Spider but equally beautiful. Unfortunately, the first 2 miles are open to motorcycles.

Built wide and hard for heavy horse use, the trail climbs gently the first
mile, steepens a bit the second mile, and at 2¼ miles, 3400 feet, comes to a
junction. The right fork climbs to the Basalt Ridge trail (Hike 68); keep
straight ahead, left. The trail, at this point some 400–500 feet above Rock
Creek, contours (with ups and downs) the next 1¾ miles, letting the river
catch up to the trail level.

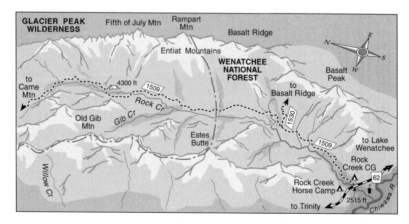

Rock Creek trail

At 4¼ miles the route enters the Glacier Peak Wilderness, drops a bit, and enters a magnificent forest of big trees. Just beyond the 5-mile marker is a choice little campsite near the stream.

Starting at about 5½ miles, the trail is no more Mr. Nice Guy, becoming rough and steep. Occasional windows open in the forest to Devils Smokestack, Fifth of July Mountain, and nameless peaks of the Entiat Mountains. At 6½ miles is a crossing—difficult until late summer—of Rock Creek. At 7 miles the way passes through the promised meadow to excellent campsites at the second crossing of the creek, 4300 feet.

For easy explorations from a basecamp here, continue upstream to more meadows or hike 5 more miles (gaining 2700 feet) to the lookout site on Carne Mountain (Hike 75). Consider a loop trip via Carne Mountain and Estes Butte (Hike 71); for this add 10 miles to the above, for a loop total of 22 miles, elevation gain of about 5000 feet.

71 | ESTES BUTTE

Round trip: 6 miles
Hiking time: 4 hours
High point: 5397 feet
Elevation gain: 2900 feet
Hikable: June to October
Maps: Green Trails Nos. 145 Wenatchee Lake, 113 Holden
Current information: Ask at Lake Wenatchee Ranger
Station about trail No. 1527

Driving directions: Drive US 2 between Stevens Pass and Leavenworth
and turn north on the Lake Wenatchee road. Cross the Wenatchee River
bridge and go straight ahead on Chiwawa Loop Road (county road No.
22) 1.4 miles, then go left on the Chiwawa River road for 15 miles. Find
Estes Butte trail No. 1527 between the Rock Creek bridge and the Rock
Creek Horse Camp, elevation 2515 feet.

A climb to a former lookout site on a 5402-foot bump on the ridge leading
to Estes Butte. Do the hike in midsummer when the forest floor is blooming with sidebells pyrola and pipsissewa, or on a crisp fall day when the
sun cheers but doesn't overheat. The trail was rebuilt in 1995 to bear up
under heavy horse traffic.

The trail parallels Rock Creek on the level along a rough old mining
road. Long switchbacks then climb to the right at a grade ideal for horses;
the slow pace gives plenty of time to look down to the pyrola and pipsissewa. The first mile has a few lookouts through chinks in the green wall to
views down the valley, and in the second mile some windows open on
green meadows of the Entiat Mountains to the east.

At 3 miles is the old lookout site. A USGS marker cemented to a rock
says "5402 feet." The USGS map shows 5397. The building was atop a tower

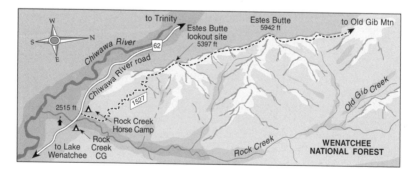

with an all-points view over the treetops. Only the concrete foundation remains, but by moving about and looking between trees the same view can be assembled from the pieces. Day-trippers should eat their cookies here and go home.

The trail continues another 12 miles, with major ups and downs, over the tippy-top of 5942-foot Estes Butte, into the Glacier Peak Wilderness, around the side of Old Gib Mountain, and to Carne Mountain (Hike 75), gaining 2500 feet on the way. The route is dangerous before the snow melts and bone-dry afterward.

Estes Butte

72 | LITTLE GIANT PASS

Round trip: 9½ miles
Hiking time: 9 hours
High point: 6409 feet
Elevation gain: 4200 feet in, 300 feet out
Hikable: Early August through September
Map: Green Trails No. 113 Holden
Current information: Ask at Lake Wenatchee Ranger
Station about trail No. 1518

Driving directions: Drive US 2 between Stevens Pass and Leavenworth
and turn north on the Lake Wenatchee road. Cross the Wenatchee River
bridge and go straight ahead on Chiwawa Loop Road (county road No.
22) 1.4 miles, then go left on the Chiwawa River road about 19 miles to
Little Giant Pass trail No. 1518, elevation 2600 feet.

Climb to the famous view of the fabled Napeequa valley. Look down on
the silvery river meandering through green meadows of the old lakebed.
See the gleaming ice on Clark Mountain and Tenpeak, glimpse a piece of
Glacier Peak. But you gotta really want it. Strong mountaineers turn pale
at memories of Little Giant in sunshine and flytime. However, this route to
Napeequa valley, though more grueling than the Boulder Pass entry (Hike
67), is 5 miles shorter and has no fearsome ford of the Napeequa to face.
Ah, but it may have a fearsome ford of the Chiwawa River. But that's at the
very beginning, so you get the bad news in time to choose another destina-

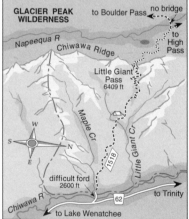

tion should the logjam be missing
and the flood be boiling halfway up
your Kelty.

Longingly think about the
bridge taken out by a flood in 1972.
Look around for a logjam—they
change every year. In 2001 a cottonwood tree had fallen across the
river, good for a tightrope walker.
Some hikers have found logjams
upstream ⅓ mile. Finding nothing
else, try the wade if you are fairly
sure you can survive it, and if you
do, follow abandoned roads
through abandoned Maple Creek
Campground and pretty soon pick
up the trail. The old straight-up

Napeequa valley from Little Giant Pass

sheep driveway of evil reputation has been partly replaced (and the sheep are long gone from here, too) by a trail that was nicely engineered if steep, but is deteriorating rapidly from lack of maintenance. The way climbs the valley of Maple Creek in pretty pine forest, crosses a saddle, and drops to South Fork Little Giant Creek at about 2½ miles from the river, 4000 feet. Campsites on both sides.

Now the way steepens and at 3 miles half-scrambles up a broad rib of bare schist that splits the valley in two and on a sunny day will fry your boots. But in ½ mile creeks begin. So do camps that get progressively better, the last on a scenic meadow knoll at 4 miles. A lovely ascent in greenery and marmots leads to the 6409-foot pass, 4⅔ miles from the river.

Better views can be obtained by scrambling up the knobs on either side of the pass, which in addition to being a sensational grandstand is a glory of flowers.

The trail down to the Napeequa has been abandoned for years, yet suffices for hikers—though not for horses or sheep, and bleached bones prove it. Watch your step—at spots a misstep could add you to the casualty list. The distance to the 4200-foot valley floor is 2 miles, and if the views don't have you raving, the blossoms will—or, in season, the flies. The abandoned trail proceeds upvalley 1⅓ miles to the site of the bridge that is gone, and the ford that remains, to cross the river to the Boulder Pass trail (Hike 67). The best camps hereabouts are on gravel bars—but watch out for sudden high water on hot afternoons.

73 | BUCK CREEK PASS–HIGH PASS

Round trip: 19 miles
Hiking time: Allow 2 to 3 days
High point: 6000 feet
Elevation gain: 3200 feet
Hikable: July through October
Map: Green Trails No. 113 Holden
Current information: Ask at Lake Wenatchee Ranger
Station about trail Nos. 1550, 1511, 1562

Driving directions: Drive US 2 between Stevens Pass and Leavenworth
and turn north on the Lake Wenatchee road. Cross the Wenatchee River
bridge and go straight ahead on Chiwawa Loop Road (county road No.
22) 1.4 miles, then go left on the Chiwawa River road some 23 miles to
the end at Phelps Creek Campground, elevation 2772 feet.

In a mountain range full to overflowing with "unique places," two things
have given Buck Creek Pass fame: an unusual richness of flower gardens
extending from creek bottoms to high summits, and the exceptional view
of the grandest ice streams of Glacier Peak, seen across the broad, forested
valley of the Suiattle River. The trail lends itself to a variety of trips short
and long: a day's walk as far as time allows, a weekend at the pass, or a
week of explorations.

Walk downstream some 300 feet to the trail bridge over Phelps Creek,
skirt the private property in the old mining (wannabe but never really was)
town of Trinity, and climb moderately along an abandoned road. At ¾ mile
enter the Glacier Peak Wilderness. In 1½ miles, at a Y where the road proceeds straight ahead toward mining claims on Red Mountain (Hike 74),

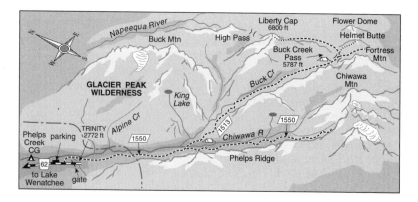

Triad Lake and Clark Mountain from the High Pass trail

the trail turns off left, going up and down within sound of the Chiwawa River. At 2¾ miles cross the "river" (here just a swift creek), then a low rib, into the Buck Creek drainage. Just beyond the bridge is a large campsite.

The trail climbs a valley step, levels out, and passes a forest camp in a patch of grass. It switchbacks up another glacier-plucked step and emerges from trees to traverse a wide avalanche meadow at 5 miles, 4300 feet. This is a good turnaround for a day hike, offering a view of the cliffs and hanging glaciers on the north wall of 8528-foot Buck Mountain.

Here begins a series of long switchbacks, climbing on a 10-percent grade to a 6000-foot high point overlooking Buck Creek Pass, 9½ miles. For camping, drop about 200 feet into the pass. Do not be surprised on weekends to find the area mobbed.

Explorations? Enough for a magnificent week.

Start with an evening wander to Flower Dome to watch Suiattle forests darken into night while the snows of Glacier Peak glow pink.

For a spectacular sunrise, carry your sleeping bag to the top of Liberty Cap.

Try an interesting sheepherders' track: Walk the main trail back toward Trinity about ½ mile from the pass to a large basin with several streams. A few feet before emerging from forest into basin meadows, go left on an unmarked way trail that sidehills flower-garden slopes of Helmet Butte, passes delightful campsites, and disappears in some 2 miles at 6100 feet, below 6400-foot Pass No Pass.

Don't miss the dead-end trail toward (not to) High Pass. Find it on the south side of Buck Creek Pass. Ascend around Liberty Cap and as far as the way is not covered with dangerously steep snow. The end, 3 miles from Buck Creek Pass, is in a 7000-foot saddle overlooking the wintry basin of Triad Lake. Getting from trail's end to High Pass is for climbers only.

74 | CHIWAWA BASIN–RED MOUNTAIN

Round trip: 16½ miles
Hiking time: Allow 2 days
High point: 6900 feet
Elevation gain: 4100 feet
Hikable: Mid-July through September
Map: Green Trails No. 113 Holden
Current information: Ask at Lake Wenatchee Ranger
   Station about trail No. 1550

Driving directions: Drive US 2 between Stevens Pass and Leavenworth and turn north on the Lake Wenatchee road. Cross the Wenatchee River bridge and go straight ahead on Chiwawa Loop Road (county road No. 22) 1.4 miles, then go left on the Chiwawa River road some 23 miles to the end at Phelps Creek, elevation 2772 feet.

Mining (prospecting and stock-peddling, actually) operations, mainly in the 1920s and 1930s but with some messing around in the 1950s, bruised and ripped and battered the fragile subalpine terrain. The old trail has been replaced by an ugly, rutted prospectors' road. Not for centuries will nature repair the damage. Keep it in mind as an object lesson next time you hear defenders of the antique mining laws bray about "free enterprise." Not all is lost, however. The surviving meadows are beautiful, and the views of the Upper Chiwawa River basin are splendid.

   Walk across the Phelps Creek trail bridge, skirting Trinity "town," and follow trail signs to the Glacier Peak Wilderness at ¾ mile. At 1½ miles,

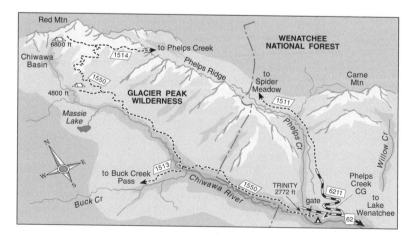

where Buck Creek Pass trail No. 1513 (Hike 73) branches left, continue on the road—officially, Chiwawa River trail No. 1550—as it steadily ascends the valley on the flanks of Phelps Ridge, the way muddy from tromping by many hooves.

At 5½ miles, 4750 feet, the route splits. The left fork trail, No. 1550, leads to the flower fields of Chiwawa Basin, offering several appealing campsites. In days past the prospectors used a loop through the basin that rejoined the other fork high on Red Mountain.

Trail No. 1550, the right fork, sticks with the road, climbing through an impossible wall of avalanche brush, then timber, in a series of long switchbacks. At the top of the last one is a fine campsite (if not recently used by horses) at the edge of a large green basin below the brightly colored rock slopes of Red Mountain.

The road–trail now cuts a broad scar across the meadows of Red Mountain, sidehilling toward the lower slopes of Chiwawa Mountain. The end is on talus, where trails branch every which way to little holes in the ground. For excellent alpine camping, descend the rubble to open benches amid the all-around splashes of waterfalls.

Camping on Red Mountain (Photo by Kirkendall/Spring)

75 | CARNE MOUNTAIN

Round trip: 7 miles
Hiking time: 7 hours
High point: 7085 feet
Elevation gain: 3585 feet
Hikable: July through October
Map: Green Trails No. 113 Holden
Current information: Ask at Lake Wenatchee Ranger
Station about trail Nos. 1508, 1509.

Driving directions: Drive US 2 to Coles Corner between Stevens Pass and Leavenworth and turn north on Lake Wenatchee road No. 207. Pass the state park, cross the Wenatchee River bridge, and go straight ahead on the Chiwawa River Loop road (county road No. 22) 1.4 miles then left some 22.5 miles on the Chiwawa River road and right another 2.4 miles on the Phelps Creek road No. 6211 to the road-end, elevation 3500 feet.

Loll around an enchanting basin, enjoying hideaway seclusion among soaring peaks. Then climb to the summit of Carne Mountain and gaze to the dark summit of mighty Mount Maude, empress of the Entiat Mountains, and around to Spider Meadow, Red Mountain, Glacier Peak, Ten Peak Mountain, and Mount Rainier.

Begin with a scant ¼ mile on the Phelps Creek trail, then turn uphill on Carne Mountain trail No. 1508, ascending a very steep slope through open forest. After the first mile occasional windows open west to the impressive massif of Chiwawa Ridge. Forest eventually is left below, and broad vistas commence. At 2½ miles is a marginal campsite, water supplied by the creek

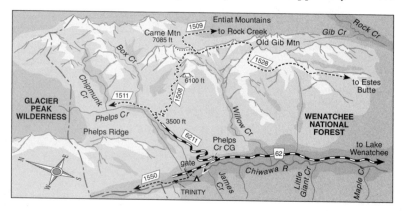

from Carne Basin, which is entered at 3 miles. The greenery of the 6100-foot floor is boxed in by rocky ridges from Carne Mountain. Camps are plentiful in the lovely alpine meadows, though some are horsey and all of them are, in season, quite buggy. The basin used to boasts one of the world's largest subalpine larches. Though now fallen, it reminds us that in October the forests hereabout turn golden and the bugs all bug out to California for the winter.

The trail disappears in the meadow and reappears as the ascent resumes on the far side. At 3½ miles the Carne Mountain trail splits in two. The right fork, Old Gib trail No. 1528, climbs to a saddle, 6500 feet, and views of the north face of Old Gib Mountain, then heads south to Estes Butte (Hike 71) and the Chiwawa River road, reached at Rock Creek.

Take the left fork, Rock Creek trail No. 1509, passing at the first switchback a steep but inviting sidetrail to the former site of a fire lookout atop Peak 6991. Continue on the full ¾ mile to a delightful open saddle with a view of the Rock Creek valley, the Entiat Mountains, and awesome Mount Maude.

The peak-grabbers should go left (north) and follow the footsteps of other peak-grabbers to the 7085-foot summit of Carne Mountain. The view is not really better at the top.

View from Carne Mountain (Photo by Kirkendall/Spring)

76 | SPIDER MEADOW

Round trip to upper Spider Meadow: 11 miles
Hiking time: 6 hours
High point: 5100 feet
Elevation gain: 1700 feet
Hikable: Mid-July through October

Round trip to Spider Gap: 15 miles
Hiking time: 9 hours
High point: 7100 feet
Elevation gain: 3600 feet
Hikable: Mid-July through October

Map: Green Trails No. 113 Holden
Current information: Ask at Lake Wenatchee Ranger
Station about trail No. 1511

Driving directions: Drive US 2 to Coles Corner between Stevens Pass
and Leavenworth and turn north on Lake Wenatchee road No. 207. Pass
the state park, cross the Wenatchee River bridge, and go straight ahead
on the Chiwawa River Loop road (county road No. 22) 1.4 miles then
left some 22.5 miles on the Chiwawa River road and right another 2.4
miles on the Phelps Creek road No. 6211 to the road-end, elevation
3500 feet.

A glorious and perhaps over-populated valley-bottom meadow in a seem-
ing cul-de-sac amid rugged peaks. Lo, the trail ingeniously breaks through
the cliffs and climbs to a little "glacier" and a pass with a grand overlook of
Lyman Basin and outlook to summits of the Cascade Crest. For hikers

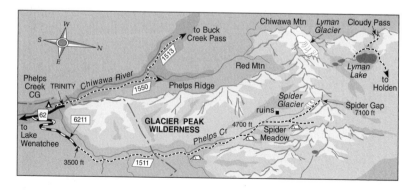

Spider Meadow

trained in use of the ice ax, this can be merely the beginning of a long and classic loop trip, described in Hike 77.

The walk begins on an abandoned road that rapidly is shrinking to trail. The gentle grade goes up and down in forest, passing the Carne Mountain trail in ½ mile, Box Creek in 1 mile, Chipmunk Creek in 1¾ miles, and the Glacier Peak Wilderness boundary in 2⅔ miles. At 3½ miles, 4175 feet, are the crossing of Leroy Creek, the junction with Leroy Creek trail, a campsite, and the end of the old road. This trail gets so much use that firewood is scarce; bring a stove or dine on crackers and cheese.

The way continues through forest interspersed with flower gardens. At 5¼ miles, 4700 feet, is the spectacular opening-out into Spider Meadow; here are good camps. Red Mountain shows its cliffs and snows; the views include other walls enclosing Phelps headwaters—no way can be seen to escape the valley, an apparent dead end. A mile of flower-walking leads to the crossing of Phelps Creek, 6 miles, 5100 feet. A bit beyond are ruins of Ed Linston's cabin. Find good camps here, too. Hikers with only a day or a weekend may turn back, content.

But there is much more, including more good camps. Follow the trail through the meadow, boulder-hop Phelps Creek, and proceed upward. At 6½ miles, 5300 feet, is a junction. The right fork follows Phelps Creek to more meadows and the end of the valley, under Dumbell Mountain.

The left fork is a steep, hot, and very dry miners' trail, climbing 1100 feet to the lower end of Spider Glacier, at 6400 feet. Here are several tiny but spectacular campsites. There's no wood, but lots of water and lots of views downvalley to Spider Meadow, Mount Maude, and Seven-Fingered Jack.

Immediately above is the narrow snowfield known as Spider Glacier. In a scant mile, either up the snow-filled gully or along the easy and scenic rock spur to the east, is 7100-foot Spider Gap. Look down to the Lyman Glacier, the ice-devastated upper Lyman Basin, and the greenery of the lower basin.

An old trail ascends ¼ mile from the pass to a mine tunnel. One must marvel at the dogged energy of Ed Linston, who hauled machinery and supplies to so airy a spot. After being badly injured by a dynamite explosion in the mine, he was helped down the mountain by his brother, who had come looking for him, and made a full recovery. His family demanded he give up his mine, but he spent many more years roaming the Cascades looking for color, and passed away in 1969 at the age of 82.

Avalanche lily

77 | SPIDER GAP–BUCK CREEK PASS LOOP

Loop trip: 44 miles including Image Lake
Hiking time: Allow 4 to 7 days
High point: 7100 feet
Elevation gain: 4800 feet
Hikable: Late July to late September
Map: Green Trails No. 113 Holden
Current information: Ask at Lake Wenatchee Ranger
Station about trail Nos. 1511, 1513, 1550; Chelan
Ranger Station about trail No.1256; and Darrington
Ranger Station about trail Nos. 789, 2000

Driving directions: Drive US 2 to Coles Corner between Stevens Pass
and Leavenworth and turn north on Lake Wenatchee road No. 207. Pass
the state park, cross the Wenatchee River bridge, and go straight ahead
on the Chiwawa River Loop road (county road No. 22) 1.4 miles then
left some 22.5 miles on the Chiwawa River road and right another 2.4
miles on the Phelps Creek road No. 6211 to the road-end, elevation
3500 feet.

Valley-bottom meadows, ridge-crest meadows, tumbling streams, quiet
lakes, crags and glaciers—the supreme sampler of the Glacier Peak Wilderness. Don't you dare so much as think of doing it as a cock-a-doodle-doo
marathon. The ups, the downs, the torrents for wading, the snows for boot-
kicking, could permanently squash the swiftness of an overweening ego.

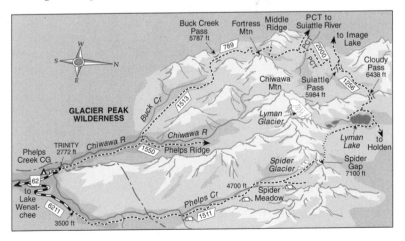

Hikers near the snout of Lyman Glacier

Besides, only a loonie would travel such country on the run. The flowers! The sunsets! The blueberries! If your feet twitch for fast action, expend spare energy on off-trail explorations. Take your time. Lots of it. Learn the difference between getting there and being there. Experience the starry nights as well as the sunny (or whatever) days. Choice campsites abound, but mostly in high country, where the little inflammable wood that exists is part of the scenery; carry a stove or save weight with cold meals.

The loop can be done in either direction. However, because the snow-field at Spider Gap may be unreasonably dangerous, counterclockwise is recommended in order to keep open a safe line of retreat if the party would rather live than be unreasonable.

Walk Phelps Creek trail No. 1511 to the Glacier Peak Wilderness at 2¾ miles, Spider Meadow at 5 miles, and Spider Gap at 7½ miles, 7100 feet (Hike 76), the highest point of the trip.

An unmaintained path, often buried in snow, descends to Upper Lyman Lake. If the snow is hard and no safe detour is apparent, *turn back* and choose another trip. Your family and friends will thank you, Mountain Rescue will thank you—only the show-biz press with its bloodthirsty helicopters will be disappointed.

The three Upper Lyman Lakes are fed by the Lyman Glacier a stone's throw away, a priceless opportunity to have your photo taken throwing snowballs in August. The unmaintained path drops to forest and Lyman Lake, 5587 feet, some 13 miles from the Phelps Creek gate.

The next stage of the loop climbs to meadows of Cloudy Pass (sidetrip toward North Star Mountain) and at 2.5 miles from Lyman Lake joins the Pacific Crest Trail at Suiattle Pass, 5984 feet. Glacier Peak will pop your eyes here, the first of many times it will do so. A scant ½ mile from the pass, the Crest Trail comes to a junction where the loop goes left—but a sidetrip to the right is mandatory, a 7-mile round trip to Image Lake (Hike 12).

Back on the loop, follow the Crest Trail a long 1½ miles and turn left on trail No. 789, dropping 1000 feet to a crossing of Miners Creek. From forest climb back to meadows of Middle Ridge—and there's Glacier Peak again, right in the kisser. Descend a bit again, to Small Creek, and climb a bit again, past Flower Dome (yes, Glacier Peak once more bigger than ever) to Buck Creek Pass, 5787 feet.

More sidetrips (Hike 73), a final goodbye to Glacier Peak, and the loop concludes in a 9½-mile descent to Trinity and (sob!) the 2½-mile walk up the Phelps Creek road to the car.

Ptarmigan in summer plumage

78 MAD RIVER–COUGAR MOUNTAIN

Round trip: 11 miles
Hiking time: 6 hours
High point: 6701 feet
Elevation gain: 2500 feet
Hikable: Mid-June through October
Map: Green Trails No. 146 Plain
Current information: Ask at Entiat Ranger Station about
 trail Nos. 1409, 1419, 1418, 1415

Driving directions: Drive US 2 to Coles Corner, between Leavenworth
and Stevens Pass, and turn north past Lake Wenatchee State Park. Just
beyond the Wenatchee River bridge, go straight ahead on Chiwawa
Loop Road. Cross the Chiwawa River at 3.7 miles. At 4.2 miles (just beyond Thousand Trails' sports facilities), turn a sharp left on (unsigned)
road No. 6100. In another 1.6 miles, at Deep Creek Campground, go
right on road No. 6101, signed "Maverick Saddle." At 0.4 mile from
Deep Creek, stay straight. At 3.2 miles turn right at a hunters' camp. After a final steep and narrow 2 miles only a 4x4 could love is Maverick
Saddle, 6.1 miles from Deep Creek. To the left is an even rougher road,
probably best walked, down 0.3 mile to the start of Mad River trail No.
1409, elevation 4250 feet.

It's a stiff climb to the top of Cougar Mountain, but the panoramas from
the old lookout site extend from Mount Rainier to Glacier Peak and out

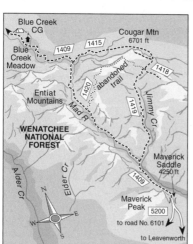

over miles of the 1994 forest fire burn
that stopped just short of the summit. The rock gardens also are
worth the effort, especially when
the snow has just melted away in
late June or early July and the very
stones seem to burst into bloom.
The trip can be done as a sortie
from a backpack base at Blue Creek
Campground (Hike 79) or, as described here, a 1-day jaunt from the
Maverick Saddle trailhead.

There is some elaboration in
Hike 79 about what Wenatchee–
Okanogan National Forest wants
for the Mad River, which is nothing
less than to serve as a crucial link in

a proposed motorcycle roadlet from Lake Wenatchee to Lake Chelan. A sign
at Maverick Saddle trailhead prohibits wheels on the snowmelt-soft tread
before it dries out, along about mid-July, duly warning us of the long-range
plans being cooked up by the rangers and their rough-riding clientele. Pedestrians should come to Maverick Saddle and return home to add their
letters to the preservationist campaign to enlarge the Glacier Peak Wilderness and thus thwart the Lake-to-Lake Raceway, which the motorcycle le-
gions are hailing as a major-league run that is sure to draw throngs of
thunderwheels from across the nation. Well, all you pilgrims out there, rise
up your wrath. Our legals are on the case and with your help will prevail.

At 1½ miles from the trailhead is a bridge wide and sturdy enough for
tanks. Paint a center stripe and it would accommodate two lanes of motorcycles, which wouldn't have to ease up a bit on the throttle to roar both
ways simultaneously across the Mad River. Then note the concrete blocks
that pave stretches of tread. Sensitivities of the rangers are offended by
seeing wheels gouge deep ruts. The gougers just hate to slow down for soft
spots. Note, too, the rubberlike water bars that divert snowmelt and rain
from the tread but can be ridden over at high speed and nary a bump felt
by the butt.

A bit past the bridge, turn right on Jimmy Creek trail No. 1419, gaining

Ice-draped cliffs on Cougar Mountain

Cougar Mountain after an early fall snowstorm

1400 feet in 2½ miles to join abandoned trail No. 1420. Keep right for ½
mile, contouring past a junction with Cougar Ridge trail No. 1418, to a junction with trail No. 1415. Turn left, climbing 500 feet, and unfold the forest
map on the sky-surrounded summit, 6701 feet, at 5½ miles from the road.

The trail escaped the 1994 burn that swept up the north and east slopes
of Cougar Mountain. The progression through an age of charcoal, snags
silvering gracefully with age, grandmothering the new forest, will add ecological interest to this century.

Happily, the Forest Service recognizes that this trail is too steep and narrow, the soil too fragile, to be "hardened" for wheels, which are banned.
Those ankle-deep (or knee-deep) trenches therefore obviously are dug by
aliens from outer space who don't give a hang about what they do to Earth.

79

MAD RIVER–BLUE CREEK CAMPGROUND–MAD LAKE

Round trip to Blue Creek Campground: 12 miles
Hiking time: Allow 2 days
High point: 5400 feet
Elevation gain: 1100 feet
Hikable: July to mid-October

Round trip from Maverick Saddle to Mad Lake:
  16 miles
Hiking time: Allow 2 days
High point: 5800 feet
Elevation gain: 1550 feet
Hikable: July to mid-October

Map: Green Trails No. 146 Plain
Current information: Ask at Entiat Ranger Station about
  trail No. 1409

Driving directions: Drive US 2 to Coles Corner, between Leavenworth and Stevens Pass, and turn north past Lake Wenatchee State Park. Just beyond the Wenatchee River bridge, go straight ahead on Chiwawa Loop Road. Cross the Chiwawa River at 3.7 miles. At 4.2 miles (just beyond Thousand Trails' sports facilities), turn a sharp left on (unsigned) road No. 6100. In another 1.6 miles, at Deep Creek Campground, go right on road No. 6101, signed "Maverick Saddle." At 0.4 mile from Deep Creek, stay straight. At 3.2 miles turn right at a hunters' camp. After a final steep and narrow 2 miles only a 4x4 could love is Maverick Saddle, 6.1 miles from Deep Creek. To the left is an even rougher road, probably best walked, down 0.3 mile to the start of Mad River trail No. 1409, elevation 4250 feet.

The Mad River country of the Entiat Mountains offers miles and miles of easy, pleasant, family-style roaming. Trails follow noisy creeks through picturesque glades, trails cross broad meadows of brilliant flowers, trails round shores of little lakes, and trails climb mountains. The hikes described here offer a wealth of fun and peace for a weekend or for a weeklong vacation, to be enjoyed by old and very young alike. Tragically, the Forest Service has dedicated the trails to motorcycles and is reconstructing and relocating routes to permit higher (noisier) speeds, deliberately converting trails to motorcycle expressways. That's the bad (dreadful) news. The good news is: Motorcycle use is moderate on weekends and virtually zero on

Old guard station near Blue Creek Campground

weekdays; wheels (and horses too) are banned until the trails dry out, generally July 15, leaving a small window between melting of enough snow to permit hiking and the onslaught of the motors. Motorcyclists seldom camp, so peace comes to backpackers at sunset.

However, how good would the news be with completion of the probably-to-be Lake-to-Lake Raceway that the Forest Service is promoting? The only practical solution is extension of the Glacier Peak Wilderness.

In 1½ miles is the monster bridge over the Mad River—at this point really just a pretty creek. A bit beyond is the Jimmy Creek trail, first of three routes to the summit of 6701-foot Cougar Mountain (Hike 78). At 3 miles is an intersection with a trail that goes right, to the top of Cougar, and left, to Lost Lake. At 4 miles cross the Mad River on a log and at 4½ miles recross near a junction with Tyee Ridge trail No. 1415, the third way up Cougar. (To avoid the damage to fragile creek banks and spawning bed for which motorcycles are infamous, expensive bridges have been purchased but not yet been put in place.) At 5 miles is a broad meadow and at 5½ miles, 5400 feet, is Blue Creek Campground, a splendid spot for the family to spread gear in the open campground or a secluded nook and set out on ramblings. (For four

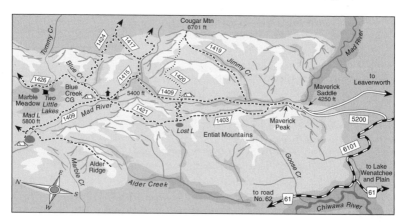

of these, see Hike 80.) The guard station located here is the last remains of the Mad River Dude Ranch, a popular resort in the late 1920s. The cookhouse stood near the present campground. The blacksmith shop and other buildings were scattered about.

The first ramble, of course, is to continue on the Mad River trail through a series of meadows. At 2 miles from Blue Creek Campground (8 miles from the road), go left on a scant ¼-mile trail to Mad Lake, 5800 feet. On the west shore are excellent camps with water from the inlet stream. As is true of most lakes hereabouts, this one is so silted that the bottom is too mucky for wading. However, the inlet stream has deposited enough sand to make a semisolid beach, suitable for cooling the feet.

A mandatory sidetrip is the romp through glorious views along the last 2 miles of the Alder Ridge trail.

Small stream near the upper end of Mad River

80

MAD RIVER SIDETRIPS: WHISTLING PIG AND KLONE PEAK LOOPS

Loop trip to Whistling Pig Meadow and Boiling Springs: 6 miles
Elevation gain: 900 feet
Hikable: July to mid-October

Round trip to Mad Lake, Two Little Lakes, Entiat Meadows, and Klone Peak: 11½ miles
Elevation gain: 1500 feet
Hikable: July to mid-October

Round trip to Lost Lake: 5 miles
Elevation gain: 500 feet
Hikable: July to mid-October

Map: Green Trails No. 146 Plain
Current information: Ask at Entiat Ranger Station about trail Nos. 1425, 1427, 1426,1409

Driving directions: Drive US 2 to Coles Corner between Stevens Pass and Leavenworth and turn north on Lake Wenatchee road No. 207. Pass the state park, cross the Wenatchee River bridge, and go straight ahead on the Chiwawa River Loop road (county road No 22). Cross the Chiwawa River bridge at 3.7 miles. At 4.2 miles (just beyond a large sports facilities), turn a sharp left on (unsigned) road No.6100. In another 1.6 miles, at the Deep Creek campground, go right on road No. 6101, signed "Maverick Saddle." At 3.2 miles turn right at a hunters' camp. The next 2 miles are steep and narrow to Maverick Saddle, 6 miles from Deep Creek. To the left is an even rougher road, probably best walked, down 0.3 mile to the Mad River trailhead, elevation 4250 feet. From here, hike the 6 miles to the Blue Creek campground as described in Hike 79, elevation 5400 feet.

Whistling Pig Meadow and Boiling Springs: A huge meadow and views across the Entiat River valley are the botanical and scenic rewards. The spice of history is provided by an ancient log cabin. As for wildlife, listen for the whistling of the pigs, as the old mountain men called marmots.

From Blue Creek Campground (see Hike 79), hike Mad River trail No. 1409 downstream toward Maverick Saddle. In 1¼ miles, at 5200 feet, the lowest point on the loop, turn left on Tyee Ridge trail No. 1415.

The trail climbs steadily ¾ mile and splits. Straight ahead is the way to Cougar Mountain (Hike 78). Go left on Hunters trail No. 1417 the ½ mile (2½ miles from Blue Creek Campground) to the edge of Whistling Pig Meadow, 5700 feet. Cross to a large grove of trees, site of the old log cabin and the campsites.

The trail enters forest and intersects Middle Tommy Creek trail No. 1424 at 5900 feet. For a mandatory sidetrip go left ¼ mile to Boiling Springs Meadow. The water bubbling from the ground is fun. The many hoof prints mean this is a great place to see deer.

Back on the Whistling Pig trail, turn left, contouring a steep hillside to a high point at 6100 feet. Near here spot a naked knoll to the right; leave the trail and climb a short bit to the edge of a cliff and views to mountains across the Entiat valley. The slope of the hillside gentles and the trail descends into the Blue Creek drainage. At 5½ miles from the start, turn left on Blue Creek trail No. 1426 and return to Blue Creek Campground, at 6 miles.

Mad Lake, Two Little Lakes, Entiat Meadows, and Klone Peak: One of the two lookout cabins that once watched over Mad River country stood atop Klone Peak, 6820 feet. The cabin is gone but the panoramas are as grand: forest, mountains, and even, on the far horizon, the Columbia River Plateau. The meadows along the way are in themselves sufficient reason to do what is, after all, not so terribly strenuous a walk, though long.

From Blue Creek Campground (Hike 79), elevation 5400 feet, hike Blue Creek trail No. 1426 the 2 miles to Two Little Lakes and drop a hundred feet to a crossing of Tommy Creek, 5400 feet. The forested way is now all up, some stretches steep, some of the switchbacks ridiculously flat, built that way to try to reduce motorcycle and horse erosion in the soft soil of

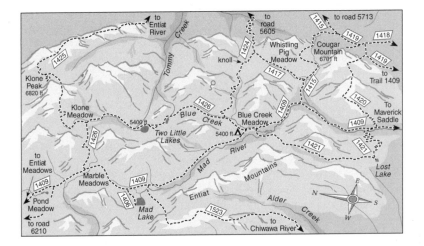

Marble Meadows

Glacier Peak pumice. At 6200 feet, 4 miles from the campsite, is a junction with North Tommy Ridge trail No. 1425 (Hike 82). Numbers on an old sign here may not be the same as on the new Forest Service map.

Turn right on trail No. 1425, pass small waterfalls, and in 1½ miles turn left on Klone Peak trail No. 1427 and hike a short distance to the summit of Klone Peak, 5½ miles from Blue Creek Campground. To the north are Glacier Peak, Clark Mountain, and Ten Peak. East are Duncan Hill and Pyramid Mountain. South is farm country. Southwest is Mount Stuart and a tiny bit of Mount Rainier.

To complete the loop, go 1½ miles back to Blue Creek trail No. 1426 and turn right, mostly through woods, 1 mile to a junction in Marble Meadows with Mad River trail No. 1409. For more meadows, go right 2 miles to Entiat Meadows. For the rest of the loop, turn right 1 mile to the Mad Lake trail, a mandatory sidetrip, ¼ mile each way (Hike 79). Proceed in a succession of meadows to Blue Creek Campground, for a total of 1½ miles.

Lost Lake: It is a shallow little lake surrounded by forest and no views, yet is a pleasant walk.

From Mad Meadows Campground head downstream 1⅓ miles, go right on trail No. 1421, and climb 1½ miles to the shore.

81 | MAD RIVER HIKING TRAILS: OLD KLONE PEAK AND THREE CREEK TRAILS

Round trip on Old Klone Peak Trail : 10 miles
Hiking time: 8 hours
High point: 6820 feet
Elevation gain: 4000 feet
Hikable: July through September

Round trip to Three Creek Trail high point: 13 miles
Hiking time: 12 hours
High point: 6569 feet
Elevation gain: 4500 feet
Hikable: Late June through October

Map: Green Trails No. 146 Plain (trail not shown)
Current information: Ask at Entiat Ranger Station about
    trail Nos. 1427, 1428

Driving directions: Drive US 97 north from Wenatchee along the west side of the Columbia River to the town of Entiat and turn left on the Entiat River road 35.4 miles to Three Creek Campground, elevation 2900 feet. The two abandoned trails are across the river.

The easy ways to the family-friendly upper Mad River have been usurped by motorcycles. Only two accesses—the original Klone Peak trail and the Three Creek trail—retain pristinity, not from any Forest Service sense of respect or fairness but by virtue of having long been abandoned, thus defended by Mother Nature's abundant wheel-barring windfalls. Hiking groups have petitioned for "foot only" status, volunteering to cut out the windfalls. The elevation gain of 4000-plus feet even so would exclude elders and youngers, who on

Signpost on old Klone Peak trail

Three Creek trail

gimpy or stubby legs still would have to dodge traffic on the Mad River ORV Speedway (Hike 79). Extension of the Glacier Peak Wilderness is in any case essential.

Wading the wide, swift stream of snowmelt is dangerous in early summer but by late summer only just wets the knees. Some years the flood is spanned by a fallen tree or logjam, so keep the eyes open downstream—the location of the trail—from Three Creek Campground as far as Spruce Campground.

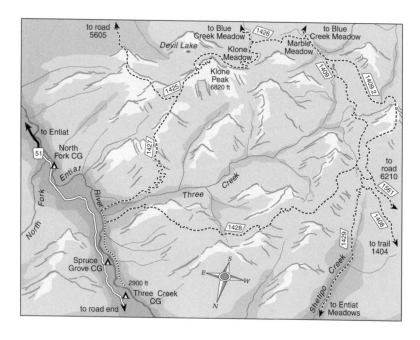

The alternative is to drive road No. 5605, cross the river on a concrete bridge, and in 0.1 mile go right on road No. (5605)125 for 2.5 miles to its end in a clearcut, elevation 2300 feet. Ribbons may mark the route 1 long mile upstream to the Klone Peak trail, close to Three Creek.

Old Klone Peak Trail: The trail sticks close to Three Creek a scant ½ mile, then switchbacks away; tread thins to nothing at a crucial spot—scout around for cutbanks and cut logs. The story from here is switchbacks, 3500 feet gained in 3½ miles, on a broad hillside that narrows to a thin ridge. Holes open in the forest, giving a good look at Pyramid Mountain and, at the ridge top, a glimpse of Glacier Peak. A short drop leads to a junction with North Tommy trail No. 1425 (Hike 82), 6300 feet, 4 miles from the river. Join the motorcycles for the final short ascent to the top of Klone Peak, 6820 feet.

Three Creek Trail: Directly across the river from the campground the Three Creek trail makes an abrupt 90-degree turn and heads uphill. Some windfalls are easily stepped over; others must be squeezed under, climbed over, or detoured around. Don't whine—this is all that keeps the motorcycles out. The trail stays in viewless forest until the last ½ mile, the dark cool a blessing on a hot day.

A conveniently placed windfall over Entiat River

82 | NORTH TOMMY RIDGE

Round trip: 13 miles
Hiking time: 7 hours
High point: 6820 feet
Elevation gain: 2900 feet in, 500 feet out
Hikable: July through October
Map: Green Trails No. 146 Plain
Current information: Ask at Entiat Ranger Station about
trail No. 1425

Driving directions: Drive US 97 north from Wenatchee along the west side of the Columbia River to the town of Entiat and turn left on the Entiat River road 30.8 miles. Turn left on road No. 5605, signed "North Tommy Trail." In 7 miles reach the road-end and North Tommy trail No. 1425, elevation 4500 feet.

Each of five high points on North Tommy Ridge has a grand panorama of mountains and farms and makes a satisfying turnaround. Of course, the farthest and highest (the old fire-lookout site atop Klone Peak) is the bestest.

Until 1986, the second mile of this trail was extremely rough, steep, and difficult. Consequently, the route was seldom used by motorcycles and ORVs; the few that did dug deep ruts into the soft pumice soil, instituting drainage channels that snowmelt trenched knee-deep, utterly destroying long stretches of tread. Rather than accepting the fact that pumice country

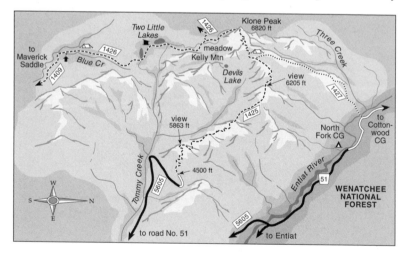

View from the first high point on North Tommy Ridge

is no place for high-speed wheels, the Forest Service obtained $87,776 (1985 dollars) of our Washington State gas-tax money to reconstruct the trail to motorcycle standards. The soft, light soil required the motorcycle trail (expressway) to be built at the 10-percent grade abhorred by hikers; endless switchbacks that even go downhill before turning up will invite shortcuts, which will become erosion channels. The switchbacks are banked and hardened with concrete blocks so the wheels won't have to slow down. A trail once almost machinefree has become a motorcycle obstacle course (with you, the hiker, as the obstacle). The cheapest and simplest answer to the damage of the past would have been to spend a few hundred dollars to fill the worst of the ruts, put in short stretches of new tread, and prohibit the machines that were ripping up the country. However, the motorcyclists persuaded the Forest Service, which never so much as gave hikers a chance to say "NO."

The first ¼ mile is on an abandoned road. The next mile gains a mere 100 feet to a creek crossing, the only water on the route. Then begins the 10-percent monotony. At 3 miles is the top of the first knoll, 5863 feet, with views from a helipad clearing.

The trail drops 300 feet, climbs 600 feet to the second knoll, loses a bit and gains 100 feet to the third, loses 100 feet and gains 200 to the fourth. You can't quit now.

The path drops 200 feet to a junction with the abandoned Klone Peak trail from the Entiat valley (Hike 81), loses 100 feet along a narrow ridge crest, and bumps against the base of Klone Peak. Climb a final 600 feet, to within a few hundred feet of the summit, and join the Blue Creek trail, a popular route from the Mad River trail. At 6½ miles from the road, step out on the lastest and bestest panorama point. The USGS map says the summit is 6820 feet; the sign on top says 6834. The cabin was destroyed by vandals in 1959, but the foundation is still there. So are the views.

83 | DUNCAN HILL

Round trip from road No. 2920: 14 miles
Hiking time: 7 hours
High point: 7819 feet
Elevation gain: 2620 feet
Hikable: Mid-July through mid-October

Round trip via Anthem Creek trail: 16½ miles
Hiking time: 12 hours
High point: 7819 feet
Elevation gain: 4675 feet
Hikable: Mid-July through mid-October

Map: Green Trails No. 114 Lucerne
Current information: Ask at Entiat Ranger Station about
trail Nos. 1434, 1435, 1400

Driving directions: Drive US 97 north from Wenatchee along the west side of the Columbia River to the town of Entiat and turn left on the Entiat River road 33 miles (to 5 miles short of the end at Cottonwood Campground). Near North Fork Campground turn right on road No. 5608. At 5.8 miles (dodging lesser sideroads) stay right at a well-traveled intersection and at 6 miles go left a short distance to trail No. 1434, elevation 5200 feet.

Sweat and pant and grumble to a former lookout site atop 7819-foot Duncan Hill, and there be richly rewarded for the suffering with views up and down the Entiat Valley, from golden sagebrush hills to the rock-and-snow giants of Mount Maude and Seven-Fingered Jack. The trail traverses the peak, making possible two quite different routes that can be combined in a superb loop, if transportation can be arranged from one trailhead to

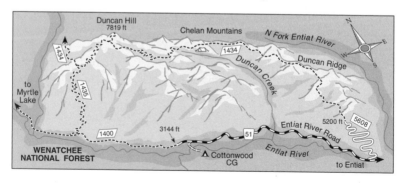

another. It is also the opening leg of another fine loop to Milham Pass. To ameliorate your death throes, carry water to compensate for Nature's stinginess.

According to a Forest Service ranger, except during hunting season this trail is so little used by machines or feet you can have a purer wilderness experience than on the Entiat River trail. However, the soft pumice of the Duncan Hill trail has been so grooved by wheels—no matter how few they may be—that one must often walk to the side of the ruined tread.

The way sets out along wooded Duncan Ridge, climbing a 5549-foot knob, dropping 100 feet, and then climbing again to 5800 feet. The grade

Glacier Peak from Duncan Hill

moderates and in about 3½ miles enters semimeadows, with water and good camps, at the head of Duncan Creek. At about 5 miles is a junction; keep right. At 6½ miles is another junction; again keep right and climb to the top of 7819-foot Duncan Hill and its solar-powered radio, 7 miles from the road.

For the second approach, drive all the 38 miles to Cottonwood Campground, elevation 3144 feet. Try this route in May or June. There likely will be too much snow to reach the summit, but the spring flowers and the abundance of does with fawns are worth it. (Look at and photograph them all you want, but never touch.)

Walk Entiat River trail No. 1400 a flattish 2½ miles and turn right, uphill, on Anthem Creek trail No. 1435. Now the fun begins—if your idea of entertainment is endless switchbacks gaining 2400 feet. At 5900 feet, 6 miles from the road, is the junction with Duncan Ridge trail No. 1434. For camping, turn left ¼ mile to water or 1 mile farther to a spot about 500 feet above the crossing of Anthem Creek. For the summit, turn right and climb open scree and flowers; the tread becomes obscure, so watch it. At 7 ¾ miles is a junction; take the upper trail to the summit, 8¼ miles.

If a party has two cars, or some other ingenious scheme, the two summit approaches make a dandy combination.

For a loop of famous flowers and views, at the 5900-foot junction turn left on Duncan Ridge trail and hike the 6 up-and-down miles to Snowbrushy Creek trail and Milham Pass (Hike 96). Descend to the Entiat River trail and then the road.

Deer on the Entiat River trail

84 | MYRTLE LAKE

Round trip: 8½ miles
Hiking time: 4 hours
High point: 3765 feet
Elevation gain: 600 feet
Hikable: Mid-June through October
Map: Green Trails No. 114 Lucerne
Current information: Ask at Entiat Ranger Station about
trail Nos. 1400, 1404

Driving directions: Drive US 97 north from Wenatchee along the west side of the Columbia River to the town of Entiat and turn left on the Entiat River road 38 miles to its end, 0.4 mile beyond Cottonwood Camp, elevation 3144 feet.

Deep forest of the lower Entiat valley provides an ambling entry to the jade-green lake hidden in a fold of ridges falling from Rampart Mountain. The trail grade is easy, the camping is pleasant, the swimming is bracing. Of all the hikes in the Entiat, this would be the ideal for a family with small children. Children? Make sure they look both ways before stepping out on the trail. Out of loyalty to its multiple-abuse to machinery the Forest Service has made it a motorcycle raceway, and now there are mosquitolike swarms of fat-tire bicycles. Your kids will be safer kept in your backyard.

Hike Entiat River trail No. 1400 through deep forest, distant from the river. Note that as a pedestrian you are a third-class citizen. The trail has been widened for swift wheels and a swath cut through the forest shadows to accommodate horses' hips; the walker must sweat in the hot sun, stifled by pine reek.

In 2½ miles, minor ups and downs netting a mere 400 feet, pass Anthem Creek trail No. 1435 and, in ¼ mile more, a sylvan camp at Anthem Creek.

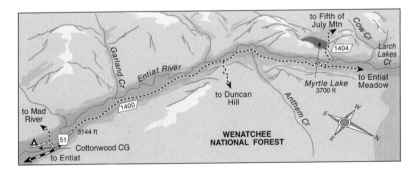

Note the wide bridge; before the trail was reconstructed for motorcycles a footlog did the job. The Forest Service has to abandon foot trails for lack of funds, but there's no shortage of money to speed the wheels.

The way pokes along the valley floor, the forest opening here and there for glimpses of Devils Smokestack and Rampart Mountain. At 3½ miles, turn left on Cow Creek–Myrtle Lake trail No. 1404 and cross the river on a bridge. In a couple hundred yards the trail splits. Both forks climb, at a slightly steeper pitch, to Myrtle Lake, 3700 feet. For camping, take the left fork, which rounds the shore to peaceful forest sites at the south end (wheels are banned). For day-hiking, take the right fork to the north end of the lake. Gaze upon the serene waters in the lovely forest bowl, greenery interrupted only by cliffs and talus on the west side, quietude only by the loud breathing of two-lung motors.

Myrtle Lake

---

85 | DEVILS SMOKESTACK

Loop trip: 22¾ miles
Hiking time: Allow 2 to 3 days
High point: 7400 feet
Elevation gain: 6250 feet
Hikable: mid-July through-September
Maps: Green Trails Nos. 114 Lucerne, 146 Plain
Current information: Ask at Entiat Ranger Station about trail Nos. 1400, 1404, 1408, 1429

Driving directions: Drive US 97 north from Wenatchee along the west side of the Columbia River to the town of Entiat and turn left on the Entiat River road 38 miles to its end, 0.4 mile beyond Cottonwood Camp, elevation 3144 feet.

Aside from the intimations of diabolism (the Hell-hued rocks of the volcanic neck thrusting ruggedly through sheer cliffs), this high-country loop has much to daunt the faint heart. The trail is extremely steep in spots and in others next to nonexistent. For much of a day you face the barren waste without the taste of water, cool, clear water (water). After the snow melts, few places on the route have so much as damp grass all summer. On the other hand, for the strong of heart the trail is full of surprises, such as flowers blooming on otherwise barren hillsides, colorful geology, and lots of solitude.

Hike 4½ miles to Myrtle Lake, 3700 feet (Hike 84). Now the climb begins, switchbacking through deep woods, over a rocky shoulder of Rampart Mountain; a bare knob off the trail to the right gives views to the Entiat

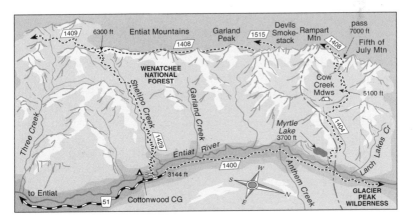

Devils Smokestack from the Garland Peak trail

valley. The way rounds the corner of the shoulder and eases off, contouring steep walls of Cow Creek valley. At 2 miles beyond Myrtle Lake, 6¼ miles from the road, a spur trail goes left over a little rise to Cow Creek Meadows, 5100 feet, a large parkland flat enclosed by cliffs of Rampart and Fifth of July Mountains. Campsites are numerous. A virtually permanent heap of avalanche snow yields meaningful water.

Again the uphill labor, ameliorated by splendid cross-Entiat views to Duncan Hill, Peak 7936, and Gopher Mountain. At 6000 feet, the trail passes a terrific viewpoint on a rock buttress, a campsite, and a path to water. Larch forest commences. At 8½ miles from the road, Cow Creek trail ends by intersecting Garland Peak trail No. 1408, 6600 feet. To the right is a little waterfall creek with several fine camps a short climb above the trail; farther to the right, and down, are the campsites at Larch Lakes (Hike 86), 1½ miles from the intersection.

The loop, however, turns left, abruptly descending a pumice slope, skirting below a band of cliffs, and climbing to Cow Creek Pass (Fifth of July Pass), 7000 feet, on the shoulder of Fifth of July Mountain. The short scramble to the summit and its commanding views is just about mandatory.

From the shoulder, drop to a 6800-foot saddle; the trail becomes vague to imaginary, the blazes the better part of a century old. Turn west, traverse to a long rib, and descend to a basin with a small meadow camp—the Ravens Roost—at 5900 feet. Water all summer, usually. A long uphill swing around the side of Rampart Mountain, then switchbacks, lead to an old sheepherders' camp. Water sometimes. The trail vanishes, reappears above a clump of trees, and proceeds around Rampart to a narrow saddle, 7100 feet.

The way levels off for a wide-open contour around Devils Smokestack to an exposed knob, 7400 feet, with views to everywhere. This is the highest elevation of the loop. Gaze to your fill, and then drop the short bit to intersect the Basalt Ridge trail (Hike 68), 13 miles from the start.

The trail sidehills open ground toward Garland Peak, the pumice soil fragile, criss-crossed with con-

Shetipo Creek trail

fusing animal traces; the correct path climbs briefly, then drops gently as it rounds Garland Peak (Hike 68), another sidetrip essential for view hogs. The way drops, climbs, and drops to a wooded saddle, 6100 feet; a sidetrail leads to Pinto Camp, an agreeable meadow with a very questionable spring.

At 17½ miles the Garland trail ends in a little pass at a junction with Shetipo Creek trail No. 1429, 6300 feet. Motorcycles are permitted to run here; at some corners the tread is rutted so deeply that multiple-use is a difficult feat. Zigging and zagging down 5 long miles, the trail enters Cottonwood Campground on the Entiat River. Cross on the car bridge and find a path heading upriver the final ¼ mile to the parking lot, closing the loop at 22¾ miles.

86 | LARCH LAKES LOOPS

Round trip to Larch Lakes: 11 miles
Hiking time: 8 hours
High point: 5742 feet
Elevation gain: 2600 feet
Hikable: Mid-July through September

Loop trip (shorter loop): 18 miles
Hiking time: Allow 2 to 3 days
High point: 6500 feet
Elevation gain: 3400 feet
Hikable: Mid-July through September

Map: Green Trails No. 114 Lucerne
Current information: Ask at Entiat Ranger Station about
trail Nos. 1400, 1430, 1408, 1404

Driving directions: Drive US 97 north from Wenatchee along the west
side of the Columbia River to the town of Entiat and turn left on the Entiat River road 38 miles to its end, 0.4 mile beyond Cottonwood Camp,
elevation 3144 feet.

Amazingly, the two loveliest lakes in the Entiat valley, surrounded by alpine parkland nestled under cliffs of Fifth of July Mountain, get virtually
no company. Indeed, neither do the miles and miles of up-and-down high
trails along the Entiat Mountains to which they are the entryway.

Hike Entiat River trail No. 1400 for 3½ miles and go left on Cow Creek
trail No. 1404. A short ⅓ mile past Myrtle Lake, go right on Larch Lakes'

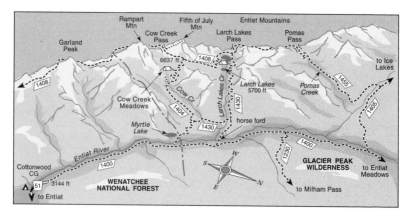

Upper Larch Lake

hiker-only trail No. 1430. The way contours to the horse trail and then begins a grueling climb of 1900 feet in 2½ miles, switchbacking up a treeless, shadeless, waterless south slope. On a hot day the best plan is to loiter by Myrtle Lake until late afternoon, when sun has left the hillside—or better yet, eat a cold dinner at the lake and make the ascent in the cool of the evening. Waiting until morning does no good; the hillside gets the first rays of sun.

Before starting up, note the waterfall high on the hillside to the west. The elevation of this falls (which comes from the lake outlet) provides a measure of how much climbing remains to be done.

The tortuous switchbacks abruptly flatten into a traverse along the shores of 5600-foot Lower Larch Lake, leading to a large meadow and acres of flat ground for camping. The trail continues a short ½ mile to Upper Larch Lake, 5742 feet, more meadows, and the junction with the Pomas Creek trail. Here is a choice of loop trips.

For the longer of the two, climb north some 700 feet to Larch Lakes Pass, then amble northward to 6350-foot Pomas Pass and down Pomas Creek to a junction with the Ice Creek trail, 6 miles from Upper Larch Lake. Go left to Ice Lakes (Hike 87) or right to the Entiat River trail.

For the shorter and more popular loop, follow the trail south around Upper Larch Lake. Tread disappears in meadows and several starts can be seen on the wooded hillside left of Fifth of July Mountain. The correct path goes into the woods at the base of the slope a couple of hundred feet from a granite "island" in the meadow.

The trail climbs steadily more than a mile with airy views down to Larch Lakes, then contours the mountain to a 6500-foot junction with the Cow Creek trail, the return route via Myrtle Lake.

The ascent of Fifth of July Mountain is a must. Though the north face of the peak is a tall, rugged cliff, there's an easy side. Leave packs at the junction and climb the Garland Peak trail a mile south to 7000-foot Cow Creek Pass (some signs say "Fifth of July Pass"). Ascend the gentle south slope to the 7696-foot summit and a 360-degree panorama of Glacier, Clark, Maude, Rainier, and other peaks beyond counting.

The Cow Creek trail descends a steep 2 miles to the edge of Cow Creek Meadows and another 2 miles via Myrtle Lake (Hike 84) to the Entiat River trail, reached at a point 3½ miles from the road-end.

Weathered wood

87 | ENTIAT MEADOWS AND ICE LAKES

Round trip to Lower Ice Lake: 28 miles
Hiking time: Allow 3 to 5 days
High point: (Knoll above lower lake) 6900 feet
Elevation gain: 4200 feet
Hikable: August through September

Round trip to Entiat Meadows: 30 miles
Hiking time: Allow 3 or more days
High point: 5500 feet
Elevation gain: 2400 feet
Hikable: July through October

Maps: Green Trails Nos. 114 Lucerne, 113 Holden
Current information: Ask at Entiat Ranger Station about
    trail Nos. 1400, 1405

Driving directions: Drive US 97 north from Wenatchee along the west
side of the Columbia River to the town of Entiat and turn left on the Entiat River road 38 miles to its end, 0.4 mile beyond Cottonwood Camp,
elevation 3144 feet.

A long trail with many byways to glory and at the two ends a pair of climaxes: a vast meadow under small glaciers hanging on the walls of a row
of 9000-foot peaks, and two high, remote lakes set in cirque basins close
under cliffs of 9082-foot Mount Maude, subalpine trees standing out starkly

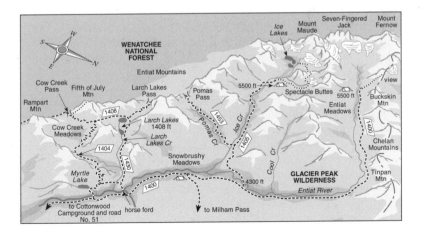

Lower Ice Lake

in a barren, glaciated landscape reminiscent of Khyber Pass. Mountain goats, too, often stand out in the open.

Hike Entiat River trail No. 1400, engineered by the Forest Service the first 4½ miles into a motorcycle expressway, which nowadays gets more bicycles than motors. At 3½ miles is the turnoff to the Cow Creek trail and Myrtle Lake, destination of most people. At 5 miles is the Larch Lakes horse trail (Hike 86), and at 5½ miles is a campsite by Snowbrushy Creek. At 6½ miles, 3900 feet, is a beautiful camp below the trail in Snowbrushy Meadow; here, too, is the Snowbrushy Creek trail to Milham Pass (Hike 96). At 8¼ miles, 4300 feet, reach the split.

Ice Lakes: The Ice Creek trail goes left a short bit to a camp and the missing bridge over the river. (The rangers lost three bridges here and gave up.) Look upstream for a log. The way climbs gradually in forest the first mile, then drops 400 feet to Ice Creek. At 1½ miles, 4300 feet, is a junction with the Pomas Creek trail, an excellent alternate return route via Larch Lakes (Hike 86).

The route follows the stream, alternating between subalpine trees and meadows. At about 3 miles is a crossing of Ice Creek; since a footlog seldom is available and the channel is too wide to jump, be prepared to wade—and find out how well the creek lives up to its name. In another mile is another crossing, but this time the creek can be boulder-hopped. At some 4½ miles from the Entiat trail, formal tread ends in a rocky meadow at a delightful campsite, 5500 feet. The noisy creek drowns the sound of a pretty waterfall tumbling from Upper Ice Lake.

From the trail-end, a boot-built path ascends the rocky meadow north to the valley head, passing the waterfall. Generally keep right of the creek, but cross to the left when the going looks easier there. The valley ends in a steep, green hillside; above, in a pair of hanging cirques, lie the lakes. From a starting point to the right of the creek, scramble up game traces, crossing the creek and climbing between cliffs to its left. The way emerges on a rocky knoll 100 feet above 6822-foot Lower Ice Lake, 6 miles from the Entiat trail. Camp on pumice barrens, not the fragile heather; no fires permitted.

Upper Ice Lake is a mile farther. Head southwest in a shallow alpine valley, below cliffs, to the outlet stream and follow the waterfalls up to the 7200-foot lake, beautifully cold and desolate.

Entiat Meadows: The way to the split is principally through forest; the final 7 miles up the Entiat River alternate between trees and meadows. Though sheep have not been allowed in the valley for years, some meadows still show deep rutting from thousands of hooves, and some native flowers have never grown back.

Entiat Meadows and Mount Maude

At 13 miles, having gained only some 2000 feet thus far, the grade steepens a little for a final 1½ miles and then, at about 5500 feet, the tread fades out in fields of heather and flowers. The camps are fine throughout the miles-long Entiat Meadows and the views are grand—up the cliffs of the huge cirque to the summits of Fernow, Seven-Fingered Jack, and Maude, all above 9000 feet, and to remnants of the Entiat Glacier, which in days of glory excavated the cirque and shaped the valley trough.

If ambition persists, scramble up grassy slopes of the ridge to the north and look down to Railroad Creek and the religious town of Holden.

88 | BIG HILL–PYRAMID MOUNTAIN

Round trip: 18 miles
Hiking time: 10 hours
High point: 8243 feet
Elevation gain: 3000 feet in, 1200 feet out
Hikable: Mid-July to mid-September
Map: Green Trails No. 114 Lucerne
Current information: Ask at Entiat Ranger Station about
    trail Nos. 1433, 1441

Driving directions: Drive US 97 north from Wenatchee along the west
side of the Columbia River to the town of Entiat and turn left on the Entiat
River road some 19 miles and turn right on road No. 5900, signed "Lake
Chelan," which is often dusty and rutted, always steep and narrow. At
8.4 miles, keep left at Shady Pass on road No. (5900)112. At 10.2 miles
pass Big Hill. Keep left on road No. (5900)113 to the road-end and trailhead, 10.7 miles from the Entiat River road, elevation 6458 feet.

Spectacular, yes, walking a ridge so high it almost touches the sky, looking
out through miles of empty air to Glacier Peak, lording it over an infinity
of icy-craggy attendants. The supreme moment is standing where once the
lookout cabin did, atop Pyramid Mountain, with an airplane-wing view
7000 feet straight down to blue waters of Lake Chelan. However, a word to
the thrifty: If the summit of Pyramid is your main goal, you do better to get
there via South Pyramid Creek (Hike 92), saving wear and tear on the family car; the road to Big Hill trailhead varies from so-so to bad to atrocious.
    Pyramid Mountain trail No. 1433 sets out on a wide firebreak the

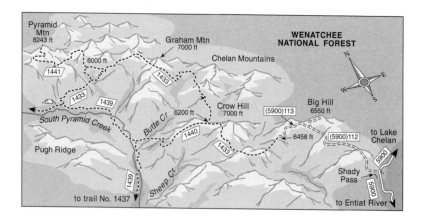

Smokey Bears slashed for exercise while waiting for the rains to come and extinguish the 1970 Entiat Fire. It climbs around the first bump, passes Poodle Dog Camp, and at about 1½ miles climbs to a 7000-foot high point on Crow Hill. A heartbreaking drop ensues, to 6200 feet. At 3 miles, pass the Butte Creek trail and a nice camp at the head of Butte Creek. A gut-wrenching climb goes to 7000 feet on flower-meadowed Graham Mountain. Again (sob!), a drop to 6000 feet. At 6 miles are a junction and another camp with water. Turn right on Pyramid View trail No. 1441 and at 9 miles step proudly onto the summit of Pyramid Mountain, 8243 feet, and enjoy your promised reward.

Pyramid Mountain trail on the side of Crow Hill

89 | NORTH FORK ENTIAT RIVER

Round trip to trail-end: 16 miles (to Fern Lake junction 12 miles)
Hiking time: Allow 2 days
High point: 6600 feet
Elevation gain: 2600 feet
Hikable: July through October
Map: Green Trails No. 114 Lucerne
Current information: Ask at Entiat Ranger Station about trail No. 1437

Driving directions: Drive US 97 north from Wenatchee along the west side of the Columbia River to the town of Entiat and turn left on the Entiat River road some 32.5 miles on road No. 5606. Drive 4 miles to North Fork Entiat trail No. 1437, elevation 4000 feet.

The North Fork Entiat River country has 43 miles of trails offering dramatic views, flower-rich meadows, and loud streams. A great area for beginning hikers who want to enjoy in peace the lovely walks in the low valleys, for intermediates ambitious to take off on a glorious ridge run starting from one of the highest roads in the state, and for experienced highlanders itching for the strenuous climb to an old lookout site. The main thoroughfare is a forest trail passing through several small meadows to a delightful camp beside a little stream with a big name—North Fork Entiat River. Here is a fine base for day hikes.

(Good news on the public-activism front: After years of motorcycles harassing the North Fork trails, 5000 letters—plus a citizens' lawsuit—got the paths returned to hikers. It's not full wilderness protection, but it's a step in the right direction.)

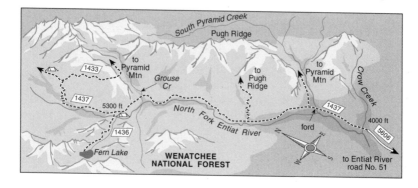

Alpine meadow near the end of the North Fork Entiat River trail

The trail immediately crosses Crow Creek and, at 1¼ miles, South Pyramid Creek, on a bridge built in 1998 by Washington Trails Association and Backcountry Horsemen volunteers. At 1½ miles, pass the South Pyramid Creek trail (Hike 92) and at 2¾ miles, the Pugh Ridge trail (Hike 90). At about 4 miles small meadows begin to break the forest; come early for the flowers. At 5 miles the trail gets very steep and stays that way to the Fern Lake junction, 5300 feet, 6 miles; here is that delightful camp by the river, the spot to lay out a mountain home.

After 1 more upstream mile the path again tilts very steeply, gaining 1000 feet in ¾ mile. At 8 miles from the road it ends at a junction with the Pyramid Mountain trail, 6600 feet. Go left a short bit to a large meadow with fine camps, more mountain homes.

Are your legs still jittering for exercise? Take the Pyramid Mountain trail 2 miles to Saska Pass, 7425 feet, and views down Snowbrushy Creek and the North Fork valley. Or continue down into the South Pyramid Valley for a loop (Hike 93).

90
PUGH RIDGE–PYRAMID CREEK LOOP

Round trip to Pugh Ridge: 12 miles
Hiking time: 9 hours
High point: 6800 feet
Elevation gain: 2800 feet
Hikable: July to mid-October

Loop trip: 14 miles
Hiking time: 10 hours
High point: 7000 feet
Elevation gain: 3200 feet
Hikable: July to mid-October

Map: Green Trails No. 114 Lucerne
Current information: Ask at Entiat Ranger Station about trail Nos. 1437, 1438

Driving directions: Drive US 97 north from Wenatchee along the west side of the Columbia River to the town of Entiat and turn left on the Entiat River road some 32.5 miles and turn right on road No. 5606. Drive 4 miles to North Fork Entiat trail No. 1437, elevation 4000 feet.

The close views of the giant peaks of the Chelan Mountains are a joy forever, and they're only part of the scenery. The meadows are very good, too. The trail is rough, at a steep angle. So much the better, giving some solitude.

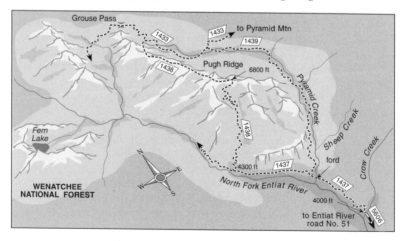

Alpine meadow on the crest of Pugh Ridge

Hike the North Fork trail 2¾ miles to the Pugh Ridge trail, 4300 feet, and turn right, steeling yourself to gain 2500 feet in 3 miles. The opening ¾ mile switchbacks 800 feet, and that average rate of gain is maintained. At 1¼ miles is a nice streamside camp. Nearing timberline the tread grows fainter and in the meadowlands is lost altogether. No matter. Continue up in the open until there is no more up. At 6 miles from the road, sit down atop Pugh Ridge, at 6800 feet. To the north is the magnificent line of Saska, Emerald, and Cardinal Peaks, all about 8500 feet. East are the naked slopes of Pyramid Mountain (Hike 88). West are the crags of Duncan Hill (Hike 83). In the middle distance is Devils Smokestack.

For the loop, cross the summit meadow. No tread here, so scout for the trail, down a bit on the west side, and do not leave the meadow until certain you really have tread underfoot. It drops several hundred feet, climbs to a 7000-foot high point, and descends to an intersection, 8 miles from the road, with trail No. 1433, called the Pyramid Mountain trail though it never goes to the mountain.

Turn downhill to another intersection. Keep straight, continuing down Pyramid Creek trail No. 1439 (Hike 93) to the North Fork Entiat trail at 1¼ miles from the road, for a loop total of 14 miles.

91 | FERN LAKE

Round trip: 15 miles
Hiking time: Allow 2 days
High point: 6894 feet
Elevation gain: 2800 feet
Hikable: Mid-July through September
Map: Green Trails No. 114 Lucerne
Current information: Ask at Entiat Ranger Station about
   trail Nos. 1437, 1436

Driving directions: Drive US 97 north from Wenatchee along the west side of the Columbia River to the town of Entiat and turn left on the Entiat River road some 32.5 miles and turn right on road No. 5606. Drive 4 miles to North Fork Entiat trail No. 1437, elevation 4000 feet.

As something of a geological curiosity, Fern Lake is the sole lake in the North Fork Entiat drainage. Why only this single cirque cupping deep water? Not enough snow in the last few "Little Ice Ages" to crank up the glaciers? The shores might be expected to be a three-deep ring of fishermen. However, the extremely difficult trail (for a mercy, signed "Hiker Only") keeps out the pikers.

Hike 6 miles to the Fern Creek trail junction, 5300 feet. The camp here is very pleasant and there's not another spot before the lake to lay your weary bones. The question, therefore, is whether to day hike from this base or carry packs the 1½ extremely steep miles to the lake, where very few bones can find space.

Cross the North Fork Entiat River—dwindled here to a creek—on an

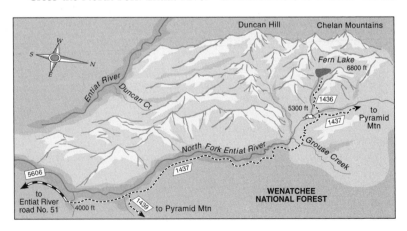

upstream log, and start the switchbacks. Don't complain about the numerous windfalls—they help keep scofflaw horses off this hiker-only trail. About halfway up, the trail leaves forest and climbs steeply beside the lake's outlet, tumbling so steeply it's practically all waterfall. The ascent ends abruptly on the shore of the lake, 6800 feet, ringed by ice-scoured cliffs and slabs and buttresses. The little campsite is such a joy you'll be sorry if you took the course of prudence and left your overnight gear below. What's a couple of hours of donkey misery beside a night and morning living in such glory?

Glacier-smoothed rocks at Fern Lake

92 | PYRAMID MOUNTAIN

Round trip: 19 miles
Hiking time: Allow 2 days
High point: 8243 feet
Elevation gain: 4300 feet
Hikable: Mid-July through September
Map: Green Trails No. 114 Lucerne
Current information: Ask at Entiat Ranger Station about
trail Nos. 1437, 1439, 1433, 1441

Driving directions: Drive US 97 north from Wenatchee along the west side of the Columbia River to the town of Entiat and turn left on the Entiat River road some 32.5 miles and turn right on road No. 5606. Drive 4 miles to North Fork Entiat trail No. 1437, elevation 4000 feet.

The views from this old lookout site extend over range upon range of snowy mountains in the Glacier Peak Wilderness, over heat-hazy plateaus of the Columbia Basin, and straight down 7000 feet to Lake Chelan, so far below that binoculars are needed to spot the tour boat. One has to wonder why the place was chosen for a fire lookout—the scenery is all rock, ice, and water, hardly anything in sight that might burn.

The two ways to Pyramid Mountain are the same length and have about the same elevation gain. The route from Big Hill (Hike 88) is spectacular, but the drive to the trailhead is so long and difficult that the recommended route, described here, is the South Pyramid Creek trail, featuring

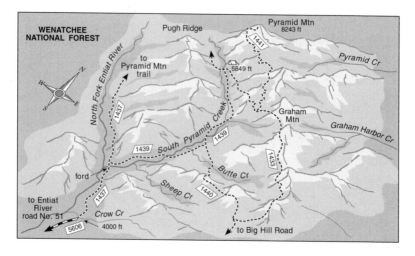

Hitching post on top of Pyramid Mountain, overlooking Lake Chelan

an interesting transition from valley forest to alpine barren.

Thanks (no thanks) to the era when the Forest Service went into a swoon over multiple-abuse machines and had more money than it knew how to use sensibly, the foot trail was widened; little creeks were provided big sturdy bridges, and the boulders that hikers hopped across big creeks were removed to let wheels splash through at full gallop.

In 1¼ miles cross Pyramid Creek and turn right on South Pyramid Creek trail No. 1439. At 5½ miles, 5849 feet, are the last creekside campsites. At the junction here, go right on Pyramid Mountain trail No. 1433, climbing 1½ miles to another junction; go left on Pyramid Viewpoint trail No. 1441. An up-and-down traverse emerges from trees, reaches a small campsite in ½ mile, and yields to steep and steeper tread climbing to the 8243-foot summit, 9½ miles from the road.

Artifacts of the vanished lookout abound: the leveled summit, scraps of metal, and an open-air privy that may have the most spectacular view of any such facility in the Northwest.

93 | SOUTH PYRAMID CREEK LOOP

Round trip: 18 miles
Hiking time: Allow 2 to 3 days
High point: 7150 feet
Elevation gain: 3200 feet
Hikable: July through October
Map: Green Trails No. 114 Lucerne
Current information: Ask at Entiat Ranger Station about
   trail Nos. 1437, 1439, 1433

Driving directions: Drive US 97 north from Wenatchee along the west side of the Columbia River to the town of Entiat and turn left on the Entiat River road some 32.5 miles and turn right on road No. 5606. Drive 4 miles to North Fork Entiat trail No. 1437, elevation 4000 feet.

Forest, meadows, views, choice camps, a babbling stream. What more? In early summer, flowers and love are in bloom. In late September, larches are old gold, the best kind. The loop can be done either way, of course, but to avoid climbing an extremely steep mile lugging a heavy pack, it is described here counterclockwise. A number of delightful campsites lie along the way and solitude is almost assured.

In 1¼ miles turn right on South Pyramid Creek trail No. 1439, whose steep sections happily are short. At about 2½ miles from the road cross the creek on a log. At a bit past 3 miles, cross Butte Creek and, soon after, South Pyramid Creek—with difficulty, repeated at a recrossing in ½ mile.

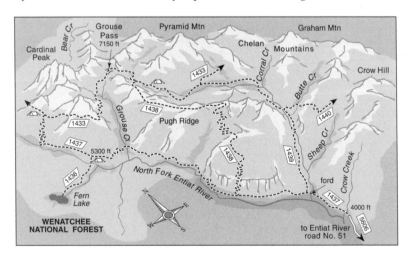

At 5¼ miles from the road, the South Pyramid Creek trail ends at a junction with Pyramid Mountain trail No. 1433. Keep straight ahead, proceeding up the valley. The way steepens and crosses the stream twice more, but the labors are more than adequately compensated by meadows, views, and choice camps.

At 6½ miles pass the Pugh Ridge trail. At 7 miles cross Grouse Pass, 7150 feet. The trail drops to a crossing of Grouse Creek, 6600 feet, at 8½ miles, traverses a steep, broad-view hillside, and at 10 miles intersects North Fork Entiat River trail No. 1437, 6600 feet (Hike 89).

If ready to camp, stay on the Pyramid Mountain trail several hundred yards to a broad meadow flat. Otherwise, follow the North Fork trail steeply down (the reason for not doing the loop clockwise) to camps at 11 miles, and more at 12 miles, at the Fern Lake junction (Hike 92). The loop continues downvalley to the junction with the South Pyramid Mountain Creek trail at 16½ miles and the trailhead at 18 miles.

View near Grouse Pass

94 | BUTTE CREEK–CROW HILL

Round trip: 13 miles
Hiking time: Allow 2 days
High point: 7366 feet
Elevation gain: 3400 feet
Hikable: Early June to mid-October
Map: Green Trails No. 114 Lucerne
Current information: Ask at Entiat Ranger Station about
trail Nos. 1437, 1439, 1433

Driving directions: Drive US 97 north from Wenatchee along the west side of the Columbia River to the town of Entiat and turn left on the Entiat River road some 32.5 miles and turn right on road No. 5606. Drive 4 miles to North Fork Entiat trail No. 1437, elevation 4000 feet.

This trail has two reputations: as one of the very best trails in the Entiat valley and one of the absolute worst. Make your own judgment as you climb with scarcely a switchback beside one waterfall after another to the view from Crow Hill, where you only need a springboard to do a swan dive into Lake Chelan, a vertical mile below, to the circle of large mountains, icy mountains, naked mountains, brown mountains, and green mountains. Yet if this view is your sole goal, you can achieve it in 1 scant mile from road No. 5900 (Hike 88)—but a lot more miles from your car if your car quails and quits. The serendipity here is gaining the views on a trail so steep it is legally closed to horses.

In 1¼ miles turn right on South Pyramid Creek trail No. 1439 and hike

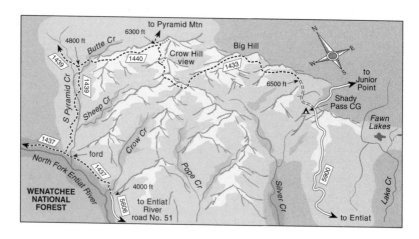

One of many falls on Butte Creek

another 2 miles to the junction of Butte Creek trail No. 1440, 4800 feet. Because of the steepness to come, it is recommended that hikers camp at the crossing of South Pyramid Creek (the nicest place) or of Butte Creek, in order to be carrying only a day pack for the morning's ascent, 1800 feet in 2 miles.

Near the top of the first steep pitch, spot a magnificent waterfall, almost hidden in the greenery. In about ½ mile cross Butte Creek, wet your face, and resume wetting your back and brow with sweat. At about 1¼ miles the trail, still steep, comes to a ridge with the beginning of views. At about 1¾ miles it levels and tread all but disappears in a short drop to a junction with Pyramid Mountain trail No. 1433, 6300 feet.

Had enough? If not, meander the short distance to the top of the 6653-foot knoll you have just passed. Great views! Not yet enough? Turn right on the Pyramid Mountain trail and hike steeply up to a 7000-foot high point. Where the path levels, leave it and stroll open meadows to Crow Hill, 7366 feet. Examine the remains of an ancient cabin. The terrain is so badly eroded that one speculates this was a sheepherder's shelter.

95 | DOMKE LAKE

Round trip: 6 miles
Hiking time: 3 hours
High point: 2200 feet
Elevation gain: 1100 feet
Hikable: June through October
Map: Green Trails No. 114 Lucerne
Current information: Ask at Chelan Ranger Station about trail No. 1280

Driving directions: Drive to Chelan town or Field Point on Lake Chelan and board a tour boat. The number of boats in service and their schedules is in a period of rapid change. For current schedules and fares, call the Lake Chelan Boat Company at (509) 682-2224 or the National Park Service–U.S. Forest Service Information Center in Seattle at (206) 470-4060. In late morning debark at Lucerne, elevation 1096 feet.

The trail has a few views of Lake Chelan. The lake at trail's end, Domke, has fish (and for each one, three fishermen). Children, for whom no summer is complete without a swim but for whom Chelan is too refreshing, find Domke sufficiently warm by mid-July for hours of splashing. Though the trip is short enough to be an easy day, families often backpack to spend a lazy week, either camping at trail's end or renting a boat to reach private sites across the lake. As for other entertainment, the odds are that one fisherman in three may get lucky.

Find Domke Lake trail No. 1280 at the boat dock. The trail parallels the road to the Railroad Creek crossing and then starts a dry and dusty climb

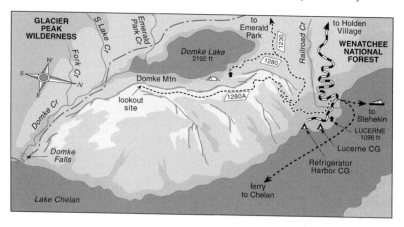

of 250 feet to a great view of Lake Chelan. Forest closes in, thinning enough at about 1½ miles for more views. At about 2¼ miles is a split. The Emerald Park trail (Hike 96) goes straight ahead; turn left. Ups and downs lead to the private concessionaire's buildings and bathing beach and rental boats at 2¾ miles. The public campground is at 3 miles, 2200 feet.

If views are the goal, at 1 mile from the Lucerne dock go left on Domke Mountain trail No. 1280A, a seldom-used 4½-mile path gaining 3000 feet to the former site of a fire lookout on the summit, 4061 feet. The building, long gone, was perched atop a 110-foot steel tower. To see the same views one must roam from side to side of the rounded mountain—rounded because the ancient Chelan Glacier rode right over the top, meanwhile gouging out the side-channel now occupied by Domke Lake.

Domke Lake

96 | EMERALD PARK

Round trip: 16 miles
Hiking time: Allow 2 to 3 days
High point: 5404 feet
Elevation gain: 4300 feet
Hikable: July to October
Map: Green Trails No. 114 Lucerne
Current information: Ask at Chelan Ranger Station
about trail Nos. 1280, 1230

Driving directions: Drive to Chelan town or Field Point on Lake Chelan and board a tour boat. The number of boats in service and their schedules is in a period of rapid change. For current schedules and fares, call the Lake Chelan Boat Company at (509) 682-2224 or the National Park Service–U.S. Forest Service Information Center in Seattle at (206) 470-4060. In late morning debark at Lucerne, elevation 1096 feet.

The jagged giants clustered about Milham Pass—Saska, Cardinal, and Emerald, all about 8500 feet—catch the eye from afar. At the base of their cliffs is a meadow valley so richly green that when seen from a distance, such as from a viewpoint in the Sawtooth Range across Lake Chelan, it seems an impossible dream. Of the many hikers who have had the vision, relatively few achieve the reality, because access from one direction, the Entiat valley, is guarded by Milham Pass, 6663 feet, often plugged up with snow until mid-August, and from the other by the expense and aggravation of travel on Lake Chelan. Though the hiking mileage from the lake makes a reasonable 2-day and easy 3-day trip, boat complications either add a day or two or keep hikers in a constant sweat worrying about connections. Lovely as the meadow is, there's not much exploring to do unless

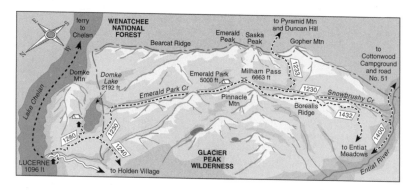

Emerald Park

one has the mountain competence to cope with Milham Pass.

Hike Domke Lake trail No. 1280. At the lake junction, 2¼ miles, go straight ahead. (You may wish to spend the first night at Domke Lake.) At about 3 miles from the dock pass the Railroad Creek trail. The way rounds a steep hillside, in spots angling upward quite strenuously, gives glimpses of Domke Lake, and turns a corner into the valley of Emerald Park Creek. The trail stays far above the water, whose sound is tantalizing as a dream on those sultry days when the flies go mad with blood lust. Openings in the forest begin and grow larger, the sun baking resins from the snowbrush, suffusing the air with ceanothus reek.

At about 6½ miles the trail levels out some and enters a meadow purple with asters, ringed by mountain ash. At 7 miles is a nice streamside camp, 5000 feet. In 1 more mile are larger meadows—the emerald gleam that so entrances the eye when seen from the high ridges across Lake Chelan.

The trail continues to 6663-foot Milham Pass, easy and safe after the snow melts. Meadows here are not so jewel-lush, are more of the rock-garden variety, but views are big across Lake Chelan to the Sawtooths. If a two-car switch can be arranged, or a friend recruited to do the pickup, the best way to do this country is with a one-way hike, exiting via the Entiat River trail (Hike 87).

97 | HOLDEN LAKE

Round trip from Holden Village: 9 miles
Hiking time: 6 hours
High point: 5278 feet
Elevation gain: 2000 feet
Hikable: Late July through October
Map: Green Trails No. 113 Holden
Current information: Ask at Chelan Ranger Station about trail Nos. 1256, 1251

Driving directions: Drive to Chelan town or Field Point on Lake Chelan and board a tour boat. The number of boats in service and their schedules is in a period of rapid change. For current schedules and fares, call the Lake Chelan Boat Company at (509) 682-2224 or the National Park Service–U.S. Forest Service Information Center in Seattle at (206) 470-4060. In late morning debark at Lucerne, elevation 1096 feet.

The lake is spectacular, the blue-green waters from the Mary Green Glacier and assorted snowfields are awesome, some summers only just melting out when the next freezing season has begun. The lake is in a deep cirque between 8511-foot Martin Peak and the "Big Banana," 9511-foot Bonanza, highest nonvolcanic peak in the state. Except for peak-baggers on their way up, up, up to the North Star (the original name before the U.S. Geological Survey lost its field notes and swapped names with a lesser peak near

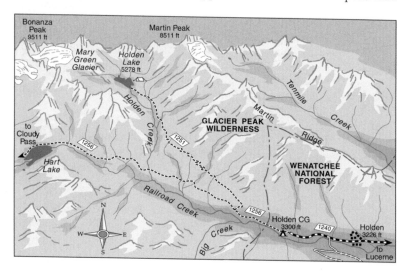

Cloudy Pass), the scene sees few backpackers, lying as it does off the cross-Cascades pilgrimage route from the Suiattle to Lake Chelan.

To experience what Railroad Creek would be had it been placed in the Glacier Peak Wilderness (as it could have been had there not been a Holden Mine, which, when played out, was "gifted" to the Lutheran Church, making for a nice tax write-off), walk trail No. 1240 some 10½ miles to Holden Village (the old mining town), elevation 3226 feet. If in a hurry, ride the church bus up the mining road, now a retreat road.

If you have the money, the bus driver will take you no matter what your religion. (Chances are that John the Baptist, famed for "returning to the wilderness where he could be alone with God," would not have liked this privatization of a national heritage for tourist purposes, operated by a church that officially opposed creation of the North Cascades National Park.)

From the village, walk the road ¾ mile to Holden Campground and trail No. 1256, 3300 feet. The path enters the Glacier Peak Wilderness (which properly should extend all the way down Railroad Creek to Lake Chelan). In ¾ forest mile is the junction with trail No. 1251, climbing steeply to the perched cirque of Holden Lake, 5278 feet, 5 miles from Holden Village.

Campsites in the forest near the lake outlet may remain snowy until nearly August. The cirque cliffs near the shore are something to look at.

Holden Lake

98

LYMAN LAKES

Round trip: 20 miles
Hiking time: Allow 2 to 3 days
High point: 6000 feet
Elevation gain: 2700 feet
Hikable: July through September
Map: Green Trails No. 113 Holden
Current information: Ask at Chelan Ranger Station about trail Nos. 1256, 1256C

Driving directions: The expensive (very) and quick (not very) access is via the boat up Lake Chelan to Lucerne and the bus ride up Railroad Creek to Holden Village (an old mining town that once was the largest single customer of the Washington State Liquor Commission and now is operated by the Lutheran Church as a Christian retreat), elevation 3300 feet. Drive to Chelan town or Field Point on Lake Chelan and board a tour boat. The number of boats in service and their schedules is in a period of rapid change. For current schedules and fares, call the Lake Chelan Boat Company at (509) 682-2224 or the National Park Service–U.S. Forest Service Information Center in Seattle at (206) 470-4060.

Ever since Professor Lyman conducted his investigations of the glaciers at the (next-to-last) turn of the century, the Lyman Lakes have been perhaps the single most popular spot in the Glacier Peak area. Long before any but a few had heard of Image Lake, pack trains with as many horses as Custer

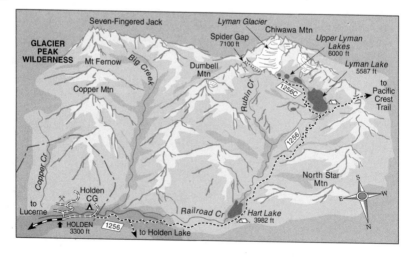

Waterfall descending to Lyman Lake

had at Little Big Horn were hauling summer-outing hordes up from Lake Chelan via Lucerne or Stehekin, or over the passes from the Entiat River and the Suiattle River. The lakes seem to be on the way to anywhere, or not far off the track. The sidetrip from the Pacific Crest Trail is short. Climbers basecamp to do the big peaks. Off-trail explorers cross the dramatic pass from Spider Meadow.

It will be well into afternoon by the time you have hiked the road the ¾ mile to Holden Campground; the notion of spending the first night here

Campground deer can be as destructive as bears

will have some appeal, though other camps are situated at short intervals up the Railroad Creek valley. A hiker in this valley will gain the impression that a major segment of the population of Holden Village, possibly outnumbering the Lutherans, is bears. At night hang food and toilet articles and anything with an interesting odor, shape, or color from the cables provided at Rebel Camp, Hart Lake, and Lyman Lake. Elsewhere, stand by to bang pots. However, if you camp off the beaten track, in a spot that is not on the bears' scheduled rounds, you may sleep in peace. If you choose a crowded camp on the principle of safety in numbers, your best chance of fun will be to have a large supply of flash bulbs to get candid photos of half-dressed campers banging pots.

At ¾ mile from the road-end campground, pass the Holden Lake trail. At 3½ miles skirt Hart Lake (camp), at 4½ miles pass Rebel Camp (good sites), and at 7 miles reach the outlet of Lower Lyman Lake, 5587 feet (camps here and at the lake inlet).

The best is yet to come. Cross the outlet on trail No. 1256C and switchback up 500 feet, from subalpine forest and parkland into wide-open meadows. Pass the several Upper Lyman Lakes and, at 10 miles from Holden, come to the toe of the Lyman Glacier, 6000 feet.

The glacier has retreated from its maximum during the "Little Ice Age," as photographed by Professor Lyman, but still flows impressively from Chiwawa Mountain, 8459 feet, and is among the safest opportunities for a hiker to touch a living glacier.

The heather meadows near the middle of the Upper Lyman Lakes cannot withstand the impact of camping; set up housekeeping on the moraine near the glacier or on any bare soil 200 feet from water. Carry a stove or eat cold; the wood here is too scarce and picturesque to waste in campfires.

99 | AGNES CREEK–LYMAN LAKES LOOP

Loop trip: 43 miles
Hiking time: Allow 3 to 7 days
High point: 6438 feet
Elevation gain: 4900 feet
Hikable: Mid-July through September
Maps: Green Trails Nos. 82 Stehekin, 81 McGregor Mtn.,
    113 Holden
Current information: Ask at Chelan Ranger Station
    about trail Nos. 2000, 1256

Driving directions: Hikes from Lake Chelan involve unusual transportation to and from trailheads. In this case there are the Lake Chelan boat service, which drops the party off at Stehekin and picks it up at Lucerne; the Park Service shuttle bus up the Stehekin road; and the Lucerne bus down from Holden Village. Drive to Chelan town or Field Point on Lake Chelan and board a tour boat. The number of boats in service and their schedules is in a period of rapid change. For current schedules and fares, call the Lake Chelan Boat Company at (509) 682-2224 or the National Park Service–U.S. Forest Service Information Center in Seattle at (206) 470-4060. The trip plan must take into account that hikers likely will spend much of the first day and the last fiddling around with all this.

From Stehekin Landing, ride the bus 11 miles to the High Bridge Ranger Station. About 500 feet beyond the bridge, on the left side of the road, is the Agnes Creek trailhead (Pacific Crest Trail No. 2000), elevation 1600 feet.

Here's a looper's favorite, ascending one of the supreme long-and-wild, low-to-high valleys of the North Cascades to Suiattle Pass, then climbing over Cloudy Pass and descending past Lyman Lake and Holden Village to Lake Chelan.

The trail drops a few feet, crosses Agnes Creek, and commences a long, easy grade in lovely forest with notable groves of cedar. Glimpses ahead of Agnes Mountain and glaciers on Dome Peak; to the rear, McGregor Mountain. A good stop the first night is Fivemile Camp, 2300 feet.

The valley forest is ever superb, featuring a fine stand of large hemlock and fir near Swamp Creek; there's another good camp here at 8 miles.

At Hemlock Camp, 12 miles, the trail splits. The new Pacific Crest Trail crosses the river, climbs to high views on the side of the valley, and at 19 miles reaches timberline campsites at a junction, 5600 feet. You can also get here via the old valley trail, which may be the better choice in early summer, when the new trail is likely to be largely in snow.

Lyman Lake, Upper Lyman Lake, Lyman Glacier, and Chiwawa Mountain

For a mandatory sidetrip, go right at the junction 6 miles to Image Lake (Hike 12), for the day or overnight.

For the loop, go left over 6438-foot Cloudy Pass to Lyman Lake and another must-do sidetrip, to Upper Lyman Lake and Upper-Upper Lyman Lake, ringed by barren moraines left by the source of icebergs, the glacier flowing from 8459-foot Chiwawa Mountain (Hike 98).

Finish the loop down Railroad Creek to Holden Village, by bus to Lucerne, and boat down Lake Chelan.

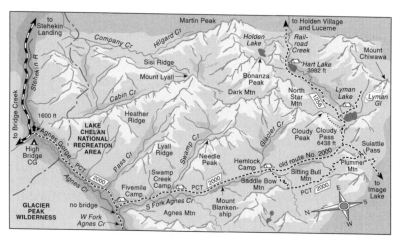

100 PACIFIC CREST NATIONAL SCENIC TRAIL

One way from Stehekin River to Stevens Pass: 98 miles
Hiking time: Allow 10 to 15 days
Elevation gain: 17,000 feet
Hikable: July through September
Maps: Green Trails Nos. 81 McGregor Mtn., 113 Holden,
112 Glacier Peak, 144 Benchmark
Current information: Ask at Chelan Ranger Station, Lake
Wenatchee Ranger Station, and Darrington Ranger Station about trail No. 2000

This stretch of the Pacific Crest Trail, traversing the west side of Glacier Peak and the ridge tops south to Stevens Pass, has some of the most flower-covered meadows and exciting scenery between Canada and Mexico.

From Chelan, take the boat up Lake Chelan to Stehekin (for current schedules and fares, call the Lake Chelan Boat Company at (509) 682-2224)

Pacific Crest Trail on the side of Indian Head Peak

and then ride the Park Service shuttle bus up the Stehekin road to High Bridge Campground. Climb the Agnes valley to Suiattle Pass (Hike 99). Continue to Glacier Peak Mines (Hike 14) on the slopes of Plummer Mountain with a choice of sidetrips to Upper Lyman Lakes (Hike 98), Image Lake (Hike 12), or the spectacular east-side Glacier Peak alternate (Hike 14).

For the recommended alternate west of Glacier Peak: Drop to the Suiattle River, climb the Vista Creek trail over ridges and down to Milk Creek (Hike 11), cross Fire Creek Pass to the White Chuck River (Hike 19), ascend the White Chuck to Red Pass, and continue via White Pass to Lower White Pass (Hike 66). *Distance from High Bridge to Lower White Pass 66 miles, elevation gain about 12,000 feet, hiking time 6 days.* The journey can be broken by trail exits to the Suiattle River road, White Chuck River road, or North Fork Sauk River road.

The remainder of the way to Stevens Pass is comparatively level, wandering along the Cascade Crest with ups and downs, frequently alternating from east side to west side, mostly through open meadows of flowers or heather. From Lower White Pass (Hike 66) the trail stays high, dipping into forest only at Indian Pass and again at Cady Pass. From Cady Pass the route contours hillsides, traversing a mixture of forest and meadows past Pear Lake (Hike 49), climbing within a few hundred feet of Grizzly Peak,

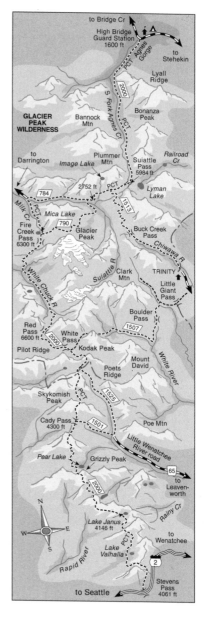

and proceeding onward to Lake Janus (Hike 51), Union Gap, Lake Valhalla (Hike 50), and finally Stevens Pass. *Distance from Lower White Pass to Stevens Pass 32 miles, elevation gain 5000 feet, hiking time 4 days.*

USGS MAPS

The Green Trails maps listed for each trail are all most hikers need. For the benefit of those who love poring over maps, 7½-minute USGS maps are listed here for each hike.

1 Sonny Boy Lakes, Cascade Pass
2 Finney Peak (trail not on map)
3 Mount Higgins
4 Whitehorse Mountain
5 Whitehorse Mountain
6 Whitehorse Mountain, Helena Ridge
7 Pugh Mountain
8 Huckleberry Mountain
9 Downey Mountain
10 Downey Mountain, Dome Peak
11 Lime Mountain, Gamma Peak
12 Lime Mountain, Gamma Peak
13 Lime Mountain, Gamma Peak, Suiattle Pass, Holden
14 Lime Mountain, Gamma Peak, Suiattle Pass, Clark Mountain, Trinity, Mount David, Glacier Peak East, Glacier Peak West
15 White Chuck Mountain
16 Pugh Mountain
17 Pugh Mountain, Lime Mountain
18 Pugh Mountain, Lime Mountain, Glacier Peak West
19 Pugh Mountain, Lime Mountain, Glacier Peak West
20 Pugh Mountain, Lime Mountain, Glacier Peak West
21 Sloan Peak, Glacier Peak West
22 Sloan Peak
23 White Chuck Mountain, Pugh Mountain
24 Sloan Peak, Blanca Lake, Bench Mark Mountain
25 Sloan Peak, Bedal
26 Bedal, Sloan Peak
27 Monte Cristo (trail not on map)
28 Monte Cristo
29 Monte Cristo, Blanca Lake

30 Meadow Mountain, Whitehorse Mountain
31 Verlot
32 Granite Falls
33 Mallardy Ridge, Wallace Lake
34 Mallardy Ridge (trails not on map)
35 Silverton, Helena Ridge
36 Helena Ridge, Silverton
37 Bedal
38 Bedal
39 Bedal, Silverton
39 Mount Stickney
40 Mount Stickney
41 Index, Baring
42 Blanca Lake
43 Blanca Lake, Bench Mark Mountain
44 Blanca Lake, Bench Mark Mountain
45 Blanca Lake, Bench Mark Mountain
46 Evergreen Mountain
47 Baring
48 Captain Point, Evergreen Mountain
49 Captain Point, Bench Mark Mountain
50 Labyrinth Mountain
51 Labyrinth Mountain, Captain Point
52 Lake Wenatchee, Mount Howard
53 Mount Howard
54 Mount Howard
55 Mount Howard
56 Lake Wenatchee
57 Labyrinth Mountain
58 Labyrinth Mountain, Captain Point

59 Poe Mountain
60 Poe Mountain
61 Poe Mountain, Bench Mark
Mountain, Glacier Peak East,
Glacier Peak West
62 Poe Mountain, Bench Mark
Mountain, Glacier Peak East,
Glacier Peak West
63 Lake Wenatchee
64 Mount David, Schaeffer Lake
65 Mount David
66 Mount David, Poe Mountain,
Glacier Peak East, Clark
Mountain, Glacier Peak West
67 Mount David, Clark Mountain
68 Chikamin Creek, Saska Peak
69 Schaefer Lake
70 Schaefer Lake, Trinity
71 Schaefer Lake, Trinity
72 Trinity, Clark Mountain
73 Trinity, Clark Mountain, Suiattle
Pass, Holden
74 Trinity, Clark Mountain, Holden
75 Trinity
76 Trinity, Holden, Suiattle Pass
77 Trinity, Holden, Suiattle Pass
78 Sugarloaf Peak, Silver Falls
79 Chikamin Creek, Silver Falls
80 Chikamin Creek, Silver Falls,
Sugar Loaf
81 Silver Falls, Chikamin Creek (not
on any map)

82 Silver Falls
83 Silver Falls, Chikamin Creek,
Pyramid Mountain, Saska Peak
(trail not on maps)
84 Saska Peak
85 Saska Peak, Trinity
86 Saska Peak
87 Saska Peak, Trinity, Pinnacle
Mountain
88 Pyramid Mountain, Big Goat
Mountain
89 Pyramid Mountain, Saska Peak
90 Pyramid Mountain
91 Pyramid Mountain, Saska Peak
92 Pyramid Mountain, Saska Peak
93 Pyramid Mountain, Saska Peak
94 Pyramid Mountain
95 Lucerne
96 Lucerne, Pinnacle Mountain
97 Holden
98 Holden, Suiattle Pass
99 McGregor Mountain, Mount Lyall,
Agnes Mountain, Suiattle Pass,
Holden
100 McGregor Mountain, Mount Lyall,
Suiattle Pass, Clark Mountain,
Trinity, Mount David, Poe
Mountain, Glacier Peak East,
Bench Mark Mountain, Labyrinth
Mountain, Captain Point

PRESERVING OUR WALKING TRAILS

AN EDITORIAL BY HARVEY MANNING

Were "civilization" to be subjected to a cost–benefit analysis, it could claim innumerable goods, such as Mozart and ice cream. Some goods, though, would have to be listed as endangered. For example, an early triumph, not of civilization itself but of an essential preliminary, was walking on our hind legs, an option that now is at risk. Wheels. Another would be the recent recognition of the need for legal protection of the church where John the Baptist went to be with God. Wilderness.

When we began publishing guidebooks in the 1960s, it was not from any delusion that penetrations by civilization—trails, that is—enhance wilderness. The good thing they do is teach us the importance of wilderness. Our books are driven by the iron law, "use it or lose it."

Books aim the feet. Feet are the artillery. Feet have fired off the broadsides that have gotten the attention of land managers and elected officials.

The turning point in the state of Washington was 1960, when we crammed down the throat of the U.S. Forest Service a Glacier Peak Wilderness that was much smaller than we sought, but far larger than the "wilderness on the rocks" that the timber industry tried to cram down our throat.

The year 1964 brought a triumph on the national scene when Congress passed the Wilderness Act.

Then 1968, the North Cascades National Park and Pasayten Wilderness.

Then 1976, the Alpine Lakes Wilderness.

Then 1984, the Washington Wilderness Act, represented in this volume by the Boulder River and Henry M. Jackson Wildernesses and additions to the Glacier Peak Wilderness.

Then—what happened? The metronomic eight-year gestation of new births stopped dead. Had the spiritual womb gone barren?

If so, it was not in one fell swoop. In chilling contrast to the grand operas staged in the Oval Office by Presidents Johnson and Ford for their bill-signings in 1968 and 1976, President Reagan signed in 1984 only under the pressure of bipartisan unanimity in our state's Congressional delegation. No convocation of smiling faces. No Marines in dress uniforms. No resounding proclamation.

The 1984 Act omitted twice as much requested wilderness as it included. An Act II was confidently expected. But 1992 passed, and 2000. Nothing. Reagan had set Washington City on a course of contumely. But he was not a captain without a crew. Go door to door in the nation's capital. Round up the usual suspects.

Frustrated preservationists, their numbers and fervor ever mounting, pursued administrative recourses, went to the courts, undertook guerrilla actions.

Yet in 2000, a president elected by a minority vote behaved as if he had won by a landslide, hunkered down in the White House with his Praetorian Guard of Reagan retreads and "think tank" brains, and declared war on the American earth. In 2003, therefore, our main forces are mustering to renew the offensive on the Wilderness Act front.

Boundaries are being studied and debated, bills drafted. Limber up your letter-writing arms. Listen to your feet.

The Foe, Too, Is Mustering

The revival of the preservation movement after World War II was energized by the hubris of the U.S. Forest Service, striving to chisel in granite the airy mantras of Gifford Pinchot. An attempt was made to glorify "multiple use" as the quintessence of the American Way; in 1964 and 1968 the American people didn't buy it. "Sustained yield" was touted as self-evidently wise, and it was, and it is; under a program of sustained over-cutting, however, the Forest Service began running out of trees.

And thus, out of money. Preservationists joined the endangered rangers in demanding that Congress make up the difference required to fund its entire spectrum of management responsibilities—wildlife habitat, species diversity, recreation. Congress wouldn't do it. Tank-thinkers who were swarming in Washington City like mosquitoes in a hot swamp had a better idea. The Plan.

The heart of it is: "Anything government can do, free enterprise can do better." The necessity of earning a profit, the "thrive or die" learned in the jungle, gives the businessman his hard head, his "know how." The "Invisible Hand" identified by Adam Smith as the superego of the marketplace wisely steers his course. These are what have made America great.

Privatization, there's the key. Politicians live for votes, bureaucrats for pensions. Together they have brought our social infrastructure to wrack and ruin. The public schools are a disgrace, the socialization of medicine a failure. An exhaustive study by civil engineers has found that most of the nation's bridges are in danger of collapsing—or, in the state of Washington, of sinking or blowing down.

As for the public lands, we waste precious tax money in tending them while MBA entrepreneurs stand ready to do the job at no cost to us. The national parks, getting the message in the era of the stagecoach, are in the jet age cloning Disneyland and Six Flags Over Texas. Taking pages from Yosemite and Grand Canyon, Mount Rainier is considering ways and means to compete with resorts on its borders, to "enlarge its service area"; one suggestion is to build a paved "skateboard trail" from Tacoma to Paradise. Real estate in the Stehekin Valley of the North Cascades National Park complex, dirt cheap in 1968, has become so pricey that luxury condos are being schemed—and what is that looming on the horizon—a casino?

Then, the national forests. . . . Cheek by jowl with loot of the Northern Pacific Land Grab, where stumps of trees gone to market are being replaced by golf course-swimming pool-cocktail lounge Gomorrahs, the future hangs heavy, heavy over their head. Scenic climaxes cry out to be freed up so the Invisible Hand can build vacation cities. Areas lacking geographical pizzazz could be converted from tax sinkholes to cash cows, "charter forests" managed by businessmen for maximum sustained yield of the revenues, at hand from the industry that lies crouched and panting, "Wreckreation."

The Plan had its inception in the think tanks about the same time that President Reagan appointed James Watt Secretary of the Interior, a position that is held in 2003 by his star pupil. A flurry of white papers from the tanks candidly detailed the exact route toward final privatization of public lands. Watt was so enthusiastic that preservationist Republicans apologized to Democratic friends, assured them that Ronnie had been misled and soon would come to his senses. He never did, not even when the largest mass rally of preservationists in Northwest history gathered at Seattle's Gasworks Park to protest the Watt intention to issue leases for geothermal power in the Glacier Peak Wilderness. When Watt was (belatedly) fired, it was not over policy but for publicly laughing at disadvantaged citizens. In 2003, Wattism waxes in the White House.

The initial step in the Plan was slyly taken by a rider to a completely irrelevant bill; few members of Congress so much as noticed. On the surface it seemed innocent, a temporary experiment to test the willingness of Americans to pay fees to use trails that had been freely walked ever since the pioneers crossed the land bridge from Asia: The Fee Demonstration Program.

Bad idea. Yet with Congress so niggardly and rangers in such danger, preservationists could not but yield to the plea, an echo of the 1933 song, "Brother, can you spare a dime?" They went along with the temporary Plan, unaware that it *was* a Plan and that the refusal of funds by Congress was fundamental to the Plan. Stupid birdwatchers? No, merely trusting. They read only the first page in the white paper, the one with the violins.

In 2002 they read the second page, where "temporary" is scratched out, replaced by "permanent." Eyes were dried, heads scratched. Some of the rangers began to look suspiciously like cops. Hikers who refused to buy the required Northwest Forest Pass were threatened with fines and/or imprisonment. What to do? Stand up for principle and at the least lose a pleasant day in the woods? Or grumble and pay up? Maybe accept the rangers' offers of free passes for serving on volunteer work crews?

The wilderness rangers on the trails were and are the best and the brightest, our very good friends. Many were obviously unhappy and told us why. They had read Chapter Two of the Plan, and Chapter Three, and this wasn't their Forest Service. Between the wilderness trails and Washington City the quality of spirit, of soul, diminished geometrically. In the vicinity of the Oval Office, the top guns of the Forest Service held secret meetings with the tank-thinkers and the wreckreationist industry. The folks in the field were being sold down the river by their bosses in the offices.

And how about this? The Northwest Forest Pass was gleefully endorsed by the snowmobilers who compel rangers to wear gas masks, by the four-wheel mud-runners of marshes and meadows and steppe, by the "vroom vroom" of motorcycles, by the log-hopping bombers of the "single-track." Paying a fee would give them a contractual guarantee, legitimize their illegitimate abuse. "We pay to play. The ones who walk on their hind legs and whine, they're the scofflaws."

The Militia Comes Marching In

For 10,000 years or so the only trails in the North Cascades were those beaten out by the feet of deer, elk, bear, coyotes, marmots, and the folks who had trekked on over from Asia. For some half a century the "dirty miners in search of shining gold" built and maintained hundreds of miles of trails, often wide and solid enough for pack trains. During the same period many a valley had a trap line and a trapper's trail and many a ridge had a sheepherders' driveway. For thirty-odd years, roughly from World War I to World War II, Forest Service rangers built trails to fire lookouts atop peaks and to give fire crews quick walking to blazes.

The rangers then began taking to airplanes and parachutes and the wannabe miners to helicopters, and the trails deteriorated. However, as recreation enlarged from a subsidiary to a central use, the management concept embraced walking.

Walking, plus whatever. . . . In the nigh-onto-half-a-century that preservationists have been saving Washington trails by creating a national park and a bouquet of wildernesses, the Forest Service has been converting *true trails* (paths for speeds up to 5 miles an hour or so) to *motorcycle roads* (trails rebuilt for machine travel) that let the off-road vehicle, the "ORV," do 10 to 30 miles per hour.

Walking is the overwhelmingly dominant travel mode in wildlands, by orders of magnitude. Yet a handful of ORVers—very loud, highly visible, reeking of hydrocarbons, heavily financed by industry and assiduously fronted by lobbyists adroit in cloakrooms and bars—have converted more miles to motorcycle roads than walkers have been able to save for trails. On federal lands of Washington State, only 45 percent of trails are machinefree by virtue of being in national parks and wildernesses; of the other 55 percent, half are wide open to motorcycles.

The dirt bike, the "revenge for Hiroshima," was welcomed on trails as a rightful and respectable multiple-abuse. Then came the "mountain" bike, exploiting the meretricious appellation to cash in on the television fad for the "extreme" and employing Orwellian "newspeak" to transform trails to "single-track."

The walker, though, if quieter and slower, is smarter. The volunteer trail crews that in the past decade have become as busy as deer flies on an August afternoon do noble work, keeping the slide alder from whipping our cheeks and the devils club from slashing our throats. They are also ingeniously political. A picture is worth a thousand words. Photos in the papers and on television of tiny children and gimpy elders whacking the weeds reach out to the hearts of the public and the campaigns of elected officials.

A person able to walk the wildlands more than a little bit ought to do some of that walking with lopper or shovel or pulaski in hand. Virtually all preservationist groups sponsor volunteer trail crews. The nagging of Congress is and must be continued; the equipment and skills of the rangers are indispensable for heavy work at a distance from trailheads. The militias, though, can serve excellently well in the several miles from the road. This "edge" wilderness is precisely the best for "green-bonding" the newcomers we must recruit as wilderness defenders.

A caveat. We revere the trail for what it does, not for what it is. We honor the volunteer weed-whackers, but not to the point of wishing to "promote" them to professionals; trail work can be a form of privatization, as it most surely is when undertaken by those who do it to facilitate their wreckreation.

No new trail should be built, for any purpose, anywhere, nor any deteriorating trail be rehabilitated, without a prior assessment of the impact on life systems. Elements of the pedestrian militia now are deconstructing— "putting to bed"—trails that are judged to do more ecological harm than re-creational good.

The wild things need their space. So does John the Baptist when he says, "Hang the slide alder and devils club," and strides into the brush to be alone with God.

> *Personal opinions of*
> Harvey Manning
> September 2002

ABOUT THE AUTHOR

Harvey Manning has been a spokesman for the environmentalist advocacy of wilderness preservation since the 1950s. He was founder and first president of the Issaquah Alps Trails Club, which led the successful campaign to obtain the Cougar Mountain Regional Wildland Park and the Tiger Mountain State Forest, with its state-endorsed wilderness, the West Tiger Mountain Natural Resources Conservation Area. He and his Trails Club initiated the Mountains-to-Sound Greenway that now connects the Issaquah Alps to Seattle west and the Alpine Lakes Wilderness and Snoqualmie Pass east. As a board member of the North Cascades Conservation Council, he participated in obtaining the North Cascades National Park and Pasayten Wilderness in 1968, the Alpine Lakes Wilderness in 1976, and other National Wildernesses from the Columbia River to Canada. His current major concern is to defeat the creeping commercialism of the public lands represented by the Trojan Horse of the Northwest Forest Pass.

HEALTHY TRAILS AND THE NORTHWEST FOREST PASS

AN EDITORIAL BY IRA SPRING

Supporters are needed—lots of supporters—to protect our wild places from an indifferent Congress that already is considering at least one bill that would allow motorcycles full access, and sightseeing helicopters to drop tourists off for an hour-long picnic by a pristine lake or a flower-covered ridge top. Healthy trails for healthy people will create green-bonded supporters to protect our wild places.

Loggers' money talked when their roads gobbled miles of trail; Washington State money talked when the Forest Service turned over a thousand miles of our trails to motorcycles. Now, at last, thanks to the Northwest Forest Pass (which Harvey detests) and volunteer trail workers, hikers have the *money* to *talk* loud enough that land managers will listen. Our Northwest Forest Pass money and thousands of green-bonded hikers is the most effective way to stop helicopters and motorcycles from invading our wilderness trails.

Revenues from the Northwest Forest Pass generate the largest fund for maintaining the trails we use. Take that away and our Northwest trails are in trouble.

Harvey and I agree on the problem, but our solutions are 180 degrees different. Harvey agrees with the Sierra Club (the most trusted environmental organization in the country), who sees the Forest Pass as a slippery slope leading to all kinds of industrial recreation. I see the Forest Pass as the best defense against industrial recreation.

So far the Sierra Club has not published their plan for funding trails. They are trying to treat the Forest Pass and trails funding as two separate issues, but in my opinion they are a single issue and cannot be separated.

Harvey believes Congress should subsidize our trails as they did in the 1980s. However, after six trips to D. C., I have given up on hoping Congress will supply full funding for trails. Eastern Congressional people I have talked to see no reason to subsidize Western trails. They said, "If volunteers can maintain the Appalachian Trail, you Westerners can maintain your own trails."

Harvey and I completely agree on the problem of industrial recreation of our public lands. Harvey's use of the term "industrial wreckreation" fits perfectly. But while Harvey and the Sierra Club are fighting to eliminate the Northwest Forest Pass, The American Hiking Society, our Washington Trails Association, and a few other hiking organizations are working with Congress to include legislation that will give users oversight on where the money will be collected and how it will be spent—nipping any industrial wreckreation in the bud.

Recent surveys by the state's Interagency for Outdoor Recreation (IAC) gives a perspective on how the forest is used (from a draft report 12/15/2002):

- 49 % road-oriented recreation (camping/sightseeing)
- 25.3 % hiking
- 12 % ORV use
- 11.4 % cross-country skiing
- 6 % mountain biking
- 1.4 % snowmobiling
- 1.4 % equestrian use

OUR LEGACY LIVES ON

The Mountaineers, Harvey, and I have had forty years of working together on some twenty guidebooks, with a mutual aim of preserving our trails and wild places.

In the 1960s, roads were being planned to crisscross what is now the Alpine Lakes Wilderness and logging roads were gobbling up trails at a fast pace.

In the first two years of the *100 Hikes* books, eight trails were lost to roads. The guidebooks brought people to trails they had never before heard of, where they could see for themselves what was happening to trails. It took a few years and a lot of words from irate hikers before the Forest Service realized what an important resource trails had become. The Mt. Baker–Snoqualmie National Forest has gradually turned from a tree-cutting forest to an urban recreation resource.

Our books played an important role in the 1984 Washington Wilderness Act. Thanks to Harvey, the Forest Service had adopted his wildlands etiquette.

I am embarrassed when strangers compliment me on our work, but I am extremely pleased when someone tells me they are the third generation in their family who have used our hiking guidebooks.

Personal opinions of
Ira Spring
February 2003

ABOUT THE AUTHOR

Photographer Ira Spring's crisp, breathtaking images of the Northwest wilderness have been inspiring outdoor enthusiasts for several decades. His creative stamp can be found on more than forty books on the outdoors, including many in The Mountaineers Books' *100 Hikes in*™series. One of the Northwest's most active trail lobbyists, Spring was given the 1992 Theodore Roosevelt Conservation Award for his volunteer efforts toward trail preservation and funding.

INDEX

THE MOUNTAINEERS, founded in 1906, is a nonprofit outdoor activity and conservation club, whose mission is "to explore, study, preserve, and enjoy the natural beauty of the outdoors. . . . " Based in Seattle, Washington, the club is now the third-largest such organization in the United States, with 15,000 members and five branches throughout Washington State.

The Mountaineers sponsors both classes and year-round outdoor activities in the Pacific Northwest, which include hiking, mountain climbing, ski-touring, snowshoeing, bicycling, camping, kayaking and canoeing, nature study, sailing, and adventure travel. The club's conservation division supports environmental causes through educational activities, sponsoring legislation, and presenting informational programs. All club activities are led by skilled, experienced volunteers, who are dedicated to promoting safe and responsible enjoyment and preservation of the outdoors.

If you would like to participate in these organized outdoor activities or the club's programs, consider a membership in The Mountaineers. For information and an application, write or call The Mountaineers, Club Headquarters, 300 Third Avenue West, Seattle, WA 98119; (206) 284-6310.

The Mountaineers Books, an active, nonprofit publishing program of the club, produces guidebooks, instructional texts, historical works, natural history guides, and works on environmental conservation. All books produced by The Mountaineers Books fulfill the club's mission.

Send or call for our catalog of more than 500 outdoor titles:

The Mountaineers Books
1001 SW Klickitat Way, Suite 201
Seattle, WA 98134
(800) 553-4453
mbooks@mountaineersbooks.org
www.mountaineersbooks.org

The Mountaineers Books is proud to be a corporate sponsor of Leave No Trace, whose mission is to promote and inspire responsible outdoor recreation through education, research, and partnerships. The Leave No Trace program is focused specifically on human-powered (nonmotorized) recreation.

Leave No Trace strives to educate visitors about the nature of their recreational impacts, as well as offer techniques to prevent and minimize such impacts. Leave No Trace is best understood as an educational and ethical program, not as a set of rules and regulations.

For more information, visit *www.LNT.org,* or call (800) 332-4100.

Other titles you might enjoy from The Mountaineers Books

Available at fine bookstores and outdoor stores, by phone at (800) 553-4453, or on the Web at *www.mountaineersbooks.org*

100 Hikes in™ Washington's North Cascades National Park Region, 3rd Edition by Ira Spring and Harvey Manning. $16.95 paperbound. 0-89886-694-4.

100 Classic Hikes in™ Washington by Ira Spring and Harvey Manning. $19.95 paperbound. 0-89886-586-7.

100 Hikes in™ Washington's South Cascades and Olympics, 3rd Edition by Ira Spring and Harvey Manning. $14.95 paperbound. 0-89886-594-8.

Best Winter Walks and Hikes: Puget Sound, 2nd Edition by Harvey Manning and Ira Spring. $15.95 paperbound. 0-89886-822-X.

Roads to Trails Northwest Washington: Mount Baker & Snoqualmie National Forests by Washington Trail Association Volunteers, coordinated by Ira Spring. $14.95 paperbound. 0-89886-875-0.

Best Old-Growth Forest Hikes: Washington and Oregon Cascades by John Cissel and Diane Cissel. $16.95 paperbound. 0-89886-839-4.

Best Loop Hikes in Washington edited and compiled by Dan Nelson, photography by Alan Bauer. $16.95 paperbound. 0-89886-866-1.

Best Rain Shadow Hikes in Western Washington by Michael Fagin and Skip Card. $16.95 paperbound. 0-89886-863-7.

Best Short Hikes™ in Washington's North Cascades & San Juan Islands, 2nd Edition by E. M. Sterling. $14.95 paperbound. 0-89886-813-0.

Best Hikes with Dogs in Western Washington by Dan Nelson. $16.95 paperbound. 0-89886-829-7.

Mountain Flowers of the Cascades and Olympics, 2nd Edition by Harvey Manning, photographs by Bob and Ira Spring. $9.95 spiral bound. 0-89886-883-1.

Animal Tracks of the Pacific Northwest by Karen Pandell and Chris Stall. $6.95 paperbound. 0-89886-012-1.

Northwest Trees by Stephen F. Arno and Ramona P. Hammerly. $14.95 paperbound. 0-916890-50-3.

Northwest Mountain Weather: Understanding and Forecasting for the Backcountry User by Jeff Renner. $10.95 paperbound. 0-89886-297-3.

Wilderness Navigation: Finding Your Way Using Map, Compass, Altimeter, & GPS by Bob Burns and Mike Burns. $9.95 paperbound. 0-89886-629-4.

Wilderness 911: A Step-by-Step Guide for Medical Emergencies and Improvised Care in the Backcountry by Eric A. Weiss, M. D. $16.95 paperbound. 0-89886-597-2.

100 Best Cross-Country Ski Trails in Washington, 3rd Edition by Vicky Spring and Tom Kirkendall. $16.95 paperbound. 0-89886-806-8.

Snowshoe Routes: Washington by Dan Nelson. $16.95 paperbound. 0-89886-585-9.